Between the Guillotine
and Liberty

# Between the Guillotine and Liberty

*Two Centuries of the*
*Crime Problem in France*

GORDON WRIGHT

New York • Oxford
OXFORD UNIVERSITY PRESS
1983

Copyright © 1983 by Oxford University Press, Inc.

Library of Congress Cataloging in Publication Data

Wright, Gordon, 1912–
    Between the guillotine and liberty.

    Bibliography: p.
    Includes index.
    1. Crime and criminals—France—History—
19th century.  2. Crime and criminals—France—History—
20th century.  I. Title.
HV6963.W74   1983    364'.944     82–12520
ISBN 0–19–503243–8

Printing (last digit):  9 8 7 6 5 4 3 2 1

Printed in the United States of America

# Preface

> Science in general . . . does not consist in collecting what we already know and arranging it in this or that kind of pattern. It consists in fastening upon some thing we do not know, and trying to discover it. . . . All science begins from the knowledge of our own ignorance: not our ignorance of everything, but our ignorance of some definite thing. . . . Science is finding things out: and in that sense history is a science.
>
> R. G. COLLINGWOOD

HISTORICAL STUDIES, like fashions in food and dress, evolve in response to changing tastes or altered social concerns. Indeed, the changes in historians' interests, and why they occur, constitute a valid subject of historical inquiry; for the topics they choose and the methods they use reflect the interests and the techniques of the society in which they live and work.

Until the last decade, crime and punishment attracted few historians in any country; monographs on the subject were rare, general works gave such matters no more than passing notice. The field was left to jurists and criminologists, whose concern with the record of the past was usually subordinated to their interest in practical problems of the present. Changes over time in attitudes toward crime and criminals, conflicting views about the purpose and techniques of punishment or treatment seemed to lie on the margins of the historian's interests, or even outside his proper realm. Just as criminals were seen as social deviants, historians drawn to such subjects were regarded in a way as professional deviants.

Things have changed of late; in fact, the study of deviants of all sorts begins to resemble a major industry. The surge of interest in social history and in *mentalités*, inspired in part by the work of the *Annales* school in France, has brought both social misfits and ordinary inarticulate people into the mainstream. History from below, concerned with the masses rather than the elites, exerts the powerful attraction of a new frontier. And while there may be a touch of faddishness in all this, the appeal of such subject matter can also be traced to genuine curiosity and valid social concerns.

Curiosity born of ignorance brought me to investigate French attitudes toward crime and punishment during the past two centuries. A dozen years ago, conversations with my son (then a legal aid lawyer involved in efforts at prison reform in California) started me thinking about the nature of prisons and the activities of prison reformers in France. The Attica riot of 1971 made me wonder whether such outbreaks had occurred in France. A brief incursion into the University library turned up few answers. General histories or studies of periods in French history ignored or barely mentioned the subject; monographs were rare and inadequate. My efforts to interest doctoral candidates in the topic fell on sterile ground, so I found myself drawn gradually into the quicksand. During a first round of investigating the subject in Paris (in 1974), I quickly learned that the topic was both rich and complex, and that a long line of French jurists, legal scholars, and criminologists had worked the field during the past century. I learned also that a whole cluster of historians, both French and Anglo-Saxon, had just descended on the crime problem, like flies attracted to carrion. No doubt good sense should have dictated abandoning the enterprise at that point, to await the fruit of others' labors. Yet I kept returning to it, driven, I suppose, by a feeling that when one's curiosity has been aroused by questions that seem interesting or important, one is somehow obligated to pursue them to the end.

Winston Churchill in his youthful days as social reformer is often quoted in support of the subject's significance: "The mood and temper of the public in regard to the treatment of crime and criminals," he declared in 1910, "is one of the most unfailing tests of the civilization of any country."[1] Churchill was certainly not aware that a French politician had said almost the same thing a century earlier (1831): "It is by the criminal legislation of a people that one can judge the level of its civilization, and the moral tendency of its government."[2] Nor would he necessarily have agreed with the French prison inspector Louis Moreau-Christophe, who asserted in 1837 (with some hyperbole) that "Crimes are the endemic malady of every social body. . . . It is into the prisons that the historian must go, if he is to make a sane judgment of a people's moral state."[3] Surely a society's crime rate and the kind of people who populate its prisons do not suffice to measure its "moral state"; nor are a society's attitudes toward crime and criminals an adequate test of its mores and values. The treatment of other marginal, deviant, or underprivileged groups is equally revealing, along with attitudes toward its more central values—work, wealth, individual rights and obligations, and so on. Still, criminality remains one of the most persistent and recalcitrant problems of any society—a problem that somehow resists every effort at control or "cure," that leads each generation to engage in the same cycle of analyses and remedies and failures, until one develops a jaded feeling of *déjà entendu*. It is not surprising that Emile Durkheim concluded at the end of the nineteenth century that crime is a normal and inescapable aspect of any society, to be accepted without shock or surprise and even (within limits) as a socially useful phenomenon. Nor is one astonished when, after two hundred years of unbroken discussion of the problems of crime and punishment, a British political leader can still say flatly: "We . . . need much more research into the causes of criminality, of which we know next to nothing."[4]

The historian's quest, of course, does not necessarily lead him toward new hypotheses about the causes of criminality, or about the proper definition and boundaries of crime, or about the best techniques of punishment or rehabilitation. His purpose, rather, is to discover and explain how a society has grappled with the problem over time, and to understand how and why attitudes toward crime and punishment have evolved, reflecting changes in values and *mentalités*. Grass-roots opinion is of course difficult and sometimes impossible to gauge; the inarticulate masses leave little formal record of their feelings and beliefs, though such beliefs can sometimes be inferred. But it is naturally easier, and not necessarily unimportant or elitist, to get at the views of the articulate minority that was able to get its opinions recorded, and that provided the leaders and activists in virtually all social reform movements over the past two centuries. Many of these activists, whose names were household vanished into historical oblivion. Some of them deserve to be rescued from that oblivion, both to show why Frenchmen of their sort became involved in efforts at penal or procedural reform, and to weigh their successes against their failures.

The book's title may seem more evocative than descriptive. It is borrowed from the title of a mid-nineteenth century drawing by an obscure French artist, whose purpose was to make an ironic comment about those reformers who exalted imprisonment as the "golden mean" of punishment techniques (see reproduction, page 74). My original title—*Criminals, Honest Folk, and Others*—grew more directly out of the subject matter, for one cannot read the record of the past two centuries without being struck by the constant repetition of the two terms "criminals" and "honest folk." At times one gets the impression of a civil war between two totally distinct and hostile races; indeed, the idea of a separate "criminal class" was long accepted, and even today recurs now and again. Only occasionally did Frenchmen suggest that there might be a gray zone rather than an impassable barrier between the world of criminals and that of *les honnêtes gens*. Such an exception was the criminologist Henri Joly, who wrote in a candid moment (1892): "There is a terrible truth that persists in the minds of prison inmates: that at bottom men do not differ much from one another, and that one can find self-styled honest folk who are no better than *galériens*."[5] Joly's purpose was not to deny the difference between guilt and innocence, but to recall the Christian view that all men are sinners, and to argue that it is safer to have offenders learn this from a chaplain than from direct observation. He neglected to add that honest folk might also do well to reflect on his "terrible truth."

My principal obligations, in the material realm, are to the John Simon Guggenheim Foundation and to Stanford University. A quarter free of teaching duties at Stanford enabled me to carry out the first stage of my research in Paris; a Guggenheim Fellowship in 1980–81 allowed me to return for the final phase and to do much of the writing. I hereby express my deep gratitude to both agencies. The manuscript was efficiently word-processed by Barbara Wawrzynski, and edited with style and forbearance by Leona Capeless of the Oxford University Press. The task of preparing the index was made easy and pleasant thanks to the help and computer expertise of Margaret H. Wright. I am greatly indebted to the eminent magistrate Henri Gaillac for permission to use two illustrations from his book *Les maisons de correction*. Nancy Lane, Editor at the Oxford University Press, provided welcome encouragement and guided the publication process throughout.

Personal obligations are more difficult to measure, but no less important. I owe a particular debt to my son Eric W. Wright, who first aroused my interest in this subject and who kept that interest alive by raising provocative questions. My wife, Louise Aiken Wright, provided the companionship and moral support that contribute so much to the completion of a long-drawn-out project. If the subject-matter were less grim, this book would be dedicated to her.

G. W.

*Stanford, California*
*January 1983*

# Contents

Between the Guillotine
and Liberty

# I

# The Challenge to Tradition

Take a moment to descend into those dark cells where the light of day never penetrates and contemplate the distorted features of your fellow men, weighed down by their chains, half naked in their tombs, barely nourished by some coarse substances sparingly doled out, constantly distracted by the groans of their unhappy companions and the threats of the pitiless guards; not so much fearful of the torture to come as tormented by having to wait for it; and throughout this long martyrdom, anticipating a death that will be kinder than their miserable lives.

JOSEPH SERVAN (1766)

WHEN THE YOUTHFUL magistrate Joseph Servan jolted his fellow judges in 1766 by his harrowing description of French prison conditions, and urged them to use Christian compassion toward lawbreakers and to push for drastic reforms in the system of criminal justice, he was voicing the sentiments of a new wave of moralists on the chronic problem of crime and punishment. For some years before Servan's passionate plea at the opening of the court's annual session, a small but influential cluster of thinkers and writers had been denouncing the excesses and inequities of the traditional system; and their cause was powerfully reinforced when a French edition of Cesare Beccaria's *Essay on Crimes and Punishments* appeared in Paris in 1765. The fact that a rising young magistrate like Servan dared to risk his career by speaking out for reform showed that something was changing in the temper of the French elite, if not in the outlook of Frenchmen *en masse*.

France's system of criminal justice had not been altered very much since the end of the Middle Ages. Most Frenchmen (like most other Europeans) accepted as natural a system of repressive justice designed to enforce law and order. "Find the guilty person, punish him, react strongly to any aggression against society"—such was the standard attitude toward offenders.[1] Such ideas as analyzing the causes of crime or trying to rehabilitate offenders scarcely existed, even in embryo. A primitive form of due process did exist, however; it was embodied in royal ordinances of 1539 and 1670, whose provisions were interwoven with doctrines drawn from Roman and canon law and were further elaborated by commentaries by the king's jurists. But if due process was respected, it was harshly conceived and enforced. The ordinance of 1670 permitted suspects to languish in prison for months or even years before trial; it allowed the magistrate to hear the testimony of accusers or witnesses without informing the suspect of either charges or evidence; it denied the accused person the right of counsel, and authorized the examining magistrate—in precisely specified conditions—to order varying degrees of torture designed to elicit a confession. Even after such a confession, the prisoner might have to undergo a second round of torture (oddly labelled *la question préalable*) to make him reveal the identity of his accomplices. The trial itself (like the investigation, conducted in secret) thus became in most cases a mere formality; the principal variable was the nature of the sentence, for judges were allowed broad discretion in fixing punishment. The ordinance of 1670 listed a series of penalties, but left it to the magistrates to apply these penalties in specific cases.

This judicial discretion was bound to produce a good deal of inconsistency; judges were restricted by no standard code, and could indulge their individual instincts. They rarely tilted in the direction of mercy, however, nor did they explicitly take into account the culprit's character or intentions, or what later generations would call extenuating circumstances. Transgressors were not viewed as tragic victims of an overpowering fate (as the ancients had once believed), or of a crime-breeding social milieu, or of some uncontrollable biological or psychological drive; they were evildoers, dangerous types who had chosen to violate society's norms and who were threats to property or life. Harsh punishment, therefore, seemed only natural, since its purpose was retribution and deterrence. If many lawbreakers escaped punishment, it was not through the mildness of the system or the generosity of those who operated it, but through the ineffectiveness of the police and through rural society's tolerance of certain infractions committed by local residents: smuggling, for example, and bloody brawls between the young men of neighboring villages. As for policing outside the large cities, the *maréchaussée*—even after it was placed under national control in 1720—was too thinly spread to function except in spasmodic fashion. The system rested on the principle of occasional arrests plus harsh punishment of those who were caught; the unlucky ones were presumed to serve as examples to deter others.

If the police and the courts of the old regime functioned sporadically and sluggishly, the punishment of those convicted was swift and sure. The ordinance of 1670 specified that sentences be carried out on the day they were pronounced—a rule that left little time for royal clemency when the penalty was death. Capital punishment might be imposed for a wide variety of offences, including such minor ones as household theft by a domestic servant. The sentence might call for hanging, burning, or breaking on the wheel, sometimes preceded by protracted torture or the lopping off of a hand or tongue. Executions were public and attracted enormous crowds. When the attempted regicide Damiens was put to death before the Paris Hôtel de Ville in 1757, the square and adjacent streets were jammed with thousands of curious Parisians; windows overlooking the scene were rented out at high rates to fashionable gentlemen and ladies who feasted and drank while watching the victim endure several hours of the most excruciating tortures, climaxed by the process known as quartering.[2] The Damiens example was not typical; most executions in eighteenth-century France were less gruesome. But at best they were brutal rituals that pandered to the most savage instincts of the crowd. It was assumed that since deterrence and social vengeance were the purposes of punishment, executions would be most effective if they were both public and horrifying.

Although death sentences were common in the eighteenth century, they amounted to less than 10 per cent of all sentences pronounced. Much more common were penal servitude in the galleys, or banishment from the region or the country. France's Mediterranean fleet in early modern times was made up in part of ships propelled by oarsmen, and manpower for this service was hard to find. From the time of Louis XIV, therefore, the government turned to the courts for *galériens*; for the most part they were petty offenders —thieves, vagabonds, smugglers, army deserters. Chained to their benches, exposed to the vagaries of wind and weather, poorly nourished, *galériens* rarely survived for more than a few years. Those hardy enough to last were often kept on well beyond the terms of their sentences; few of them returned to freedom unless they managed to escape. When the galleys were decommissioned in 1748, they were replaced by what eventually came to be known as *bagnes*: shore-based prisons (sometimes using moored vessels for nighttime confinement) in various seaports, where the navy utilized the prisoners for hard labor to maintain port facilities and arsenals. In the nineteenth century the term *galérien* gradually gave way to *bagnard* (though the two words were long used interchangeably) ; but whatever the label, these prisoners remained legendary figures, objects of fascinated horror among the general population. When the semiannual shipment of *bagnards* departed from Bicêtre prison near Paris for the long journey (on foot or, later, on open carts) to Toulon or Brest, crowds gathered to watch as iron collars were riveted around their necks; and in every village en route, the locals came out to hoot or stare.[3] Escaped *bagnards*, bearing the telltale brand on the shoulder and often betraying their condition by a characteristic limping gait (the effect of years weighted down by ball and chain), were sources of terror in the countryside, rivaling the werewolf in the disciplining of unruly children. The *bagnes* held about 4000 prisoners in 1748; there were 5400 by 1789, and 16,000 by the end of Napoleon's rule. When the English reformer John Howard visited the Toulon *bagne* in 1785–86, he was told that some inmates had been there for forty, fifty, even sixty years. One of them, aged fifty-six, had been there since the age of fourteen, when he was given a life sentence for stealing.[4]

For lesser offenses, banishment from the area of the court's jurisdiction was the commonest penalty; it might be for a term of years or for life. Since other countries also resorted to this easy solution, the effect was a kind of multilateral trade in malefactors. Alternative punishments (sometimes in combination) included whipping, branding, public exposure in the pillory, and, less often, prison terms or monetary fines. Prisons, however, were rarely used for punishment, but were places of detention for arrested or indicted persons awaiting trial; the ordinance of 1670 did not even mention a prison term (except for penal servitude in the galleys) in its list of penalties. Prison as punishment was reserved mainly for women and juveniles whose offenses would, if committed by men, have led to galley service. There were also two special categories of prisoners: debtors incarcerated on the demand of a creditor,[5] and persons detained by a royal order (*lettre de cachet*). These latter unfortunates—victims of court vendettas or family disputes—were locked up without trial or sentence, usually in an old fortress or abbey such as the Bastille, Vincennes, or Mont-Saint-Michel.

Such prisons as existed during the old regime were invariably grim places: "sewers of infection," said Voltaire; "inhuman and indecent," as described in one of the cahiers submitted to the Estates-General in 1789. A Parisian magistrate complained in 1789 that prisoners brought before his court "resembled spectres or cadavers rather than living men"[6]; another in 1783 reported thus on the condition of one inmate who had finally come to trial:

> The prisoner remained recumbent night and day, possessing neither trousers nor stockings nor shoes, deprived of heat for two winters, lacking fresh air, wine, and adequate nourishment, tightly confined by iron bars and locks, exposed to the most intense cold, and for three years, whether healthy or ill, denied the right to present himself for confession.[7]

Over the years, some officials had made sporadic efforts to correct the worst abuses. The drafters of the ordinance of 1670 had discussed prison conditions, but without result. The *parlement* of Paris tried again in 1717, ordering that the sexes be separated, that prisoners be provided with bread and water and with clean straw for beds, and that jailkeepers be forbidden to charge inmates for special amenities. In fact, nothing of consequence changed. When the Petit Châtelet prison in the heart of Paris was demolished in 1783, Parisians had their first chance to observe how suspects had been housed for centuries: the dank subterranean cells, below the water level of the nearby Seine, resembled tombs rather than living quarters for human beings.[8] And in 1788 they could read the newly translated work of the English reformer John Howard, who set forth in sober detail the record of his visits to dozens of prisons throughout France.

Some Frenchmen justified the dreadful state of the prisons on the ground that living conditions for a great many free citizens were not much better. (This latter argument was to be echoed frequently throughout the nineteenth and into the twentieth century.) But there were other grave flaws in the traditional system of criminal justice, flaws less easy to explain away. They included the class character of justice, which ensured special treatment for privileged offenders; the slow and costly nature of the judicial process; the often arbitrary and capricious nature of judgments, especially in the lower courts; the persistence of jurisdictional conflicts in a system that lacked an ordered hierarchy of courts; and the want of a clear and uniform legal code. Indeed, Voltaire was led to remark ironically that a traveler in France changed his law code more often than his horses.[9]

Yet until the eighteenth century, there was no serious or generalized protest against the system of criminal justice. Law and order was, after all, a condition to be valued by those Frenchmen who had property or privilege to protect; and it was valued also by those who possessed little but who feared for their personal safety. In Paris before the eighteenth century, police protection was still rudimentary, and the streets were dangerous after dark. The countryside was even less effectively policed, and many regions were infested (especially in periods of famine) by roving bands of vagrants and beggars who preyed on isolated farmsteads and extorted food and shelter from the peasants. Brigandage was endemic in certain mountainous or forested areas, so that travel involved risk to both property and life. In a society where, despite the splendors of the court and the brilliant culture of the capital, the manners of the common folk were rude and the struggle for survival a desperate reality, it is easy to understand why violent crime was common and why its severe repression was demanded by all those who called themselves *les honnêtes gens*. True, this attitude was counterbalanced by a strain of popular sympathy for the local poor and for wanderers down on their luck. A kind of informal system of charity operated in much of rural France; peasants shared what little they had with vagrants and gave them shelter in a corner of the barn. Indeed, at times a sense of common humanity and of resentment toward authority caused the small peasant to feel a closer bond with the vagrant than with state officials, who were often seen as rapacious oppressors rather than protectors. There was even an undercurrent of admiration for certain social deviants— notably those colorful leaders of roving bands who became heroes of popular literature. Yet it was more often the poor and the weak rather than the wealthy and powerful who suffered from criminal depredations; and the poor and weak therefore saw virtues in a harsh law-and-order system. Evil men, like dangerous animals, were generally believed to deserve what they got.

Nevertheless, a few lonely voices of protest did begin to question the system toward the end of the seventeenth century, and they were to swell into a resonant chorus by the mid-eighteenth century. At first, their principal target was the use of judicial torture for obtaining confessions. As far back as Montaigne's day, that practice had already drawn criticism on utilitarian grounds. Montaigne, ex-magistrate and moralist, had pointed out that torture was an ineffective way to separate the guilty from the innocent. Some of the framers of the ordinance of 1670 had shared this opinion, but they were outvoted. A provincial magistrate, Augustin Nicolas of Dijon, boldly espoused Montaigne's view. Why, he asked, should anyone imagine that the ability to resist pain was a sign of innocence? The abolition of judicial torture, Nicolas admitted, might permit some rascals to escape punishment, since French rules of proof required a confession unless there were two corroborative eye-witnesses. One eye-witness constituted only half-proof, and circumstantial evidence was given little credence. Yet a Christian's duty, Nicolas argued, would be as well served by sparing some innocent persons as by ensuring punishment of the guilty.[10]

Criticism of judicial torture continued sporadically during the first half of the eighteenth century, and other themes of protest were added as well. Montesquieu, in his *Persian Letters* (1721), broadened the issue to include the general brutality of punishments, and in *The Spirit of the Laws* (1748) he developed this idea into a full frontal attack on the crime-control system. Harsh penalties, he contended, did not serve as the best deterrent to crime; experience in the most enlightened countries proved that moderate ones were just as effective. Indeed, in a nation that had not been brutalized by savage repression, the infamy of conviction for crime would be enough to deter most offenders. Certainty of punishment was a better deterrent than severity. Punishments should be varied to fit the crime, and should bear some analogy to the offense committed. Even more original was Montesquieu's contention that any enlightened government should concern itself more with the prevention than with the punishment of crime. But his concept of prevention was narrowly rational; he advocated laws so simple and precise that they would be generally understood by all citizens, and would leave no room for arbitrary judgments by the courts.[11] Montesquieu's ideas were to recur, with further elaboration, in Diderot's *Encyclopédie* during the 1750s. The encyclopedists added the idea that punishments should vary not only according to the nature of the crime but also according to the particular circumstances surrounding it. This suggestion anticipated by more than a century such conceptions as extenuating circumstances and "individualized penalties."

But the real surge of interest in the reform of criminal justice was to come in the 1760s with the publication of Beccaria's essay *Dei delitti e della pene* (1764; French edition 1765), and with Voltaire's conversion to the cause. Voltaire's interest had been lukewarm until it was aroused in 1762 by the Calas affair. Jean Calas, a Protestant, was accused of having strangled his son when the latter abjured his faith in favor of Catholicism; the father's contention that the son had committed suicide was rejected by the court, and Calas was broken on the wheel. Voltaire's passionate crusade to clear Calas's name was inspired mainly by his intense dislike of religious bigotry, but it developed into an attack on current criminal procedures—notably the secrecy that shrouded the investigation and trial, and the obvious lack of safeguards for the defendant.

Voltaire's new concern about the malfunctioning of justice led him to greet Beccaria's treatise with enthusiasm. The young Italian aristocrat (he was only twenty-six when he wrote the essay) had received a traditional Jesuit education, but in the process he had immersed himself in the writing of the *philosophes*; his treatise summed up their outlook in lapidary prose. Society's effort to control crime, Beccaria argued, must be balanced by a concern for the rights of the accused. The principle of punishment only on the basis of an existing law (*nulla poena sine lege*) must be absolute. There must be an end to arbitrary detention before trial, to the secrecy of legal proceedings, and to social inequalities before the law. Judgment should be by one's peers, as in the English jury system. The gravity of a crime should be measured solely by the injury done to society; the only purpose of punishment should be to prevent the culprit from repeating his offense and to deter others by example. A precise calculus of pain and pleasure should ensure that the pain of punishment would barely exceed the advantage gained by the crime; any excess of punishment beyond this minimal level would be both "superfluous" and "tyrannical." Cruel penalties, including torture, should be abolished; so should capital punishment, but only because it was "neither necessary nor useful." Judicial torture was a remnant of barbarism; it assumed guilt even before sentencing. Certainty rather than severity of punishment was the true deterrent.

For Beccaria, prevention rather than punishment should be the central goal. The path to prevention lay through simplifying and codifying the laws, reforming the magistracy, educating the citizenry, establishing a system of rewards for virtuous conduct, and ensuring that punishment be quick, certain, and just. His position reflected the rationalist temper of the age: it rejected tradition as a guide and left no room for the idea that criminal motivation might sometimes be irrational or abnormal in nature. Nor did it show any awareness of the possible social origins of crime. One might question, too, the depth of Beccaria's humane instincts. Although he attacked excessive and cruel punishments, it was on utilitarian rather than humane grounds. Laws should not only be clear and simple, but should inspire a "salutary fear." So should punishments. The most effective deterrent is not "the terrible but momentary sight of a rascal's death but the sustained example of a man deprived of his liberty, transformed into a kind of beast of burden, recompensing society, through a lifetime of hard labor, for the injury that he has done to society." As for thieves too poor to pay a fine, it was plain justice to impose a kind of penal slavery during which the culprit's person and work would belong "absolutely" to society.[12] The humane impulse, even in the Enlightenment era, evidently had its limits.

Beccaria's essay had an immediate and powerful impact in France; and during the next quarter-century there was a steady drumfire of reform agitation. The subject became a popular one with French and Swiss learned academies, which organized frequent essay contests on such topics as "How to soften the rigor of French criminal laws without endangering public security." Voltaire and Diderot lent their prestige to the cause, though they quibbled a bit on certain details of Beccaria's argument. Since a hanged man is good for nothing, wrote Voltaire, why not condemn able-bodied offenders to hard labor for life on public works or transport them to the colonies where, forced to work, "they will be transformed into honest folk?"[13] Rousseau's stance was as usual more ambiguous. Frequent punishments, he declared, were evidence of a government's weakness; "there is no miscreant who can't be rendered good for something."[14] But malefactors who violated the social contract were dangerous to society; as public enemies and traitors to their country, they deserved the death penalty or exile for life.

The activists who picked up the Enlightenment view of criminal-justice reform included not only marginal intellectuals like the journalist J.-P. Brissot and the physician Jean-Paul Marat, but also some successful members of the establishment. One such figure was Joseph Servan, the twenty-seven-year-old magistrate whose oratorical talent led his colleagues in Grenoble to select him in 1766 as keynote speaker for the opening of the new court session. Servan, drawing his inspiration from Beccaria and Rousseau, made his oration a stirring manifesto for change.[15] In 1781 F.-M. Vermeil, a lawyer attached to the *parlement* of Paris, published a sober work that embodied all of Beccaria's principles except the abolition of capital punishment. "The preferable punishment, even for grave offenses, would at the same time cause the least suffering and make the deepest impression on the multitude."[16] An even more eminent figure was Charles Dupaty, son of a royal bureaucrat, who rose to be presiding officer of the Bordeaux *parlement* but resigned that post in frustration when his colleagues blocked reform. In 1786 Dupaty went onto the offensive with a pamphlet attacking a recent court judgment by which three convicted offenders were to be broken on the wheel. Dupaty's impassioned appeal was addressed to the king; it urged the monarch in the name of humanity to transform the system of criminal justice. "Sire . . . , do not believe those who tell you that it is dangerous to diminish the respect for law by open criticism—as if anything could dishonor those laws more than the mildew of barbarism that covers them, or the innocent blood that drips from them."[17] Dupaty's pamphlet was burned by the authorities, but two years later he returned to the attack. "How is it possible," he demanded, "that the most refined nation in Europe whose mores are the gentlest and the most accommodating, should still have laws . . . suited to a people plunged into the last degree of ignorance and barbarism?" Dupaty called for drastic changes in criminal procedure, an end to excessive and cruel punishments, and a codification of the laws to ensure "an exact proportion between crimes and punishments." For offenders who might benefit by a second chance, he proposed transportation to the colonies; for the few incorrigibles, why not sell them as slaves to the North Africans or the Turks?[18]

Among the crusaders for reform, there was more interest in altering procedures and penalties than in seeking out the causes of crime. Yet the idea that crime might have social roots did begin to seep through in a limited way. The august *parlement* of Paris, in a memorial to the king, blamed the unbearable tax burden for at least some crime. No doubt the *parlement* had ulterior motives; it was engaged in a protracted struggle for power with the king's entourage. But there were others as well who suggested a possible relationship between inequality, misery, and crime: the jurist Montyon, the journalist Brissot, the pamphleteer Marat, and the observer of Parisian mores Louis-Sébastien Mercier. Brissot, in his prize memoir addressed to the Academy of Châlons-sur-Marne, drew on Montesquieu and Beccaria to argue that governments should focus on prevention rather than punishment. Man is not born an enemy of society; it is circumstances that make him so: indigence, ill fortune. To make citizens happy is to prevent the birth of crime. Build hospitals and asylums, give aid to the poor, purify mores, allow the free expression of public opinion, improve popular education—with such reforms, you will hardly need a penal code. Some criminals, like venomous insects, will still turn up, but "they should be reformed rather than punished, conserved and not destroyed."[19] Louis-Sébastien Mercier, whose colorful *Tableau de Paris* fascinated French readers in the 1780s (and who was to be elected a member of the Convention in 1792), found in the contrast between luxury and misery the source of most crime. A kind of chronic civil war resulted: "When palaces proliferate, it's necessary to build vast prisons." Punishment was nothing more than useless vengeance, so long as the causes of crime remained.[20]

Had the idea of reforming the system of crime control penetrated by 1789 beyond the educated elite, to become a matter of general public interest? The evidence permits no clear answer; eighteenth-century mass opinion on any subject is largely a matter of inference from inadequate data. We do know that when the call for an Estates-General went out in 1788, the *cahiers de doléances* summarizing the grievances of the time gave a prominent place to the flaws in criminal justice. The most frequent demands were for a clear and uniform law code; an end to such abuses as the *lettres de cachet*; protection of defendants' rights, notably through open and public proceedings; milder and more humane penalties; more rapid and less expensive justice; and even in some cases the election of judges and introduction of the jury system. It is hardly surprising that the issue was one of the first to come before the National Assembly in 1789. But the cahiers were, of course, drafted and adopted by members of the educated elite; they provide no clue to what French commoners were thinking.

We do know also that the educated elite was by no means united on the need for criminal-justice reform. As the reform movement gathered strength, the partisans of law and order fought back energetically in defense of the traditional system and its central bulwark, the ordinance of 1670. Spearheading the traditionalists' campaign was the jurist and royal counselor P.-F. Muyart de Vouglans. Muyart's reputation rested on his *Institutes of Criminal Law* (1757), which won quick acceptance as the standard commentary on the existing system of justice. Muyart reacted at once to Beccaria's treatise; in a pamphlet published in 1767, he challenged and ridiculed almost every aspect of Beccaria's argument. It was shocking, he declared, to find anyone pleading on behalf of "that portion of humanity that is its scourge and destroyer." Beccaria's ideas were "dangerous for the Government, for Mores, and for Religion." "Systems born of a spirit of contradiction and innovation" are bound to fail. No substitute for capital punishment —not even perpetual slavery—would be either effective or just. Judicial torture, which was carefully circumscribed by the ordinance of 1670, was absolutely essential; for every innocent victim of the procedure, one could cite a thousand examples of guilty men who, without torture, would have gone unpunished. Beccaria's idea of equal punishments for high and low alike was dismissed as "dangerous and absurd." Indeed, French jurisprudence had reached "a degree of perfection" that made it a model for many other nations.[21] Muyart persisted in his anti-reform campaign until the eve of the Great Revolution; "Leniency," he wrote in 1781, "breeds crime; harsh punishments alone will diminish it."[22] Muyart's opinions were echoed by a battery of other royal jurists; Attorney-General Louis Séguier went so far as to declare that the French system of justice was not only the most perfect yet achieved, but represented the highest stage of perfection attainable by mortal man.[23] "If you have read one French *criminaliste*," jeered the reformer Brissot, "you have read them all."[24]

The most emotional issue in the controversy between traditionalists and reformers—the practice of judicial torture to extort confessions—was to some extent a false issue. Muyart insisted that the ordinance of 1670 had rigorously restricted that practice, confining it to culprits against whom there was already a strong presumption of guilt. Recent scholarship suggests that resort to judicial torture was in fact dying out during the eighteenth century, largely due to changes in the law of proof that made it possible to convict offenders on the basis of circumstantial evidence, thus bypassing the old requirement of two corroborative eye-witnesses or a confession by the accused.[25] The royal administration itself gave legal force to this changing practice; in 1780 an edict abolished the *question préparatoire* (torture used to induce a confession), and in 1788 a further edict outlawed the *question préalable* (the second round of judicial torture, designed to reveal accomplices). On this issue, therefore, the Enlightenment reformers were beating a dying horse.

Indeed, the royal administration showed signs of slow and reluctant retreat all along the line. In 1780 the king forbade the use of the frightful underground *cachots* at Bicêtre prison, to which some unfortunates had been consigned for years on end.[26] And in May 1788, a royal declaration ordered a series of immediate reforms—notably procedural changes to protect defendants' rights, and a reorganization of the court system to simplify its structure, reduce jurisdictional conflicts, and make justice more rapid and less costly. In the preamble to this declaration, the king declared that the time had come to overhaul the ordinance of 1670, and "to seek all means of reducing the severity of punishment without compromising public order and general security. . . . Our unalterable purpose is to prevent crime through the certainty and the example of punishment; to reassure the innocent . . . , to make punishment inevitable by eliminating that excess of rigor that leads men to tolerate crime rather than denounce it . . . , and to punish malefactors with all the moderation that humanity demands and that the interests of society will permit. . . ." The king's minister, presenting this declaration to the *parlement* of Paris, frankly attributed the action to the pressure of public opinion: "The entire nation," he declared, "is calling for this important legislative action . . . , and His Majesty has resolved in council to accede to the wishes of his people."[27]

No doubt the royal officials, in speaking of "the entire nation," really meant the active elite that had been urging such reforms for a generation. The edict, in any case, was a classic example of too little and much too late; before it could take effect, the Revolution had swept it away. Furthermore, the traditional system had already been in process of change for a generation, despite the efforts of law-and-order jurists like Muyart. The magistrate P.-L. Roederer, reminiscing in 1798 about the latter years of the *ancien régime*, recalled that Beccaria's treatise "had so changed the spirit of the old criminal courts in France that ten years before the Revolution they had been completely transformed. All the young magistrates— and I can attest to it since I was one of them—handed down their judgments more in accordance with this work than with the laws."[28] It would be the task of the Great Revolution to speed and expand a process of change that was already under way.

It is usually easier to narrate what happened than to explain why it happened. Why did the traditional crime-control system come under attack in the mid-eighteenth century, inaugurating the modern era of controversy and experimentation in matters of crime and punishment?

The commonest answer, by those historians who have offered

any answer at all, has been that the spread of humanist and rationalist ideas from the Renaissance onward gradually produced a deepened sensibility, a new morality that placed greater value on the individual's rights and on the rationality of institutions. This development, which culminated in the eighteenth-century Enlightenment, has been viewed as a largely autonomous process—a change in attitudes and values that may have been influenced by socioeconomic factors, but that developed its own inner dynamic as the new outlook penetrated the consciousness of a reflective and increasingly sensitive European elite.

In our day, explanations of this sort are seen as unsophisticated and even simple-minded; we have become conditioned to the idea that changes in fundamental value-systems are never autonomous, but are mere reflections of deeper changes in the substructure of society. Any modern historian must, therefore, look further for a more persuasive explanation.

One possible hypothesis might be that a growing sense of security, a decline in the intensity of social fear, led Frenchmen (and other Europeans) to take a more dispassionate view of the problem of crime and to consider more humane procedures. Such an hypothesis would require evidence of a noticeable decline in the incidence of crime—or at least of a widespread belief, justified or not, in such a decline. If there were such a reducton in the crime rate, it would presumably be the product of a general improvement in the quality of life and a consequent refinement of manners—or, alternatively, it might result from more effective policing.

The piecemeal evidence now available does not offer much support for this hypothesis. It is true that the eighteenth century was a time of economic growth and enrichment, though progress was jerky and did not bring equal benefits to all segments of society. It is true also that the death rate fell and life expectancy lengthened: fewer children were left fatherless or motherless, to join the population of drifters and "the army of crime."[29] But there is no convincing evidence that improved conditions brought a decline in the overall crime rate or a lessened degree of social fear. In recent years, a number of historians have begun the arduous task of sifting through surviving court records, along with the records of poor relief and police activity. Their findings to date are still fragmentary, and their conclusions often ambiguous or even contradictory. The nearest approach to consensus is on the changing pattern of crime, with offenses against property rising while offenses against persons declined. Several microscopic studies focused on Paris or on provincial areas show that after mid-century a large majority of court cases were concerned with theft rather than personal violence.[30] But this changing pattern was not the universal rule; some provinces still showed a persistently high level of crimes against persons, and it is likely that much rural violence continued to be accepted as "normal" and went unreported.[31] As for trends in the overall crime rate, generalizations are even more risky. Magistrates steadily complained about the rising case load in the courts, but this can be interpreted in a variety of ways. At least it does not suggest an absolute decline in the crime rate and a growing sense of security.

It is true, of course, that the incidence of crime and the level of social fear do not always follow the same trajectory. Waves of panic about the breakdown of public order do not always reflect reality. Public emotions can be consciously manipulated by men in power or in search of power; the evidence can be faulty or misunderstood; or a deep collective neurosis may find its outlet by fixing on a supposed crime threat. In most such cases, social fear probably outruns the reality. But there may be times when the reverse phenomenon occurs—when social fear lags behind the incidence of crime.

For eighteenth-century France, the evidence once again is inconclusive. The contemporary observer Louis-Sébastien Mercier asserted in 1783 that "the streets of Paris are safe both night and day, save for occasional incidents"; and a modern scholar tells us that eighteenth-century Paris was generally regarded as the safest of European cities.[32] In the same vein, Louis Chevalier contrasts pre-Revolutionary Paris with what he sees as the much more dangerous city of the 1830s: before 1789, he declares, Paris may have been "unhealthy and brutal . . . , but it was not a Paris threatened by crime and haunted by fear."[33] And in the provinces, Emmanuel Le Roy Ladurie suggests that by mid-century the large marauding bands of outlaws had disappeared, leaving only small and less dangerous groups.[34]

But if there was indeed a growing sense of security after

mid-century, it was apparently confined to Paris—and even there the evidence is shaky. Mercier spoke of an orderly Paris but also claimed that the authorities managed to suppress most news of violent crimes that might terrify the population.[35] In the provinces, public concern about the crime problem seems to have been persistent or even on the rise. Officials there continued to report a climate of widespread insecurity, and a steady flow of pamphlets and memoirs commissioned by various learned academies focused on the threat posed by hordes of vagrants and beggars. The magistrate G. Le Trosne, in a memoir dated 1764, called this "the most terrible plague for the countryside; they are voracious insects who infect and devour it." Virtual outlaws, "they live in society without being members of it"; they form a breeding ground for thieves and assassins. In some areas, Le Trosne declared, their exactions equalled or exceeded those of the tax-gatherers. He urged tougher policing, and even the use of bounties for the capture of outlaws, as was done for the slaughter of wolves. The only effective punishment for vagrants was a life sentence to the galleys, for such "ferocious beasts" could not be tamed by gentleness.[36] Yet even a law-and-order advocate like Le Trosne was affected by the reform spirit of the time. In another pamphlet a dozen years later, he echoed Beccaria's call for fundamental changes in the crime-control system.[37]

The government's response to the wave of social fear among rural Frenchmen was to step up repression. In 1764 it ordered that able-bodied vagabonds aged sixteen to seventy be sent to the galleys rather than banished, and in 1767 it directed that places of detention called *dépôts de mendicité* be set up throughout France.[38] Some *dépôts* were created, and sentences to the galleys became more frequent for a time; but the new measures had only marginal effect. The rural police (the *maréchaussée*) was too undermanned to provide consistent enforcement; and a downturn in the economy during the 1770s and 1780s put more vagrants onto the roads and increased peasant fears. In some areas the locals organized vigilante patrols and even formed convoys through dangerous sectors; false alarms of "brigand bands" about to pounce were frequent.[39]

The government's turn toward increased repression and the growing sense of social fear in rural France coincided strangely with the rising momentum of the reform movement. Beccaria and Le Trosne published their quite different essays in the same year

(1764). None of the reformers, however, based their arguments on the idea that crime was on the decline. Their thesis, in most cases, was that harshness was ineffective as well as inhumane, and that a turn toward a milder and more equitable system would check the rising tide. Judges would be more likely to punish, citizens would be more supportive, if penalties were seen to be fair and just. It seems clear, in any case, that the reform movement cannot be traced to a decline in the crime rate or a lessened public sense of insecurity.

Marxist scholars have advanced a second hypothesis: that the reform movement was merely a by-product of socioeconomic change. "Every system of production," according to two Marxist analysts, "tends to discover punishments which correspond to productive relationships. . . . The origin and fate of penal systems, the use or avoidance of specific punishments, and the intensity of penal practices . . . are determined by social forces, above all by economic and then fiscal forces."[40] The motive of the Enlightenment reformers was, quite simply, the urge to protect the interests of the rising bourgeoisie. That social class had not yet achieved political power; its goal therefore was to protect itself against arbitrary actions by the royal courts. "The pioneers of reform were . . . concerned first and foremost with limiting the power of the state to punish . . . by creating fixed rules and subjecting the authorities to rigid control."[41] But in addition, the bourgeoisie wanted more effective repression of those lawbreakers who threatened property or the social order; it "was more interested in the completeness, rapidity, and reliability of criminal justice than in its severity." Beccaria, like other reformers of his era, wanted to "humanize" punishment because he feared that the continued use of brutal and unequal penalties might boomerang and bring on social revolution.[42]

There is an attractive simplicity and an apparent logic about this thesis, especially in an age that is inclined to believe that human motives are never what they are professed to be. The dominant value-systems of any epoch are surely connected in some way with the socioeconomic realities of the time and with the interests of those who possess political and economic power. The eighteenth-century reformers were clearly concerned about the security of property and about the costs and hazards of an arbitrary, inefficient system of criminal justice. Yet the Marxist hypothesis suffers from the lopsidedness that marks all reductionist theories, and from an exaggerated confidence that their theory can detect "real" motives. Single causes rarely suffice to explain human behavior in all its complexity. If the rising bourgeoisie supported drastic changes in the crime-control system, that support found no vocal expression and was mild at best; spokesmen for commerce and industry, then as now, showed more interest in other spheres of reform. None of the leading advocates of criminal-justice reform came from the business class. The Marxist hypothesis thus seems more plausible than persuasive.

A third hypothesis, even more ingenious and much more complex in nature, has recently been advanced by the French philosopher-historian Michel Foucault in his study called *Surveiller et punir: naissance de la prison*. For Foucault, as for the Marxists, the Enlightenment reformers were impelled by bourgeois interests clothed in humanitarian phrases. The reformers' concern was the rising threat to property manifested in the changing crime pattern from violence to theft, and the belief that harsh punishments caused magistrates to acquit offenders and led the masses to sympathize with criminals as victims of the system. The old ritual executions accompanied by torture no longer frightened people (if, indeed, they had ever done so) ; they produced a kind of solidarity between criminal and populace, and sometimes turned into violent demonstrations of hostility toward the authorities. The bourgeoisie, in Foucault's version, was also determined to close those legal loopholes ("margins of tolerated illegalities") that favored the poorer classes, and to widen those loopholes that would be useful for enterprising businessmen.

Even more fundamental, according to Foucault, was the bourgeoisie's urge to create what he calls "the disciplinary society," adapted to the needs of an industrial age. Individuals would be transformed into regimented and docile robots, largely shorn of their human qualities. The process of creating this new society and this new type of man had been under way for a century, through such institutions as the hospital, the barracks, the school, and the workshop; after 1789 the prison would emerge as the ultimate capstone of the disciplinary society. And the prison would endure, despite its glaring defects and its chronic failure to rehabilitate offenders or even to reduce crime, because it was useful to the dominant bourgeoisie. The prison, replacing the old public punishments with their elaborate rituals, made it possible to drive a wedge between the working class and the so-called "criminal class," thus breaking the link of solidarity between them.[43]

Foucault's hypothesis, unlike that of the Marxists, avoids the appearance of reductionism by being made part of an elaborate and ingenious theory of cultural change. The dazzling brilliance of his work has made him a cult-figure, and his ideas are echoed in a number of recent monographs on the crime problem. The trouble is that while complex theoretical structures in the hard sciences can be tested, those in the human sciences or in cultural history usually cannot. Foucault boldly asserts his ideas as facts, and just as boldly attributes motives to the criminal-justice reformers. If one accepts his analysis of the eighteenth-century reform movement, it must be more on the basis of faith (and admiration for intellectual brilliance) than on the basis of compelling evidence.

Perhaps it is likewise a matter of faith to return to an older orthodoxy—the traditional hypothesis that a gradual and partially autonomous change in values occurred in France and Europe during early modern times, culminating in what we call the Enlightenment and initially affecting a segment of the educated elite. Undoubtedly the spread of these "humanist" and "rationalist" values had a structural base; they were connected, in some complex way, with the socioeconomic changes of the time. But to take Enlightenment ideas as no more than a reflection, a dependent variable, of economic change is to take hypothesis for fact. It is more likely that the relationship between values and socioeconomic base, then as now, was reciprocal—that base and value-system combine to shape a society's view of man and the world.

Condorcet, a leading Enlightenment thinker, offered this definition of the humane impulse: "a feeling of tender, active compassion for all the sufferings that affect the human spirit, and of horror toward everything in our public institutions that . . . adds new sufferings to those to which all flesh is heir."[44] Such phrases, in our tough-minded age, strike us as lachrymose and hypocritical effusions suited only for the tender-minded and the soft-headed. Even in the Enlightenment era, they represented only an outer fringe of the movement for criminal-justice reform. Most of the reformers took a more restrained view of the possibilities of humane punishment, and operated mainly on utilitarian principles. Beccaria's substitute for the death penalty—perpetual slavery—hardly reflected a profoundly humane sentiment. But if the humane impulse fell far short of Condorcet's definition, the Enlightenment reformers' campaign for change did constitute the first major challenge to a traditional system of brutally repressive justice. It was the initial phase in a debate that has not yet ended, in France or in the Western world.

# II
## Laboring on a Volcano
### 1789–1814

> Let these houses of blood, misery, shame and corruption vanish from the surface of France, let these premature tombs restore to the light of day the unfortunates buried within them, let the law be inflexible and no longer barbarous, and let society, following nature's example, be an indulgent mother who corrects and pardons but does not destroy her children when hope remains that they can be saved.
>
> MIRABEAU, reporting to the National Assembly
> on prison reform (1790)

> The Penal Code of 1791 was undoubtedly a magnificent monument raised to humanity and to reason upon the ruins of barbarous institutions; but it must be admitted that its authors labored on a volcano, and that they were not always able to hear the voice of reason.
>
> COMTE RÉAL, reporting to the Corps Législatif
> on Napoleon's Penal Code (1810)

REVOLUTIONS suffer from a built-in paradox. They break what Walter Bagehot once called the cake of custom, and permit bold innovations in the rules and mechanisms that govern human societies. But they also shake and temporarily weaken the foundations upon which the new institutions rest; and even innovations require some stable base if they are to survive. Thus the very conditions that open the way to drastic social experiments pose an immediate threat to the success of those experiments. One is reminded of the

French ironist who, reacting to nineteenth-century lamentations about the evil effects of urbanization, exclaimed: "How many problems might have been avoided if only the cities had been built in the countryside!" The same paradoxical logic may apply to reforms adopted in a revolutionary era when the reformers find themselves "laboring on a volcano."

When the Estates-General convened in May 1789, the opening speeches by royal officials showed that even the king's top advisers were reconciled to the idea of fairly fundamental changes in the traditional system of crime control. Barentin, the official in charge of the judicial establishment, spoke of the need "to make penalties more proportionate to offenses, and to rely on the offender's sense of shame as a surer and more decisive deterrent than punishment." The king's chief minister Jacques Necker, toward the end of his interminable speech, mentioned plans for "the amelioration of civil and criminal laws; a softening of penalties; a reduction in the costs of justice," and a series of reforms designed to speed and simplify the judicial process. But both officials warned the assemblage that such reforms were not in the competence of the Estates-General; they were matters, rather, for bureaucratic action.[1] Events, however, had already outrun the bureaucracy; the Estates-General, shortly transformed into the National Constituent Assembly, seized the initiative and plunged at once into the task of transforming the system of criminal justice.

The basic principles of the new system were promptly enshrined in the Declaration of the Rights of Man. "No man can be accused, arrested, or detained except in cases determined by the law, and according to the forms prescribed by the law. . . . The law must establish only such penalties as are strictly and clearly necessary, and no one may be punished except on the basis of a law established and made public prior to the offence. . . . Every man being presumed innocent until he has been declared guilty, if it is judged indispensable to arrest him, any severity beyond that necessary to ensure his detention must be rigorously repressed by the law."[2] These guarantees were based on the new principle of equality before the law, and on the tenet that "the law has the right to forbid only those actions that are harmful to society." The echo of Beccaria's essay and of the eighteenth-century *philosophes* resounded clearly through the Assembly's manifesto.

Assembly committees were appointed at once to draft criminal codes and to study such special problems as the *lettres de cachet* and the ancient plagues of vagrancy and begging. Pending their reports, the legislators adopted a series of interim measures to correct the worst of the old abuses. To protect the rights of accused persons, they ordered that criminal investigations and trials be conducted publicly, with the defendant assured the right of counsel throughout. They abolished the practice of "chain responsibility," by which the dishonor visited upon a convict might be legally extended to cover his whole family; and they put an end to confiscating the property of major offenders—a procedure that had quite literally visited the sins of the father upon his children. They ordered that all victims of arbitrary imprisonment who were currently confined should be set free within six weeks, and that the sentences of all currently detained long-term convicts be reduced to a maximum of fifteen years. They provisionally suspended the functioning of the provostial courts, which had been the judicial arm of the provincial police (the *maréchaussée*) and which had exercised final jurisdiction, without appeal, over certain categories of offenders (vagrants, beggars, ex-convicts) and certain types of offenses (highway robbery, counterfeiting, treason). The provostial courts, summary in their procedures and ruthless in their judgments, had become one of the central mechanisms in the old regime's crime-control system.[3]

More permanent reforms were hammered out during 1790–91; they were embodied in laws of August 16, 1790 (on reorganization of the court system), September 16, 1791 (on criminal procedure), and September 25, 1791 (the Penal Code).[4] Long and impassioned debate preceded the adoption of these new codes; it demonstrated both the profound impact of Enlightenment ideas on the legislators and the sharp differences that persisted on crucial matters of both principle and practice. The least controversial reform was the restructuring of the court system. In place of the traditional tangle of jurisdictions, a simple and coherent hierarchy was established: in each canton a justice of the peace (empowered to arbitrate disputes, to order arrests, and to rule on minor offenses), and in each department a criminal court. Judges and public prosecutors would no longer inherit or purchase their office but would be elected. Responsibility for ferreting out and reporting crimes would henceforth be left to individual citizens; the *gendarmerie nationale* (the new label for the old *maréchaussée*) would confine itself to arresting persons accused by a victim or witness.[5]

The Code of Criminal Procedure (law of September 16, 1791) produced far more controversy, especially on the idea of jury trial. Adrien Duport, a former magistrate of the Paris *parlement* and chief drafter of the bill, argued forcefully for the adoption of the jury in both criminal and civil cases; he and his supporters on the progressive wing of the Assembly pointed to the English example as proof that the jury system was not only workable in practice but was also a mark of a nation's enlightenment. A vocal minority of legislators put up strong resistance, warning against dangerous foreign innovations and urging that the historic ordinance of 1670 be retained with appropriate amendments. In the end a compromise was reached: the jury would be introduced in serious criminal cases but not in civil cases.[6]

The Code's section dealing with prisons, on the other hand, sailed through without discussion. It called for a national network of prisons that would rigorously separate persons awaiting trial from convicted criminals serving sentences. To corral them together, it was argued, would be likely to corrupt young and possibly innocent detainees. All prisons would be inspected at least twice weekly by municipal officials, to ensure that they were clean, healthful, and secure. Guards would be chosen for their irreproachable morality, and would be required to treat prisoners in gentle and humane fashion.[7] The contrast between these prescriptions for the future and the harsh reality of past practice was breathtaking. The legislators were surely aware that they were prescribing not merely a set of reforms but a quantum leap from one age of penal practice to another. Their unanimity did credit to their good intentions if not to their realism.

The central importance of prison reform became more obvious during discussion of the new Penal Code, which proposed to adopt imprisonment as the standard technique of punishment. The committee's rapporteur for the Code, L.-M. Le Pelletier de Saint-Fargeau (*"ci-devant de Saint-Fargeau"*, as he was listed in the official records) was, like Adrien Duport, a former magistrate of the *parlement* of Paris—one of those who had most thoroughly absorbed the Enlightenment spirit. Le Pelletier prefaced his long and impassioned report with a dramatic catalog of the abuses of old regime justice—that collection of "incoherent provisions without system or unity, adopted at different epochs, mainly in response to circumstances of the moment . . . , whose ferocious absurdity was tempered only by another abuse—arbitrary interpretation and modification by the judges." The Assembly's goal, declared Le Pelletier (again echoing Beccaria), should be to simplify and humanize the system of crime control, and to prevent rather than punish crime. For a start, the list of crimes should be pruned back drastically. The criminality of an act should be determined by two simple criteria: its immorality and its danger to society. The nature of punishment should also be shaped by two simple tests: will it deter potential offenders, and will it rehabilitate the guilty? Since inhumane penalties were likely to do neither, they should be abolished: capital punishment should go, along with the galleys, branding, whipping, and banishment. The galleys were not only inhumane but ineffective as well; they were not really deterrent since few citizens could observe what went on there, and they diverted convict labor from more useful public works. Banishment was completely irrational, since it amounted to no more than an exchange of criminals between nations or jurisdictions, and thus spread the "infection" of crime.[8]

In the committee's simplified and rationalized scheme of punishments, prison would henceforth become the standard mechanism. That decision was based not so much on Enlightment doctrine as on pragmatic considerations. The eighteenth-century reformers had not argued for imprisonment as a substitute for traditional penalties. On the contrary: they had viewed prisons as symbols of arbitrary injustice and sewers of infection, whose only proper function should be the temporary detention of persons awaiting trial or of vagrants considered dangerous to public security. But if all of the traditional penalties were to be swept away as inhumane or ineffective, a practical problem emerged: what penalty except imprisonment could take their place? Deportation to a distant penal colony was one possible alternative, already practiced by the English. Monetary fines would bear unequally on different classes, and would therefore be unjust. Release into the custody of the offender's family or village community would have seemed too utopian in that era. If imprisonment struck no one as ideal, it had at least one negative virtue: the alternatives were few, and they seemed even more flawed.

Other motives, more complex and less respectable, have recently been suggested to explain the sudden "birth of the prison" in this era. Some Marxist scholars have argued that imprisonment was a bourgeois device to provide forced labor for cheap mass production. "Of all the forces that were responsible for the new emphasis upon imprisonment as a punishment, the most important was the profit motive. . . ."[9] The argument rests, however, on doctrine rather than evidence. Some reformers (Voltaire among them) did advocate using convict labor on public works, but at open-air sites rather than in prison workshops. A more elaborate thesis, that of Michel Foucault, links the prison to the emergence of what he calls "the disciplinary society" of the modern age. It was, according to Foucault, one of several social institutions (along with the barracks, the hospital, the school, and the factory) designed to transform free and creative individuals into docile and regimented workers in the bourgeoisie's technological system. As a by-product, it provided the ruling elite of the bourgeois age with a useful category of "delinquents"—ex-convicts who were rejected by society and were therefore available to manage profitable enterprises (such as prostitution and various rackets) outside the law.[10] The theory is both ingenious and unprovable; its aesthetic appeal to intellectuals is perhaps best explained by the semi-ironic remark of one Foucault admirer: "I like fancy footwork." The simpler idea that the reformers saw no workable alternative to the adoption of the prison perhaps calls for little imagination, yet it may nevertheless be true. Sometimes, in human affairs, things are what they seem.

Enlightenment doctrine called for a rational correlation between crimes and penalties, and a mathematically accurate gradation of crimes. "It is essential," declared Le Pelletier, "to punish an offense in the precise proportion that it bears to another offense." Penalties and crimes should also be linked by analogy: "thus physical pain will punish offenses marked by ferocity; hard work will be imposed on the person whose crime springs from sloth; infamy will punish the actions that have been inspired by an abject or degraded soul." More than a touch of the old moral concept of retribution was revealed here, diluting the drafters' utilitarian emphasis on deterrence and rehabilitation. Finally, the committee recommended that the penalty for each offense be fixed and invariable, leaving no scope for judicial capriciousness.[11]

A precise calculus of the gravity of crimes was easier to assert in principle than to work out in practice. Le Pelletier's committee fell back, therefore, on an essentially pragmatic solution, classifying offenses as either *crimes* (felonies), *délits* (misdemeanors), or *contraventions* (petty violations). *Délits* and *contraventions* were to be the business of the justices of the peace, who might order fines or prison sentences of up to two years. *Crimes* would be in the province of the new departmental criminal courts, and would carry prescribed prison terms ranging from two to twenty-four years. Life sentences must be abolished, Le Pelletier explained, because it was essential to leave every prisoner with a glimmer of hope. Convicted prisoners would be required to work, but (except for those sentenced to hard labor) might choose the type of work they preferred; their earnings would be apportioned between the institution, their own immediate need to supplement the basic prison diet, and a reserve for use after release from prison. To reinforce deterrence, convicts would be imprisoned near the scene of their offense, and the public would be admitted to the prison once a month to observe the wages of misconduct. Before entering prison, convicted offenders would be exposed to public view for three days in the town square, tied to a stake and loaded with the chains they would wear in prison.[12]

Although the committee proposed to abolish capital punishment, it felt the need for a substitute that would be equally or more effective as a deterrent. "A prolonged series of painful privations," declared Le Pelletier, "while sparing humanity the horror of tortures, will make a deeper impression on guilty men than a momentary instant of pain." The public likewise would be inspired to "salutary terror" by the spectacle of protracted punishment, whereas the one-day spectacle of execution was quickly forgotten. To this end, the committee proposed to replace capital punishment by what it called *le cachot*: solitary confinement in a pitch-dark cell, body and limbs loaded with chains, "bread, water and straw providing the prisoner with the absolute minimum of nourishment and painful rest." But this new penalty would be "worse than the cruelest death" if not softened a bit; therefore no one should be sentenced to more than twenty-four years of *le cachot*. And after the first few years, the prisoner should be allowed to work in his cell: two days a week at first, then three. On working days, the prisoner's chains would be removed and his diet supplemented; but his solitude would remain complete. Intermediate between this fearsome penalty and ordinary imprisonment would be *la gêne*: solitary confinement in a lighted cell with less burdensome chains, and with work permitted daily—five days alone in the cell, two days in common work with others.[13]

While the committee proposed the prison as the key institution in the new crime-control system, it also opened the door slightly to a second penalty—deportation. The English had long transported petty offenders to the American colonies and had recently substituted Australia for that purpose. The French monarchy had experimented briefly with transportation to Louisiana in 1718-22, but had abandoned the practice because of protests from the *parlements* and from the free colonists in Louisiana.[14] The idea of exporting offenders continued to appeal to some eighteenth-century reformers and to Revolutionary pamphleteers after 1789, and it was picked up rather hesitantly by Le Pelletier's committee. Second offenders, it proposed, would be deported for life after serving their second prison term.[15]

That Le Pelletier's report inspired vigorous and varied dissent in the National Assembly is hardly surprising. Partisans of the traditional system, whose goal was to preserve the ordinance of 1670 with some amendments, found the new code outrageously idealistic; but even those deputies who favored reform were suddenly confronted by a whole battery of issues that had never been seriously discussed in France and that would continue to provoke controversy for generations to come. Partisans of corporal punishments such as whipping and branding insisted on the effectiveness of both practices, but were beaten back by the reformers. Those who favored capital punishment, on the other hand, put up a resolute fight and managed after lengthy debate to retain the death penalty for a shortened list of offenders. Decapitation was chosen as the method of execution, though some legislators favored hanging or strangling. The new "scientific" machine for decapitation, the guillotine, was subsequently adopted and first used in 1792.[16]

Some legislators launched emotional attacks on the principle of imprisonment as the standard punishment; they denounced it as likely to be tyrannical, corrupting, costly, difficult to police, and ineffective as a deterrent. The idea of requiring prisoners to work was also challenged as involving a kind of double punishment, or as a profanation of the sacred character of labor. In the end, Le Pelletier was forced to accept some changes in the committee's draft, though its substance remained intact. *Cachot* punishment was eliminated as too extreme, and this was balanced by making *gêne* somewhat more severe (to require uninterrupted solitary confinement, though without the use of chains). The Code ordered that most offenders would be condemned either to hard labor with ball and chain (*peine des fers*) or to confinement (*réclusion*) in a *maison de force*.[17] As a temporary expedient, the shorebased galleys or *bagnes* were maintained for hard-labor convicts. The temporary, as usual, was to become quasi-permanent: the last seaport *bagne* was not to be liquidated for another eighty years.

The Penal Code of 1791, along with its twin the Code of Criminal Procedure, was greeted with enthusiasm by reform-minded Frenchmen and with apprehension by the traditionalists. Its authors may have nursed exaggerated hopes, yet they recognized that it would not resolve the crime-control problem in one dramatic blow. Le Pelletier, in the peroration of his report on the Code, insisted that the reformers saw it as only a long first step. Penal laws were necessary for any state, he declared. "for crime, that deadly malady of the body social, too often requires a painful and unfortunate remedy; but in politics as in medicine, the art that prevents illness is a thousand times more certain and more beneficial than the art that cures it." Supplementary measures were needed: effective policing, the repression of vagrancy and begging ("the richest source of crimes"), work for the needy and security for the old and infirm. Even more important were long-term goals: to correct France's "monstrous inequality in the contrast between wealth and poverty," and to educate all citizens to make them "free and virtuous." "These useful institutions," he concluded, "can do much more than all our penal laws."[18]

The Great Revolution's reform of the criminal-justice system has been variously judged over the years since 1791. Were its authors farsighted statesmen, woolly visionaries, or hypocritical spokesmen for the propertied elites? All three positions have found vigorous support. Critics have observed, for example, that these men of the Enlightenment showed an excessive faith in the power of example as the best deterrent from crime, and that they presumed all criminals to be morally responsible individuals who committed offenses by conscious and rational choice. Their belief that a twenty-four-year prison term would, unlike a life sentence, spare the culprit a feeling of despair suggests at least some lack of sensitivity. Dubious likewise was their idea that long years of incarceration, through the effects of silent meditation and disciplined work, would somehow rehabilitate the prisoner. Some of the Code's reforms were also double-edged: for example, the establishment of a fixed penalty for each offense, leaving no margin of flexibility to the judge. The Assembly was of course reacting against the capricious judgments of some old regime magistrates and was aiming at what it thought would be equal and absolute justice. But the reform also straightjacketed the judges, making it impossible to consider special circumstances and to make the punishment fit the criminal as well as the crime.[19]

Yet the landmark nature of the Revolutionary Code seems hard to deny. It embodied a fundamental change in attitudes toward the nature of crime and the way to control it. From the old idea of public vengeance and deterrence through fear alone, France's governing elite had turned toward somewhat less barbarous penalties, toward the concept of rehabilitating offenders, and toward the idea that over the long run, creating a more equal and just society might do more than ex post facto repression in reducing the incidence of crime. For the next two centuries, these would be among the central issues that would dominate debate about the crime problem.

For most Frenchmen, of course, the test of the new system would not be the noble intentions of its authors but its practical effectiveness in ensuring even-handed justice and controlling crime. The record in this respect was to be disillusioning. Within two years, the Jacobin government suspended the procedural guarantees embodied in the new codes; special summary courts made a mockery of due process, and public executions by the newly invented guillotine (first used in April 1792) became a production-line business.[20] It is true that after the Terror ended in 1794, the Convention reasserted the principles that had guided the reformers, and even went farther in one respect by decreeing an end to capital punishment—though this action's effect was suspended pending the end of the national emergency, and in fact never became operative. But in the conditions of the time, it was easier to assert principles than to make them stick. In a nation that was deeply divided, even traumatized by the experience of the Terror, and that was still plagued by civil and foreign war, the time was hardly auspicious for a test of an "enlightened" system of criminal justice. The shortcomings of the Directory, which attempted to stabilize the country from 1795 to 1799, further undermined the experiment. During those final years of the century, France lived through what was probably its worst crime wave of modern times.

No accurate measurement of that wave is presently possible; the statistical evidence is deficient and has not been carefully analyzed. Virtually all of the contemporary evidence, however, suggests a serious and generalized threat to public security. Most historians have ascribed this breakdown to the disruptive effects of domestic political turmoil and foreign war. Some, however, have  seen it as the consequence of a well-meaning but impractical experiment that partially dismantled the old system of crime control and failed to create an effective new one. The reforms of 1791, these critics contend, had a cumulative effect in the years that followed. They required longer and more elaborate pre-trial investigations, so that more detainees were jammed into the overcrowded prisons: many culprits managed to postpone or evade punishment. Effective policing of the prisons became difficult, escapes were common, and discipline was so lax that in some prisons counterfeiters managed to carry on their activities. During the Terror, common criminals sometimes had to be turned out into the street to make room for political suspects. The suppression of the old provostial courts allegedly left the government disarmed in face of the rising disorder; bands of brigands reappeared in many areas, reinforced by new recruits—political dissidents and army deserters. The new court system broke down under the pressure; jurors and elected magistrates, threatened with reprisals by offenders on trial, often acquitted dangerous malefactors.[21]

Nature added to the crisis caused by the failings of institutions and men. The terrible winter of 1794–95—the coldest since 1709, which had deeply scarred French memories—had disastrous consequences. Thousands of destitute and desperate men roamed through the countryside, singly or in groups, terrorizing isolated farmsteads and attacking travelers or peasants returning from market. Organized bands of brigands such as the notorious *bande d'Orgères* virtually controlled some areas and attained a kind of Robin Hood fame (though their victims were more often the poor than the rich). Murders reached epidemic proportions; in Lyon alone, Richard Cobb estimates that more than a thousand bodies were dumped into the Rhône during the later 1790s. Panicky reports and appeals for help poured into Paris from government officials throughout much of France. The police seemed incapable of coping with the crisis—especially when the malefactors they did manage to arrest often escaped from local jails or were acquitted by juries.[22]

Officials of the Directory made some effort to play down the gravity of the situation and to reassure the public. "The time has not yet come," editorialized the official *Moniteur Universel* in December 1796, "to refute in detail the exaggerated rumors that are being repeated everywhere about the state of France and the disorders that are being committed. At the proper moment we will bring forward solid proofs to show the role of party spirit and thirst for power in these declamations . . . about the ineffectiveness of our laws for the repression of crime."[23] The legislature, added the *Moniteur*, must not succumb to panic, or to ideas such as those recently expressed by one legislator: "The more terrible the law, the more humane it becomes, for it inspires salutary terror in the souls of evil-doers, and instead of having to punish crime, it anticipates and prevents it!" [24]

But the government's assurances could not counter the mood of social fear that gripped the country. Beginning in 1797, the Directory undertook a series of measures designed to tighten the crime-control system. The gendarmerie was reinforced; the death penalty was decreed for those found guilty of highway robbery, armed housebreaking, and certain personal injuries; emergency courts-martial were set up to deal with offenses committed by bands of three or more persons; jailers were subjected to severe penalties for allowing inmates to escape; the elected judges and public prosecutors of the criminal courts were replaced by appointed ones.[25] A few legislators tried to resist this piecemeal return to repressive justice and spoke up for the importance of due process; but their voices were faint in the clamor for law and order that resounded throughout the country and in the legislative halls.[26] Yet the turn to severity was apparently ineffective; during 1798 and 1799, provincial officials continued to plead for more police and troops and to report the spread of a kind of creeping anarchy.[27]

This state of affairs—and even more this state of mind—prepared the way for a return to a more authoritarian regime, and led many Frenchmen to welcome Bonaparte's coup d'état in November 1799. The First Consul moved at once to restore public order, often in ruthless fashion. A centrally appointed prefect was named for each department of France, with extensive powers over the entire departmental administration. Tough-minded men were chosen for these posts in areas where brigandage had been rampant. In the southern department of Var, for example, the new prefect organized mobile squadrons of troops to patrol dangerous areas, and expanded the system of extraordinary courts-martial to try and execute not only brigands but villagers who had given them aid and comfort. To enforce compliance, ten hostages were taken from each village suspected of harboring outlaws; their property could be confiscated if further depredations occurred. Bounties were offered for brigands, dead or alive. Local units of the National Guard, which had remained passive until now, were prodded into action. In 1801 a government inspector reported from the backwoods of the Var *"un beau spectacle"*: seventy-four communes had organized against the brigands, and had assumed the burden of policing their respective areas.[28]

The dramatic turnaround in the Var epitomized what was happening throughout France. By 1802, the prefects' reports had taken on a new and optimistic tone; public order was returning, and public confidence with it. But law and order had been achieved at some cost, and even certain Frenchmen who had welcomed Bonaparte's seizure of power began to ask whether the cost was not too high. They objected especially to the First Consul's proposal early in 1801 to short-circuit the regular processes of justice by establishing *cours spéciales* in certain regions, empowered to deal with threats to public order posed by outlaws, vagrants, and anti-Bonapartist conspirators. Critics saw in this proposal a resurrection of the old provostial courts that had been such an important cog in the traditional crime-control system, and that had been one of the first targets shot down by the reformers in 1789. Like the provostial courts, the new special courts were designed to deliver summary justice: they would operate without a jury and with minimal procedural guarantees, and their verdicts could not be appealed. Each court would consist of three magistrates and five non-professional appointees—three army officers, two civilians.[29]

The special-courts proposal evoked a long and impassioned debate in both houses of the legislature. Many representatives, including such eminent politician-intellectuals as Pierre Daunou and Benjamin Constant, argued that even in times of public disorder and widespread social fear, abridging the rights of accused persons could not be condoned. If due process had any importance at all, Constant declared, that importance was greatest when many citizens were being charged with the most serious crimes. Furthermore, exceptional measures could open the way to generalized abuse. Law-and-order representatives struck back with emotional descriptions of a nation in the grip of malefactors and a public whose patience was exhausted: ". . . there exists a conspiracy of brigandage, vast in its scope, profound in its organization, atrocious in its effects . . . , feeding on pillage and assassination. . . ." "The existing laws are powerless against these brigand hordes who are ravaging France." "The whole society is calling for punishment." The advocates of due process were accused of conjuring up "horrible phantoms" of future abuse, and were reminded that "the honorable man . . . is [most] secure when criminal institutions and penal laws are most severe."[30] Over the next two centuries, partisans of repressive justice were to echo this latter theme again and again. The special courts finally won legislative approval, though by a narrow margin in both houses, and with the understanding that the legislation would lapse no later than two years after the end of the national emergency. In fact, it was to endure throughout Napoleon's rule and even beyond: the restored Bourbons retained the special courts, and even revived the old label—provostial courts.[31]

Two other actions supplemented this return to a law-and-order stance: in 1804 a Ministry of General Police was reestablished, and in 1810 a kind of *lettre de cachet* system without the name was revived. The Ministry of Police was vested with extensive powers and broad autonomy of action; its chief, Joseph Fouché, quickly achieved a kind of legendary status as the unscrupulous but effective creator of modern secret-police methods. The decree of 1810 authorized the government to imprison without trial certain individuals who were considered dangerous. They were consigned to specially-designated state prisons (*prisons d'état*), most of which were old fortresses that had housed *lettre de cachet* prisoners before 1789. These victims of arbitrary detention were held to be threats to national security or public order—men who could not safely ("*convenablement*") be brought to public trial. The decree of 1810 in fact legalized a Napoleonic practice that had been in operation for several years. A private council named by the Emperor was empowered to order incarcerations and to review the list of prisoners once a year; but this latter safeguard was mere window-dressing. The list in 1811 contained 810 names; it included such political dissidents as Jules de Polignac and General Malet together with a number of high churchmen and an odd cluster of vagabonds and "*hommes vicieux*."[32]

Early in his rule, Napoleon felt the need to provide a permanent base for his system of repressive justice by substituting new criminal codes for those of 1791. A small commission of legal experts began work in 1801, with Napoleon himself participating actively in its deliberations. After lengthy examination by the Conseil d'Etat and an interruption from 1804 to 1808, the draft was finally split into two parts: a Code of Criminal Procedure and a Penal Code. Both drafts were rubber-stamped by the legislature (in 1808 and 1810 respectively) without a single question or a word of debate.[33] The drafters took a tough-minded, no-nonsense position; they spent little time on theoretical questions such as the causes of crime or the basis of the state's right to punish. Their goal was social defense, the protection of the existing order, rather than due process for defendants or the rehabilitation of offenders. The reformers of 1791, rapporteur Jean-Baptiste Treilhard told the legislators, had been estimable men, but "they had not always managed to resist '*l'enthousiasme du bien.*'" Many of their innovations, Treilhard continued, were beyond challenge: the right of defendants to counsel and a public trial, the abolition of excessively brutal corporal punishments, and the principle that it was better to prevent than to punish. But twenty years of experience, said Treilhard, showed the need to correct the illusions of the men of 1791, who had "considered men not as they are but as they would like them to be."[34]

The authors of the new Penal Code obviously took a somewhat jaundiced view of men "as they are"; severe repression alone could restrain their evil impulses. The death penalty was extended to thirty-six offences, and the old practice of cutting off the right hand of a parricide prior to execution was revived. Life sentences were once again legalized; so were banishment, the branding of major offenders, confiscation of property in certain cases, and lifetime police surveillance of ex-convicts who had served out their prison terms. To the complaint that confiscation of an offender's property was unfair to his innocent children, Teilhard responded bluntly: "But who will suffer for the sins of the fathers if not the children?" Many offenses that had been classified in 1791 as misdemeanors were upgraded to the category of felonies. Penalties for second offenders were made more severe; so were those for vagrancy and begging.[35] Abortion would henceforth be punished by imprisonment for the woman and hard labor for the doctor (whose guilt, said Treilhard, was greater). A "gap" in the 1791 Code was filled by penalizing "violations of conjugal vows": adultery by a wife would draw a prison term, adultery by a husband might be punished by a fine, but only if the offender brought his concubine into the home. In one respect alone, the new Code was less repressive than the old: it restored to magistrates some flexibility in sentencing. Judges might now vary the length of prison terms (though within precise limits), thus taking some account of the character of the offender and the circumstances of the crime. But the motive for this retreat from "the blind inflexibility of the 1791 Code," declared the rapporteur Comte Réal, was not humanitarian; with less rigid penalties, fewer offenders would be acquitted.[36]

The new Code of Criminal Procedure (1808) also represented a partial retreat from the guarantees of 1791. It restored in part the secrecy of the pre-trial investigation: suspects could once again be interrogated before being informed of the charges against them and of the accusations of witnesses. The Code reinforced the powers of the investigating magistrate (*juge d'instruction*) and the state prosecutor (*procureur-général*) ; they were authorized to search out and prosecute offenders. The summary-procedure special courts set up by the decree of 1801 were given renewed official sanction.

The most divisive procedural issue concerned the retention of the jury in criminal cases. Even in 1791 there had been strong opposition to the adoption of the jury system, and experience since then had intensified this negative view. The law-and-order forces had steadily opposed it, but even some spokesmen for due process now believed that the system had not worked in France. One of them, J.-P. Chazal, had charged during the 1801 debate on the special courts that jury decisions, far from being "judgments of God or of the people," were most often handed down by "groups of ignoramuses" or by "factious types who brazenly acquit their most rascally accomplices and remorselessly slaughter their innocent enemies."[37] When the Conseil d'Etat queried magistrates throughout France, it found a majority in favor of abandoning the use of the jury. To some extent, anglophobe sentiment was at work here. In 1791 English institutions had been the rage among reformers, whereas a decade of warfare had turned public attitudes around. Napoleon also disliked the jury system, but was finally persuaded to retain it for major criminal cases.[38] His apparently liberal concession rested on his expectation that most cases would continue to go to the special courts, and that the selection of jurors would henceforth be carefully controlled by the prefects.

The Napoleonic codes, with some significant retouches from time to time, were to provide a permanent base for France's system of criminal justice from that day to our own. Like many of Napoleon's other innovations in government, they drew sporadic criticism from later reformers who found the codes too rigid and repressive as attitudes toward crime and punishment changed. For most Frenchmen, however, the codes were a source of pride and even veneration, too sacred to be seriously challenged or drastically altered.

Napoleon's crime-control system called for a dual set of penal institutions: a nationwide network of prisons suited to graduated degrees of punishment, and one or more penal colonies overseas. Napoleon's predecessors since 1789 had also intended to develop such institutions but had managed to do little more than impro-vise. The Empire, though considerably more efficient, proved to be hardly more successful in this realm.

The codes of 1791 had called for a total transformation of France's prison system. For accused and indicted persons awaiting trial, there would be a *maison d'arrêt et de justice* in the vicinity of each criminal tribunal. For hard-labor convicts, the seaport *bagnes* would be provisionally maintained. For most persons con-victed of felonies or misdemeanors, cell-type prisons would be de-veloped: *maisons de force* and *maisons de correction*, respectively.[39]

This program remained little more than a blueprint during the Revolutionary decade. Successive governments, diverted by other concerns and hard pressed to cope with the rising flood of prisoners, confined themselves to expanding the ramshackle pseudo-system inherited from the past. The old prisons remained in use, and additional buildings (mostly vacated convents) were com-mandeered as they became available. Most prisons were disgraceful makeshifts, crowded and uncomfortable, poorly administered, and insecure. Persons awaiting trial and convicted felons continued to be herded together in common quarters; there was no separation by age, and sometimes not even effective separation of the sexes. Many institutions housed not only lawbreakers but the sick, the infirm, the mentally ill, simply for lack of adequate facilities. Idleness was the general rule, since few prisons had space or equipment to set up workshops. As in the past, jailkeepers continued to sell favors to the more affluent prisoners: private cells, beds instead of damp straw on the floor, food and drink to supplement the basic diet. In the spring of 1795, the concierge of Bicêtre prison (where hard-labor convicts from northern France were collected for semi-annual shipment to the *bagnes*) complained that many of the con-victs died en route to Bicêtre because of prior mistreatment in the provincial jails:

> Along with the health officers, I undertook to find out why these prisoners were in such deplorable state; all of them informed us that the major cause was the misery they had experienced in their pris-ons, where they were deprived of everything, sleeping on the floor on straw that was changed only once a month, without blankets, chained in most cases, allowed no exercise, crowded 30 to 34 persons in sleeping quarters of about 30 square feet which they were never allowed to leave.[40]

By the time Napoleon seized power, only four large *maisons de force* with facilities for convict labor were in operation, while two others were in course of construction; and most of these were old prisons that had undergone some renovation. The total prison population of about 20,000 was scattered through some nine hundred places of incarceration, most of them small makeshift jails totally unsuited to their purpose.[41]

In 1800, only a few months after Bonaparte's coup d'état, his government made its first move to put some order into the prison system. That move, however, only made things worse, for its aims were merely to save money and to tighten prison discipline by putting an end to idleness. The order restricted the daily diet of persons awaiting trial to one and one-half pounds of bread and a bowl of soup; for convicted criminals, the regime was bread and water only. In theory, all prisoners would henceforth be required to work and could supplement the basic diet through their earnings.[42] In practice, no work was available for most prisoners. A second directive in 1801 shifted the costs of prison maintenance and operation from the central government to the departments. The effect of this action was also purely negative. A detailed report submitted in 1803 by a high official of the Ministry of Interior indicated that the starvation diet ordered in 1800 had led to a sharp rise in attempted and successful escapes; that few prisons had been able to install workshops for the inmates, due to cramped quarters; and that the transfer of operating costs to the departments had caused hard-pressed prefects to close a number of prisons, so that overcrowding was getting worse. The report was a depressing litany of misery and inefficiency; it spoke of poor and inadequate food, insufficient space, dampness, lack of security, idleness, illness, deteriorating buildings. The government, declared the reporting official, had an obligation to correct all these deficiencies, and to provide proper care for offenders who would eventually resume their places in society. An annual appropriation of six million francs, he added, would be needed to correct the worst shortcomings, and additional funds should be provided to build more prisons large enough to contain workshops.[43]

The plain-spoken report of 1803 seems to have produced no improvement during the years that followed. In 1806 an official who had traveled widely through provincial France reported thus to the Minister of Justice:

> The prisons that the writer has just visited, from Strasbourg to [Lot-et-Garonne] in the southwest, are in general poorly maintained and poorly administered: lack of straw, bread ranging from good to bad, bad sleeping quarters infested with vermin and mold, bad water, no change of shirts or jackets. . . . Many inmates therefore die each year of hunger and misery, without help or visits from outside since it seems that faith and charity no longer exist. . . . The prisoner would prefer less bread if he could have a little soup, but to live so long with only dry bread and water—even dogs could not value such an existence.[44]

In 1808 the emperor at last took decisive action: he ordered the development of a nationwide system of modern prisons to be called *maisons centrales,* large enough to provide work facilities for the inmates. France was to be divided into regions of nine departments each, with a *maison centrale* in each region.[45] The prefects were instructed to look for buildings that might be adapted to the purpose; and a second circular in 1810 directed that all existing prisons be brought up to proper standards without delay.[46] But once again the results were meager. An official report in 1813 demonstrated mainly that the prefects had become experts at bureaucratic evasion. Most of them, in responding to the 1808 order, reported that no state-owned buildings in the region were available, or that such buildings were too small or too dilapidated to be suitable. The 1810 order produced even more obfuscation; much correspondence flowed back and forth between Paris and the provinces, but it amounted to little more than excuses by the prefects (mainly based on financial stringency) for their failure to act.[46] Two further decrees in 1810–11 attempted to simplify the classification of prisons. Long-term prisons or *maisons centrales* (for sentences of more than one year) were to be the property and responsibility of the central government; short-term prisons, the property and responsibility of the departments.[47] This division was to endure until 1944, with baneful results for the short-term prisons. Whatever the accomplishments of the Napoleonic regime in other realms, there is little evidence that anything constructive was done about the nation's prison system. The number of prisons had increased since 1789, but so had the number of prisoners; and the condition of inmates remained appalling. If imprisonment was henceforth to be the standard penalty for lawbreakers, France by 1814 had hardly made a start toward grappling with the problems involved. Those problems were passed on intact to the restored Bourbon monarchy.

One other scheme for the punishment of offenders—deportation to an overseas colony—attracted the sporadic interest of reformers and governments during the Revolutionary and Napoleonic years. A mixture of motives fed into this scheme: the tempting idea that France might export one of its social problems by shipping dangerous criminals to distant shores; the more charitable conception that idle and lazy types might undergo a change of character if allowed to start afresh in a new country, one that could be made fruitful by hard work; and the impulse, in times of civil strife, to find a dumping-ground for political dissidents. The principle of deportation was adopted early, being written into the Penal Code of 1791 as a punishment for second offenders; but the practical question of identifying a destination was postponed for a time. Le Pelletier, responding to a legislator who warned against sending deportees to any colony already peopled by French settlers, indicated that his committee had been thinking of some isolated stretch of the African coast. The National Assembly's Committee on Mendicity had meanwhile suggested Corsica as a convenient location, since it was underpopulated and underdeveloped.[48] Some pamphleteers were active in support of Guiana, where only a few French colonists had managed to survive the climate and endemic disease. One enthusiast nevertheless wrote lyrically of this "superb and excellent" land of "eternal springtime," perfectly suited (he declared) to realize the dream of Plato's republic.[49]

It was not this illusory vision, however, that led the Legislative Assembly in 1792 to designate Guiana as the dumping-ground for non-juring priests (who were regarded as dangerous subversives). This proposal was adopted after the briefest of debate; but no action followed, due to the costs involved and to preoccupation with domestic political turmoil. Pending shipment of the non-jurors to Guiana, several hundred of them were rounded up and confined in various prisons, notably to the old abbey of Mont-Saint-

CELL-BLOCK OF THE *MAISON CENTRALE* AT EYSSES IN SOUTH-EASTERN FRANCE. Originally a 17th-century Benedictine abbey, it was converted into a long-term prison by Napoleon, and has remained in use ever since. For a time it housed incorrigible juveniles; currently it holds medium-term convicts. (Roger-Viollet)

Michel, which had served intermittently as a state prison since the fifteenth century. Some of these priests were freed after a time by Chouan rebels; some were eventually transported to Cayenne; the remainder had to await Napoleon's rule before being released from this glamorous but chilly and isolated place of detention.[50]

The newly elected Convention in 1793 reasserted the principle of deportation to Guiana, and broadened its scope to include not only seditious priests but persons accused of *incivisme* as well. Several months later it added a new category: vagrants and beggars arrested for a third time were to be transported for a term of at least eight years, after which they would be eligible for a grant of land in the place of deportation, where they might make a new start in life.[51] This time, however, the legislators shifted their attention to Madagascar as the most convenient outlet; the voyage would be a natural port of call en route to the colony of Ile de France (Mauritius). But once again, implementation of the order was delayed; British control of the seas made the venture too risky.

Some action came at last with the arrival in power of the Directory. That regime, faced by threats of subversion from both left and right, began in 1795 to ship off political dissidents to Guiana; the first two were prominent Jacobins, Billaud-Varenne and Collot d'Herbois. Two years later, a larger batch of sixteen royalists followed, and in 1798 a third batch, even larger and more variegated. It totaled 393 persons, most of them nonjuring priests, together with some dissidents and a few common criminals. Hardship and disease were to decimate their ranks; fewer than half of the Directory's deportees lived to see France again.[52]

After Bonaparte's seizure of power, deportations continued for a time, but in more scattergun fashion. The largest group of seventy-one was sent to the Seychelles islands in the Indian Ocean; but they met a hostile reception from the resident population, and half of them were soon transferred to a small island off Madagascar, whence they gradually scattered in various directions. Only a handful of these exiles eventually returned to France.[53] Further shipments were soon cut off by the British navy, which eventually (1808) captured Cayenne itself. The principle of deportation was nevertheless reiterated in Napoleon's Penal Code of 1810, but it remained inoperative during the later years of the empire. For the next forty years, deportation continued to be a legally sanctioned form of punishment in France, but in practice it remained a dead letter. From time to time the idea was to emerge for brief debate, but it drew little sustained attention until the accession to power of another Napoleon in mid-century. Then, in a more serious and more permanent way, it would become the most important alternative to imprisonment in France's panoply of punishments.

# III

## Age of the *philanthropes*
## 1814–1848

There are in America as well as in Europe, estimable men whose minds feed upon philosophical reveries, and whose extreme sensibility feels the want of some illusion. These men, for whom philanthropy has become a matter of necessity, find in the penitentiary system a nourishment for this generous passion. Starting from abstractions that deviate more or less from reality, they consider man, however far advanced in crime, as still susceptible of being brought back to virtue. . . . They hope for an epoch when all criminals may be radically reformed, the prisons be entirely empty, and justice find no crimes to punish. . . . Philanthropy has become for them a kind of profession; and they have caught the *monomanie* of the penitentiary system, which to them seems the remedy for all the evils of society.

GUSTAVE DE BEAUMONT and
ALEXIS DE TOCQUEVILLE (1833)

THERE ARE TIMES in the history of any society when a given social problem suddenly breaks through the surface of public consciousness, provokes passionate discussion and even some action, and then subsides once more into relative neglect. Such a burst of interest in the problems of crime and punishment occurred in France during the post-Napoleonic era. Never before had there been so much talk about these issues in the press and the political arena; never again thereafter (in France, at any rate) would there be such sustained and broad-based debate. Prison inspector Louis Moreau-Christophe grumbled in 1846 that everybody in France had his own ideas on the subject and was thinking of writing a brochure about it; prison doctor Arthus Vingtrinier counted up the works on prisons published between 1818 and 1840 and reached a total of 142.[1] The weight of words considerably exceeded the yield of results, but that is hardly surprising. Problems that are so complex as to be almost insoluble are likely to inspire unending discussion and, eventually, a high level of frustration.

Why were so many Frenchmen of that era drawn to the subject of crime and prison reform? Was it the product of some striking change in the incidence of crime—either a rapid rise in the crime rate that focused French minds on the problem and intensified social fear, or a sharp downward trend that relieved public anxiety and encouraged humanitarian experiments? The social-fear hypothesis is strongly implied in Louis Chevalier's provocative study of Paris in that era, *Classes laborieuses et classes dangereuses*. Paris in the early nineteenth century, he contends, became a city "menaced by crime and haunted by fear"; the rapid influx of provincials into the city, the physical conditions in the slum quarters, the tensions that resulted, produced a kind of generalized neurosis to which was joined a morbid bourgeois fascination with the criminal underworld.[2] This fixation on crime was reflected in the work of leading novelists of the time (Balzac, Hugo, Sue), in the publishing success of such ventures as the daily *Gazette des Tribunaux* (1825) and the memoirs of ex-*bagnard* Eugène Vidocq, and in the public's avid interest in the poet-murderer Pierre-François Lacenaire.[3]

The thesis of rising social fear is plausible for Paris, if not for the rest of France; the city's growth in this period was explosive, and rapid urban growth is sometimes (though not always) accompanied by a rise in the crime rate.[4] But such crime statistics as are available for the years 1814–48 do not suggest the kind of dramatic upsurge that would provoke public panic, or the kind of decline that would encourage growing tolerance. There was indeed a sharp burst of crime from 1813 to 1817; convictions rose from 5,343 to 9,431 during those years.[5] But such a phenomenon is a standard aspect of the transition from war to peace; the rate normally levels off or declines thereafter, as it did from 1818 to 1830. The number of prison inmates dropped from 38,450 to 34,766 during those years.[6] The crime rate did rise again after 1830, but most of the increase was in misdemeanors rather than felonies.[7] It was another phenomenon, however, that caused increasing alarm: an apparent rise in the rate of recidivism. Alexis de Tocqueville reported to parliament in 1840 that 40 per cent of the inmates of the *maisons centrales* had prior prison records; Minister of Interior Duchâtel in 1844 raised the ante to 45 per cent.[8] These figures fed the growing sentiment that crime was the work of an incorrigible "criminal class"—a race apart, "born and bred to the outlaw life, with its own special habits, instincts, and mores."[9] Most reformers drew a different conclusion: the rise of recidivism proved that the existing prisons served neither to deter nor to reform offenders, but were in fact breeding-places of crime; therefore they should be drastically changed. Hard-liners retorted that recidivism demonstrated the need for harsher punishments; at Clairvaux, alleged Louis Moreau-Christophe, 506 of the 655 recidivist inmates had committed new crimes for the sole purpose of returning to the excessive comforts of captivity.[10] The rising concern about recidivism thus fed the controversy about prison reform, but it surely was not its original stimulus.

If the explosion of interest in the crime problem after 1814 was not the product of changes in the crime rate, some other explanation must be offered. Some historians have argued that it was part of the fallout from the great upheaval that had shaken French society from 1789 to 1814: "great political commotions," one of them remarks, "have always resulted in drawing attention to the disinherited elements of society."[11] The record does indeed suggest that wars and revolutions in France have usually provoked both talk and action about the system of criminal justice; new surges of interest (though less profound) would occur in 1871–75, and 1945. The Great Revolution had brought a variety of inconclusive experiments; France emerged from the Napoleonic era with a durable criminal code but with a makeshift prison system that urgently demanded attention. Furthermore, the Revolution gave many members of the French elite their first direct experience with prisons, and inspired in some of them a new interest in prison reform. Even those aristocrats who fled abroad usually had relatives or friends who had spent time behind bars. One stray émigré who found asylum for a time in the United States happened onto an American experiment that struck his imagination and launched him onto a notable career as prison reformer. This was the duc de Rochefoucauld-Liancourt, who visited the Quaker-inspired Walnut Street prison in Philadelphia and promptly published an enthusiastic brochure about it—a work that went through four editions between 1796 and 1819 and drew the attention of a whole generation of French reformers to the American example.[12]

Another possible source of the lively French interest in crime and punishment after 1814 may have been the intellectual climate of the age. This was the era of romanticism, with its stress on sensibility, on the colorful and the bizarre. The fact that so many of France's leading writers were fascinated by crime, chose to portray it in their novels, and entered actively into the public debate on prison reform suggests a connection with the prevailing mood of the age. There was of course a strain of sheer morbid curiosity in this literary interest in criminals and prisons; it was demonstrated by the lionizing of the murderer Lacenaire by Parisian society and the inclination of some romantic writers to see him as a kind of artist of crime. Maxime du Camp went so far as to obtain the embalmed hand of the guillotined Lacenaire and to display it on a cushion in his drawing room.[13]

But the aspect of the romantic temper that fed most directly into the interest in prison reform was its religious side. The post-Napoleonic years brought a surge of intense religious feeling, especially marked among those aristocrats who had been drawn to rationalism before the Revolution. This religious impulse, with its stress on moral uplift and on the expiation of sin, suffused the reform movement during the Bourbon Restoration and carried over to some extent into the July Monarchy as well. Yet the link between the Catholic revival and the wave of interest in the crime problem should not be exaggerated. Within the reform movement, one important segment continued to find its inspiration in the rationalist thinkers of the Enlightenment, and some leading reformers were Protestants. Conversely, many fervent participants in the Catholic revival were inflexibly hostile to the reformers; they looked for guidance to the mystical reactionary Joseph de Maistre, who preached the divine origin and the social necessity of retributive justice. Evil, according to Maistre, was omnipresent in the world, and had to be constantly repressed: "the sword of justice has no scabbard. . . . The entire race of men is kept in order through punishment, for innocence scarcely exists. . . . When

Punishment, with his black countenance and flaming eye, comes forward to destroy crime, the people are saved. . . . All greatness, power, subordination are based upon the executioner; he is both the object of horror and the linchpin of human society; remove him, and order instantly gives way to chaos, thrones decay and society disappears."[14] Maistre's dark vision, and its attraction for many Catholics of the romantic age, obstructs any attempt to show a direct connection between the religious revival and the burst of activity in penal reform. The link existed, but it must be qualified.

One further hypothesis about the post-Napoleonic generation's interest in the crime problem has been advanced by Michel Foucault and his followers. Foucault points out that severe criticism of the prison as an institution began from the very moment when the prison was adopted as the standard punishment technique. Although it was denounced from the outset as either inhumane or ineffective (or both), Foucault contends that the ruling elite found it too useful to abandon. For one thing, the prison reflected the prevailing values of the liberal bourgeoisie, for whom individual freedom was the highest good; it would naturally punish deviants by depriving them of that cherished liberty. Much more important, the prison was an essential cog in developing "the disciplinary society"; it was a necessary device for the more thoroughgoing repression of property crimes; and it created as a kind of by-product an outlawed category of ex-convicts who could be used to operate devious but profitable enterprises. Furthermore, the technique of imprisonment made it easier to drive a wedge between the working class and the newly baptized "criminal class," with a view to more effective social control. In earlier times, poor but honest workers had been inclined to identify with offenders as brothers in misery; by replacing the old public rituals of punishment by the grim secrecy of prison, it was possible to portray convicts as a race apart and to turn the honest poor against their erring fellows.[15] The Foucault thesis seems to imply that an institution so fundamentally flawed as the prison was bound to become the focus of bitter controversy from the very outset, as the bourgeois elite was confronted with its flagrant shortcomings even while clinging to it as a necessary mechanism. If Foucault's inferences about bourgeois motives are sound, perhaps we need look no further for an explanation of the wave of interest in crime and punishment after 1814. Once again, however, imputing motives is easier than demonstrating their validity.

Only a few weeks after the return of the Bourbons in 1814, Louis XVIII's minister of interior, the abbé de Montesquiou, ordered the establishment of a small experimental prison in Paris and named the duc de Rochefoucauld-Liancourt as its unsalaried director. Liancourt, scion of one of the oldest aristocratic families in France, was a notable example of the breed that came to be called "the philanthropists"—a term that was sometimes used with respect but more often with a strong tinge of irony. Liancourt was one of those born crusaders who are drawn to every progressive social cause—"*patron banal de toutes les philanthropies de la terre,*" in the words of an unsympathetic police spy.[16] In his youth he had visited England and had returned fired with zeal for agricultural and educational reform. As a member of the Estates-General in 1789, he became a leading constitutional moderate and chaired the important Committee on the Extinction of Mendicity.[17] Forced into exile in 1792, he returned in 1800 with two new passions: vaccination and prison reform. His brochure on the Quaker penitentiary in Philadelphia exalted its goal of rehabilitation through penitence.[18] Work there was seen as rehabilitative rather than as a supplementary punishment. Daily visits by dedicated Quakers, according to Liancourt, helped turn tigers into lambs; "firmness and reason have replaced chains and blows." Inmates left the prison, he was told, purged of their evil impulses; recidivism had almost disappeared, and the crime rate had been reduced by half. The death penalty had been replaced by day-and-night solitary confinement; this isolation was supposed to punish but also to encourage self-examination and repentance. Liancourt's enthusiasm was premature; the Walnut Street experiment was shortly to turn sour. But his brochure attracted wide interest in Europe and focused attention on the allegedly protective and curative aspects of solitary confinement.

The return of the Bourbons seemed to offer Liancourt his chance to try a small-scale Philadelphia-style experiment. His experimental prison or *maison d'amendement* was designed to begin with one hundred long-term offenders aged twenty-one or below; it was intended to prove that even the most dangerous criminals, if still young enough to be reformed, could be persuaded to "abandon all of their vicious ways and to substitute gentle, disciplined, laborious habits. . . . The healthy and useful ideas that are to be inculcated must be absorbed, so to speak, through every pore, and quite unconsciously."[19] To encourage this happy result, Liancourt laid out the most elaborate specifications, ranging from the design of the prison uniform (with insignia for good behavior) to the organization of small workshops where prisoners would learn the joys of productive labor and would build up savings for use after release. Along with work there would be moral uplift, tinged with religious sentiment but not bathed in it; Liancourt was, after all, still a man of the eighteenth century. The prison chaplain would serve as friend and counselor; he would seek to "reawaken the religious sense" but would be cautioned to refrain from "thoughtless zeal." If time allowed, he would also teach inmates to read and write; education, in Liancourt's view, was useful but no guarantee against criminal behavior. The prisoners would be visited daily by members of a corps of volunteer inspectors chosen from the well-to-do bourgeoisie; these inspectors might initiate proposals for pardons. ("Crowds of estimable citizens," Liancourt later recalled, "flocked around to volunteer for this service.") [20] The jailers were to be chosen for their qualities of fairness, humanity, and kindness; but kindness would be tempered by discipline and austerity. "A prison in which the inmate would be so contented as to prefer detention to freedom would be the most absurd and ill-advised of institutions"; therefore the rule must be "constant submission to orders, to routines, to obligatory silence—that continuous surveillance that never leaves a man to himself, that demonstrates at every moment both his condition of captivity and the mistrust that he inspires."[21] Reluctantly, Liancourt postponed his goal of providing each inmate with an individual cell; since the cost would be excessive, he settled for rooms holding eight to ten men, with monthly changes of cellmates.

Liancourt's elaborate plan epitomizes the ambitions of the *philanthropes*; but it was to end in frustration. Only a few weeks before the new prison's opening day, Napoleon escaped from Elba, and the king fled into a second exile. When Louis and his court returned after the Hundred Days, the project was permanently shelved. Other needs were now more pressing; and besides, Liancourt's influence was tarnished by his mild collaboration with Napoleon's ephemeral government.

His ideas, however, continued to provoke discussion, for it was clear that something drastic had to be done about France's prison system. Without exception, the prisons were under-equipped, overcrowded, and miserably administered. The political purge of 1815–17 made things even worse; ex-émigré judges and the revived provostial courts imposed ruthless vengeance on their former persecutors. Critics were prompt to speak up. Liancourt brought out a new edition of his famous brochure; and a young jurist named Alphonse Bérenger inaugurated a long and distinguished career as penal reformer with a weighty tract denouncing political justice and challenging the current crime-control system. "Our penal laws," he declared, "are a thousand centuries [!] behind the epoch in which we live"; it was time to stop thinking of criminals as monsters rather than as men suffering from a moral malady, in need of pity and correction. Bérenger praised the humanitarian reformers of 1791 and criticized Napoleon for returning to a system based on repressive justice. Frenchmen, he declared, might think that they had abolished torture, but in fact it persisted in a different form; now it took the shape of isolation for months on end in damp and dark disciplinary cells. In the prisons, inmates of all categories were mixed indiscriminately, spreading corruption; jailers were brutal, the mortality rate appalling.[22]

Both the king and his chief minister Elie Decazes were sensitive to this growing criticism; they responded in 1819 with some important reform moves. Decazes pushed through parliament a financial subsidy to upgrade the departmental prisons, where conditions were most disgraceful; and he set out to channel and utilize the energies of the *philanthropes* by persuading the king to create a Royal Prison Society, with the king's nephew the duc d'Angoulême as its president.[23] The Society was made up of 320 carefully-screened notables of philanthropic bent: aristocrats such as Liancourt, Lafayette, and Barbé-Marbois (the only member who had once been transported to Guiana), bankers such as Mallet and Rothschild, intellectuals such as Guizot and Royer-Collard. The king contributed an initial subsidy of 50,000 francs from his personal funds; members of the Society paid annual dues of 100 francs.

From the Society's membership was drawn a new official body called the *Conseil général des prisons*, with authority to carry out inspections and to draft prison budgets and rules. Subsidiary committees were set up in the provinces to supervise local prisons.

This curious bureaucratic-philanthropic hybrid got off to a vigorous start during its first few years. Its principal goal, declared the duc d'Angoulême at its first meeting, must be the rehabilitation of offenders—to restore the purity of souls "degraded by vice and evil passions." On his initiative, the Society voted to begin by providing prisoners with better bread, woolen winter clothing, and the consolations of religion, and by printing up collections of books appropriate for moral uplift.[24] Members were delegated to inspect prisons throughout the country and brought in detailed reports that showed appalling conditions almost everywhere. At the Grande Force prison in Paris for men awaiting trial, some two hundred inmates were crowded into a large room, most of them barefoot and ragged, their nourishment bread and water and "a spoonful" of soup; the average length of stay in this branch of Dante's Inferno was six months. In the filthy infirmary of Sainte-Pélagie in Paris, prisoners suffering from the itch slept two or three in a bed.[25] Barbé-Marbois, who visited thirty-five prisons in Normandy, reported that in most of them prisoners slept on straw without blankets and were fed only bread and water. Some prisons continued to house madmen as well as criminals: "I observed one," Barbé-Marbois reported, "confined to a secret cell; he was completely naked, crouched on a bit of straw as savages do; around his neck was an iron collar from which a long chain was attached to the ceiling joist."[26]

At the Society's strong urging, the government issued an elaborate new set of prison regulations drafted by the *Conseil général des prisons*. Some abuses were corrected, but the ministry put its main effort into expanding the *maisons centrales* so that long-term convicts might be transferred out of the crowded and ramshackle departmental prisons. By 1830 this task had been virtually completed; the *maisons centrales* held 17,378 long termers, while the departmental prisons held an equal number of short-termers and persons awaiting trial.[27] Meanwhile, however, the Society's wings had been clipped. The assassination of the king's nephew the duc de Berry in 1820 turned the monarchy sharply toward reaction;

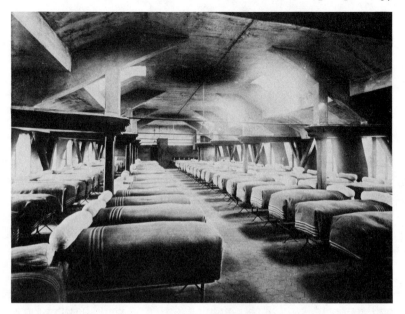

DORMITORY OF THE SAINT-LAZARE PRISON FOR WOMEN IN PARIS. An example of the common prison denounced by the advocates of cellular isolation. Converted from a pre-Revolutionary convent, it was finally demolished in 1941. (Roger-Viollet)

Decazes was dismissed as chief minister, and the reform impetus slowed. In 1823 the government carried out a drastic purge of the *Conseil général des prisons* and stripped it of most of its authority. Both the *Conseil* and the Society vegetated obscurely until 1828, when King Charles X was reluctantly forced to appoint a more moderate ministry headed by the vicomte de Martignac. In this altered atmosphere, the Society enjoyed a brief renaissance; Martignac himself appeared at its session in 1829 to present the most detailed report the Society had ever received.

The Martignac report, if taken at face value, showed that the Bourbon monarchy had made notable improvements in the prison system. It had spent 28 million francs to upgrade central and departmental prisons. Sixty-eight departmental prisons had been repaired or reconstructed, nine others were in process; only a few,

said Martignac, still needed attention. Of the local (arrondisse-
ment) jails, 198 had been refurbished, 17 were in process, and
only 59 still awaited renovation. The remodeling and expansion
of the Paris prisons and the *maisons centrales* was nearing completion; they were now able to hold almost all of the long-term
convicts. A standard diet of bread and soup was now provided
everywhere; clothing was furnished for the most indigent; camp
beds were gradually replacing straw; work was being provided for a
growing proportion of inmates; chaplains had been appointed,
chapels and infirmaries set aside in most prisons. The most notable
progress, according to Martignac, had been achieved in the *maisons
centrales*. There, private contractors now employed about three-
quarters of the convicts at an average wage of thirty-three centimes
a day. Corporal punishment had been eliminated; disciplinary
confinement in the *cachots* was strictly regulated; a new Catholic
order, the Sisters of Charity, was beginning to provide nursing
care. The regime, Martignac concluded, had not received proper
credit for all its achievements: "the past in certain respects weighs
on the present." Although London and Geneva could boast of a few
"de luxe prisons" that were beyond France's means, "it is well
known that the mass of inmates are better treated in France than
anywhere else."[28]

Martignac's rose-tinted report left some of his hearers skeptical.
Decazes, still a member of the Society, rose to challenge the minister
on a whole series of points: neglect of provincial needs in favor of
Paris, inadequate separation of sick from healthy prisoners, the
continuing detention and ill-treatment of madmen in many prisons,
the abusive practice of imprisonment for debt, shameful conditions
in the seaport *bagnes*. Decazes's criticism infuriated the duc d'Angoulême (who was now the dauphin); he lectured the Society on
its proper role, which was not to discuss administrative practices.
Evidently its only function, as the government saw it, was to serve
as a sounding board. Even for this limited purpose, its life was
almost over. It met for one final session in 1830 to hear another
detailed and self-satisfied report from the Bourbons' last minister
of interior, Baron Guillaume de Montbel. The material upgrading
of the prisons, Montbel declared, had now been completed; "we can
go no further in this respect without wounding public morale." Yet

grave problems of another sort persisted. Recidivism was on the rise; the prisons had lost their power to deter through fear; they no longer punished but were not yet able to reform. The next effort, Montbel declared, must be to regenerate offenders—though he failed to offer much constructive advice on how to achieve that goal.[29] Before he could give serious thought to the problem, the regime had fallen.

The Bourbon monarchy can hardly be credited with brilliantly innovative or humanitarian accomplishments in the realm of criminal justice. On the other hand, it was not a time of complete stagnation; material conditions in many prisons were measurably improved. Buildings were made less uncomfortable and insecure; sanitary conditions got some attention; most long-term convicts were separated from the short-termers and those awaiting trial; more prisoners were provided with regular work (though hardly in ideal conditions).[30] Indeed, some Frenchmen were beginning to complain about pampering malefactors. For the *philanthropes*, however, only a bare beginning had been made: the Napoleonic codes were much too harsh, the prison system was still a disgrace to a civilized nation, the failure to rehabilitate offenders could no longer be condoned. It was this reform-minded group that welcomed the fall of the Bourbons in 1830 and that hoped for far more fundamental changes under Louis-Philippe.

The Bourbons' turn toward reaction during the 1820s had alienated virtually all of the men who were loosely labelled *les philanthropes*. Although most of these reformers were Christian believers, they were still marked by the Enlightenment spirit; they abhorred the fanaticism of the religious revivalists who surrounded Charles X and who hoped to reimpose a single orthodoxy of belief in France. In 1821 these moderate liberals organized the *Société de Morale Chrétienne* as a center for the discussion and advocacy of their social reform ideas.[31] The duc de Rochefoucauld-Liancourt became its first president; the membership included such future luminaries as Charles de Rémusat, the duc de Broglie, François Guizot, Alexis de Tocqueville, Adolphe Thiers, and Alphonse de Lamartine. This circle of liberal Catholics and Protestants was to

ALEXIS DE TOCQUEVILLE (1805–1859). Tocqueville's study mission to the United States (accompanied by Gustave de Beaumont) did much to stimulate the long French debate about solitary confinement. (Roger-Viollet)

provide the July Monarchy with much of its leadership; indeed, the duc d'Orléans (who became King Louis-Philippe) was himself a member of the *Société*.

The Bourbon authorities had viewed the *Société*'s activities with truly paranoid alarm. Police spies submitted panicky reports on the subversive goals of these "unbelievers, agnostics, and hypocritical deists," whose talk of visiting prisons obviously concealed a revolutionary purpose.[32] The official press denounced the *Société* as "a vast league organized by the Protestants and liberals . . . with the aim of de-Catholicizing France."[33] The government abruptly dismissed Liancourt from several official advisory posts, inaugurating a feud that culminated at Liancourt's funeral in 1827. The funeral procession was disrupted by a squad of soldiers under police command, and the coffin, jolted from the grip of the pallbearers, fell to the street and was smashed open.[34] Parisians were scandalized.

In fact, the *Société*'s concerns were philanthropic rather than political. It met to discuss a wide variety of social ills ranging from the slave trade to gambling and alcoholism, and its members undertook charitable activities on behalf of the underprivileged. Among its concerns was the problem of crime and punishment, and particularly the issue of capital punishment. Guizot published a forceful brochure urging an end to the death penalty for political offenses, and a twenty-four-year-old lawyer named Charles Lucas achieved overnight fame in 1826 by winning the *Société*'s prize for an essay entitled *Du système pénal et de la peine de mort*. That success drew Lucas into an unintended career as prison reformer that was to extend over the next sixty years, and that was to invest him (in the eyes of his admirers at least) with a kind of historic stature rivaling that of Beccaria and John Howard.[35]

Alongside the *philanthropes* of the *Société de Morale Chrétienne*, other voices too were beginning to be raised in favor of reform. Some of the early socialist thinkers (and even more, their disciples of the 1830s and 1840s) challenged the current orthodoxv about the causes and nature of crime as well as the proper treatment of offenders. The Saint-Simonians put forward the idea that crime was not a moral transgression but a social fact, changing in its definition and expression as society itself evolved; they argued that offenders should be re-educated rather than subjected to society's vengeance. The followers of Fourier put their faith in a re-organized society that would allow free expression of men's naturally healthy passions and that would make crime obsolete. Louis Blanc blamed crime on misery and called for a cooperative economy; Etienne Cabet preached the idea of utopian communities in which abundance would reduce crime to occasional aberrations, properly treated in a hospital rather than a prison. Some individual Catholic thinkers such as Pierre-Simon Ballanche and the abbé de Lamennais, some novelists such as Victor Hugo, were beginning to share the view that the roots of crime were mainly social.[36] Such ideas were too unorthodox to get a serious hearing outside the limited circle of socialist believers, but they would persist henceforth as an undercurrent expressing the hopes of some idealists and the disillusionment of many thoughtful Frenchmen with the standard techniques of crime control.

At the level of popular consciousness, the memoirs of François-Eugène Vidocq (1827) had broader and more immediate effect. Vidocq's considerably embroidered account of his life as *bagnard*-turned-policeman became an instant best seller; his account of the corrupting effect of the *bagne* focused attention on that peculiar survival from a more barbarous age and spurred an interest in prison conditions generally.[37] Vidocq also exposed the consequences of the system of police surveillance of ex-convicts; those who wanted to go straight were given no chance to escape their flawed past, and were often forced back into crime through social ostracism. The interest in crime and prisons aroused in part by Vidocq was kept alive during the next generation by leading French novelists—Balzac, Hugo, Eugène Sue. Balzac and Sue consulted Vidocq as a kind of technical adviser, and Balzac modeled one of his principal characters after this colorful figure.

Louis-Philippe's accession to the throne in 1830 thus seemed likely to introduce a bright new era for the reformers of criminal justice; the subject was prominent in the public mind, and the new monarch was personally involved with the leading *philanthropes*. Many of the king's ministers were chosen from the ranks of the social reformers. In 1830 the government created a new post of inspector-general of departmental prisons and, in a symbolic action, appointed the young activist Charles Lucas to the office.[38] In 1831 two youthful magistrates, Alexis de Tocqueville and Gustave de Beaumont, cajoled the minister of justice into granting them leave to visit the United States and to report on various prison experiments there.[39] In parliament, a resolution was adopted requesting the king to initiate changes in Napoleon's harsh criminal codes.

Liberals had for some time been critical of the Napoleonic heritage in criminal justice. As humanitarians, they objected to certain penalties that seemed excessive or even barbarous; as practical men, they observed that juries were inclined to acquit defendants rather than impose penalties that struck them as unreasonable. The king shared the humanitarian view, especially with respect to capital punishment. As a young man in 1792, he had expressed shock at the bloody September massacres and had been scolded for this by Danton. Inhumane acts, said Danton, were sometimes necessary: "You must recognize that in politics, when you have enemies, you must exterminate them to the last man if you don't want to suffer the same fate yourself." Instead, the young Louis-Philippe had resolved to outlaw such atrocities as the taking of human life.[40] He responded favorably, therefore, to parliament's resolution; his government in 1831 brought in a bill to revise the criminal codes (though the king was reluctantly persuaded to postpone his idea of abolishing capital punishment).

A long parliamentary debate followed. Some deputies wanted a complete overhaul of the codes rather than patchwork revision; some wanted to suppress the *bagnes* and substitute transportation to a penal colony; some were determined to outlaw capital punishment without further delay. The idea of transporting criminals enjoyed considerable vogue at the time; almost half of the departmental *conseils-généraux* had recently adopted resolutions in its favor.[41] In the end, however, government supporters beat off most of the amendments. The law of 1832 reduced the number of capital crimes, abolished such "odious débris of barbarism" as branding and mutilation, and restricted the practice of public exposure of newly convicted offenders. But the most important change authorized juries to consider extenuating circumstances and to recommend reduced penalties. This reform was intended to make the punishment fit the criminal as well as the crime, but even more, to increase the rate of convictions by juries. That aim was in fact accomplished; there were fewer "scandalous" acquittals in the years that followed. But the new system outraged the partisans of repressive justice, who complained that juries now took the easy route of finding extenuating circumstances in almost every case. The lower penalties imposed, they contended, were responsible for the continuing growth of crime and the rising incidence of recidivism.[42]

Shortly after the revision of the Napoleonic codes, Beaumont and Tocqueville returned from America with their report on transatlantic experiments in prison reform. The government showed little interest in their findings, and both men soon resigned their bureaucratic posts.[43] But the document quickly drew the attention of prison reformers (despite its rather scornful reference to the *philanthropes*); it was to influence the course of the long debate that ensued, a debate that occupied much of the time and attention of France's political elite from 1832 until 1848.

Beaumont and Tocqueville reported that after a generation of experiment, the Americans had groped their way to two rival models of what they called "the penitentiary system": Cherry Hill in Philadelphia, and Auburn in New York state. The older Walnut Street prison, praised so uncritically by Liancourt, had failed in its purpose; solitude without work had proved to be corrupting, but so had work without solitude. Cherry Hill had therefore been organized on the principle of solitary confinement night and day for all prisoners, with work provided in each cell. Auburn was based on the individual cell at night but work in common during the day, with absolute silence rigorously enforced through the use of the whip. Both experiments, the travelers observed, rested on the necessary combination of solitude and work; that combination alone would allow prisons to be converted into penitentiaries, in which rehabilitation would be combined with punishment as twin goals. After weighing the fitness of the two sytsems to French traditions and needs, the authors came out strongly for some form of the penitentiary idea, but waffled on the choice of model. Cherry Hill type prisons, they suggested, would be easier to administer but costlier to build; the Auburn type would require trained and talented personnel not available in France. Besides, French susceptibilities would not allow the use of the whip to enforce silence. The authors added a warning, however, that neither model would fulfill the "reveries" of the *philanthropes*; no sensible person could expect the "radical reformation" of depraved criminals except in rare and accidental cases. But they believed a more modest kind of regeneration to be possible: the penitentiary might instill moral and disciplined habits through essentially pragmatic techniques, not through a kind of spiritual rebirth. The American experience, they contended, gave substance to this more realistic hope, for recidivism among ex-inmates of Auburn and Cherry Hill was far lower than among those released from the older prisons. As footnotes to their report, Beaumont and Tocqueville recommended the use of agricultural colonies for liberated convicts who found it hard to get honest work, and they flatly rejected the idea of transportation to an overseas penal colony.[44]

Central to the Beaumont-Tocqueville thesis was the need for isolating prisoners, either physically or by the rule of silence. Only thus, they believed, would prisons cease to be breeding-places of corruption. This issue of isolation was to stand at the center of the debate that filled the next fifteen years. Was solitary confinement a new form of torture, more refined but more agonizing than the old? Was it likely to make men better, or would it merely prevent them from becoming worse? Was it unsuited to the sociable and volatile French temperament? Was the Auburn rule of silence unenforceable among Frenchmen? Did the cost of building cellular prisons outweigh their possible merits? Long before a formal proposal to create a penitentiary system in France finally came before parliament (in 1840), the battle lines had been drawn and the reformers had taken sides.

The largest faction favored the Cherry Hill system of absolute solitary confinement; even Beaumont and Tocqueville came down on that side when the debate began.[45] The pro-Auburn minority, headed by Charles Lucas, was equally intransigent. A third group clung stubbornly to the tempting alternative of transportation; and there were some lonely campaigners for penal farm colonies—especially for rural offenders, whom the journalist Léon Faucher held to be "a distinct race," less corrupted and more docile than city-dwellers.[46] There were even a few defenders of the traditional common prison with some improvements added—notably marquis Gaetan de Rochefoucauld-Liancourt, son of the noted *philanthrope*.[47] Journalists and novelists entered actively into the controversy; doctors were recruited on both sides to testify on the connection between solitary confinement and madness; statistics were marshaled to prove each faction's case. But consensus remained elusive; the argument merely reinforced each group's convictions.

While the reformers battled over these issues, the proponents of law and order kept up their own barrage of attacks on the "tearful school of philanthropy." They referred derisively to one *philanthrope* in formal dress who, they alleged, had chained himself to a *bagnard* in a gesture of solidarity.[48] They ridiculed the Catholic philosopher Ballanche, whose essay called *La Ville des expiations* (1832) made him an easy target. Ballanche had sketched out a detailed plan for abolishing prisons in favor of a city of refuge in which criminals and sinners voluntarily seeking redemption would be rehabilitated through ritual, music, prayer, and lovingkindness. Conservative critics leaped on this scheme as the ultimate example of the philanthropic spirit: they described Ballanche's Utopia as "an Eldorado for rascals," where each malefactor would be provided with a house and garden, would dine at an abundant and varied table, would drink only milk, and would be led back to morality by the ministrations of a white-haired tutor.[49]

More serious were the anti-reform tracts published by two prison inspectors-general, Alexandre de La Ville de Mirmont and Louis Moreau-Christophe. Mirmont's book was a direct rejoinder to the Beaumont-Tocqueville report; it rejected both of the American models, and it was prepared to accept only some cautious experiments in prisoner education and in the use of the nascent science of psychology in classifying inmates.[50] Moreau-Christophe, writing a few years later, used his expertise and his wicked pen to ridicule the do-gooders; in the Maistre tradition, he frankly asserted his belief in man's innate perversity (*"Je crois aux monstruosités de l'âme"*). Already, Moreau-Christophe charged, the *philanthropes* had gravely damaged France's crime-control system; the reformed code of 1832 had jumbled the hierarchy of punishments by providing the best treatment for the worst offenders and had undermined the "granite base" of repression, Napoleon's admirable criminal codes. Prison's purpose was not to moralize but to repress and punish; but thanks to "subversives" like Charles Lucas, prisoners now enjoyed "a well-fed, warm, comfortable, well-paid captivity in place of a freedom of suffering, hunger, cold, idleness, misery." "It is *criminal* heresy to say that a penalty does not represent *vengeance,* that punishment should not involve *suffering. . . . Vengeance,* in this case, is a synonym for *justice.*"[51]

Moreau-Christophe's philippic was echoed the next year (1839) by the keynote speaker at the opening session of the royal court of Paris. *Avocat-général* Delapalme passionately denounced the humanitarians for rendering life in prison more comfortable than that outside, for finding excuses for criminal behavior and even investing it with a kind of "savage mystery," and for destroying the old structure of morality without putting anything in its place. It was no wonder, Delapalme told his fellow magistrates, that justice had become powerless, that "crime [was] winning an awful triumph."[52] François Guizot, who had been associated with the reformers before 1830, startled the Chamber of Deputies in 1835 by declaring that "there is no morality, no *true* morality, without fear"; "preventive and general intimidation" was the principal purpose of punishment, for without it, men would slide into "the dementia of individual egoism." One must choose, cried Guizot, "between the intimidation of honest folk and the intimidation of dishonest folk."[53] Honoré de Balzac denounced the "philosophers, philanthropists and publicists [who were] incessantly occupied with diminishing all social authority"; the alleged horrors of French prisons, he declared, were "exaggerations that exist only in the theater."[54] There were even some self-styled reformers whose humanitarian impulse was tempered at best. Thus the popular novelist Eugène Sue, who favored abolition of the death penalty, could find no better substitute than to blind the culprit and commit him to a solitary cell for life.[55] And the eminent lawyer and deputy André Dupin found in an eighteenth-century tract another substitute for the guillotine that caught his fancy:

> I would wish for . . . an enclosure surrounded by thick walls, accessible only through a single entrance equipped with a triple iron gate. This place would present a lugubrious appearance, its interior walls would be painted black, and the eternal silence that reigns there would be disturbed only by the noise of chains and the frightful baying of the dogs that would stand guard within. There, clothed in rags, nourished on bread and water, denied the right to speak, the criminals attached to stakes would be subjected during the day to hard labor, and would rest at night on straw in separate compartments. Each one would bear on his forehead the brand of his crime, and the atrociousness of awful crimes would be more starkly revealed by the greater horrors that surround these guilty men.[56]

While the reformers disputed and the hard-liners cried havoc, Louis Philippe's ministers had been proceeding with their own piecemeal experiments, directed for the most part toward a tightening of prison discipline and toward the gradual adoption of solitary confinement. In 1836 the minister of interior, comte Adrien de Gasparin, infuriated the anti-cell group by ordering that all new or reconstructed departmental prisons be built henceforth on the cell principle. Gasparin accepted the argument of most reformers that the inmates of these prisons, being short-termers or accused persons awaiting trial, were most in need of protection against the corrupting effects of the common prison. His critics complained, however, that the administration was usurping parliament's authority to decide on the principle. Two years later a new minister, comte Bachasson de Montalivet, ordered the conversion of the new Paris prison for juveniles, La Petite Roquette, to the cellular model. This imposing star-shaped structure, reminiscent of the architecture of Cherry Hill, was mistakenly thought to be inspired by Bentham's famous Panopticon scheme.[57] From the time of its completion in 1836, La Petite Roquette stoked the fires of controversy: critics voiced outrage at the enormous cost of this "palace for rascals," while the pro-cell enthusiasts after 1838 claimed almost immediate evidence of its rehabilitative success.[58]

More rigorous discipline in the prisons was a second goal. Montalivet in 1832 ordered prison directors to cease utilizing work as a device to keep prisoners quiet or contented. Instead, it was to be regarded as an aspect of punishment, coercive in nature; each convict must be required "to work steadily, without interruption, and up to the limit of his strength."[59] Such a standard was difficult to enforce, however, since almost all prison work was organized by private entrepreneurs who contracted for the use of prison labor and ran the workshops as they saw fit. In 1838 Montalivet tried again, ordering a renewed effort to provide work in the short-term prisons (where facilities were usually lacking) but warning once more that work must be seen as part of the punishment, and that inmates must not be better off than free workers outside. He also sought to resuscitate the visiting committees that had been created in 1819 but had quickly withered, and he ordered that mayors and prefects visit and report regularly.[60]

More severe and more durable was the so-called Gasparin decree of 1839, imposing a new disciplinary code in the *maisons centrales*.[61] The rule of absolute silence was imposed for the first time; the use of alcohol and tobacco was forbidden; and prison canteens, where inmates were accustomed to buying small luxuries, were virtually suppressed (they could sell henceforth only a few unpopular items such as bread and boiled potatoes). The new rules responded to the complaints of law and order advocates and of some reformers as well. Hard-liners claimed that the prisons had become the scene of shameful drunken orgies; Moreau-Christophe described the canteens as "magnets that attract all the odious and vile passions produced by crime and debauchery."[62] He was especially outraged by reports that some female prisoners even managed to get their morning coffee served with cream. Some reformers

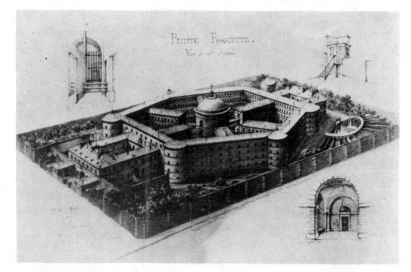

**LA PETITE ROQUETTE PRISON IN PARIS.** Built in 1825–36 and demolished in 1974, it was used until 1865 to house juvenile offenders in day-and-night cellular isolation. Thereafter it went through a series of transmutations, including a spell during World War I when one wing was leased to the American army for erring doughboys. (Roger-Viollet)

(Beaumont and Tocqueville among them) had also been arguing that the canteens encouraged intemperance, gambling, favoritism, and profiteering by prison directors and entrepreneurs.[63] The new austerity caused bitter debate during the next few years; one faction insisted that it had ended chaos and disorder in the prisons, while critics charged that it drove many inmates to despair, caused many cases of malnutrition, and even led some prisoners to assault or murder fellow inmates or guards in order to be transferred to the fearsome but less puritanical *bagnes*. The charge was so commonly repeated that the government in 1842 ordered sentences for such offenses to be served in the prison where they occurred rather than in the *bagnes*.[64]

Although the trend of the times was toward tighter prison discipline, the government also acted to correct some abuses that had been denounced by certain *philanthropes*. Rochefoucauld-

Liancourt the younger charged in parliament that unruly prisoners were confined for weeks on end in pitch-dark *cachots* (notably at Mont-Saint-Michel), where some of them died of scurvy or malnutrition. He also cited cases of "torture" of obstreperous children in Rouen; one twelve-year-old, he asserted, had died after being confined for fifteen days to a tiny box in which he could neither move nor lie down. The child's offense, according to Liancourt, had been a mere peccadillo; he had burst out laughing in the prison schoolroom.[65] Testimony by the prison doctor at Rouen seemed to corroborate the charge, but prison and ministry officials were outraged at the accusation. The lawyer-deputy André Dupin defended the Rouen authorities, pointing out that "even the best *collèges* and pensions" needed some sort of *cachot* to keep children in line.[66] But the criticism did lead the minister of interior in 1842 to order that the *cachot* be used henceforth "only in extreme circumstances."[67]

Most of the government's experiments during the 1830s were controversial, but one change caused general satisfaction: namely, the abolition of *la chaîne*. By long tradition, hard-labor convicts destined for the *bagnes* had been shipped off twice a year to Toulon, Brest, or Lorient from the collecting point at Bicêtre prison. On the appointed day, crowds of Parisians—sometimes as many as 100,000—gathered to watch the process of chaining the prisoners together and riveting the iron collars around their necks; and as the *bagnards* passed through the countryside en route, conveyed on open carts, the scene often resembled a carnival sideshow. This barbarous ritual offended the reformers, some of whom (notably Charles Lucas) campaigned to substitute a new form of transport, the *voiture cellulaire*. In 1836 Minister Gasparin adopted this scheme; *bagnards* would henceforth travel in a twelve-cell wagon, where they would be hidden from onlookers and where they might while away the time with books of "religious morality." The first trial of the new system in 1837 proved instantly successful; the journey to Brest was shortened from twenty to three days, the convoys passed unnoticed.[68] So ended the last of the public punishment rituals left over from the old regime.

This overdue reform, however, touched only the margin of a larger problem—the existence of the *bagnes* themselves. Ever since 1791 there had been sporadic proposals to abolish these relics of a past era; some *bagnes* had been closed (at Lorient, Le Hâvre, and Cherbourg), but Toulon, Brest, and Rochefort remained in operation, housing some 7000 hard-labor convicts. The naval ministry, which administered the *bagnes*, had long chafed at this onerous responsibility, and complained that there was not sufficient work in the ports to keep all these men busy.[69] Even the defenders of the *bagnes* admitted that they were grim places. At Brest, wrote the *bagne* official Vénuste Gleizes, most inmates were assigned to heavy work in the open air; despite three hundred days of rain annually, no change of clothing was provided on return to barracks. Prisoners were herded into three large rooms holding some six hundred men each, and chained at night to "camp beds" large enough for twenty-four men. There they ate and slept, according to Gleizes, "*serrés, pressés, entassés*", indulging in unnameable, shameful practices. The diet was frugal, and the most important reward for good behavior was promotion to *la chaîne brisée*, which meant substituting a half-chain attached to the belt and the ankle for the standard chain joining prisoners in pairs. Such a concession was rare and was granted only after four or five years. Severe treatment was essential, Gleizes believed, for these were hopeless incorrigibles—"ferocious and bloodthirsty men, insensitive to remorse and pity, dreaming only of murder, theft, and pillage. . . ."[70]

Ironically, Gleizes's grim description was intended to defend the *bagnes* against those critics who wanted to liquidate them because they were allegedly too attractive. André Dupin, deputy and former government prosecutor, argued in 1846 that "the *forçats* have been treated with scandalous kindness, better even than the sick." Visiting Toulon, Dupin observed a barrel of wine destined for the inmates, while the guards, he complained, got none. "Our *forçats* enjoy the open air; they work very little. The *bagne* is no longer a punishment. . . . If there were more rigor and hardship, there would be more moral improvement."[71] In one sense Dupin was right; many hardened criminals preferred the *bagnes* to the closed prisons because much of the work was done in the open air, there was no rule of isolation and silence, and wine or beer was supplied with meals (an essential supplement, it was believed, for anyone engaged in hard labor). Most hard liners were nevertheless determined to retain the *bagnes* unless something equally intimidating could be found to replace them. The reformers found it hard to come up with an alternative; some favored closed prisons with facilities for hard labor, others fell back on the simpler solution of transportation to an overseas penal colony. The controversy thus remained stalemated, and became part of a broader discussion of penal methods.

The issue that emerged to dominate debate throughout the 1840s was the one that Beaumont and Tocqueville had introduced in 1833: should France adopt an American-style penitentiary system with rehabilitation as an important secondary goal, and, if so, which of the two American varieties would best suit France? The Beaumont-Tocqueville report had stimulated so much discussion that it finally impelled the government to act. In 1836 Minister of Interior de Gasparin dispatched a second study mission to the United States, composed this time of magistrate Frédéric Demetz and architect Abel Blouet (famed for his restoration of Fontainebleau palace and his completion of the Arc de Triomphe). This mission was designed to update the earlier report and to test its validity. The new investigators fully reaffirmed the findings of their predecessors; Demetz, who had departed from France as a strong opponent of solitary confinement, returned a vigorous convert to the Cherry Hill experiment.[72] A new minister of interior, Montalivet, sought further advice by polling the departmental *conseils-généraux*. The returns were overwhelmingly in favor of the Cherry Hill model: fifty-five *conseils* favored day-and-night solitary confinement as compared with fifteen for the Auburn plan and only one for the traditional common prison.[73] In 1840 a new cabinet reshuffle brought to the ministry of interior Charles de Rémusat, and this former member of the *Société de Morale Chrétienne* promptly submitted a prison reform bill to the Chamber of Deputies. From that moment (May 1840) until the revolution of 1848, the issue of penal reform was to remain the most persistent and contentious item on the parliamentary agenda.

Rémusat's bill reflected his traits of character; he was once described as an "indeterminate eclectic liberal." His presentation of the measure to the Chamber was a fine example of high principle tempered by equivocation.[74] He assured the deputies that he would not think of proposing blind imitation of a foreign model or some illusory dream of perfection. Although he expressed a cautious preference for solitary confinement, he suggested that the government be authorized to try various experiments before settling on an "irrevocable" commitment. In the same spirit, he spoke out for the abolition of the *bagnes* but then backed off by suggesting that precipitate action might offend the public. The bill thus sketched out a dim and distant vision of a penitentiary system based on solitary confinement, to be established if and when experimental evidence and public opinion were to come to its support. Rémusat's prudent proposal was quickly transformed into something much more sweeping. The Chamber referred it to a committee chaired by Alexis de Tocqueville (who had been elected a deputy in 1839) ; and his report (June 1840) went far beyond Rémusat's draft.[75] There was no time, he argued, for further delay and time-consuming experiments; the rising crime rate and the growth of recidivism called for immediate decisions. The crucial choice must be the adoption of the Cherry Hill model, for reasons both moral and practical. That model was more likely than the Auburn system to encourage moral improvement or at least to prevent further corruption; it would not require jailers of outstanding quality; it would make a more profound impression on the sensibilities of both prisoners and public; and it would (according to Tocqueville's Philadelphia informants) improve rather than injure prisoners' health. Furthermore, the French public clearly favored it, as shown by the survey of *conseils-généraux* in 1838. Since solitary confinement was a harsh penalty, the maximum sentence (except for life terms) should be reduced from twenty to twelve years; and the few "lifers" should be transferred to a common prison after their twelve years of solitary.

Neither Rémusat's bill nor Tocqueville's drastically revised version ever reached the floor for debate. Another cabinet crisis, followed by the dissolution of the Chamber, forced delays and a new start. In April 1843 another minister of interior, comte Charles Duchâtel (a faithful lieutenant of Guizot) , presented a revised bill that borrowed heavily from the Tocqueville version of 1840.[76] Once again the Chamber referred the bill to a committee chaired by Tocqueville, who naturally reported it out with very few changes.[77] Discussion on the floor finally began on April 23, 1844; it occupied most of the Chamber's time during the next four weeks, and brought into the open virtually every argument and every prejudice inspired by a generation of debate about penal methods.

"THE GOLDEN MEAN BETWEEN THE GUILLOTINE AND LIB-
ERTY." A forgotten 19th-century artist's stylized conception of prison life
at the time. (Roger-Viollet)

Few other debates in French parliamentary history dealt in such
detail with the broad issue of criminal justice or evoked the talents
of so many notable orators.

The heart of the revised bill was its acceptance of the Cherry
Hill system of cellular isolation, modified by Tocqueville's pro-

vision limiting solitary confinement to a maximum of twelve years. The bill also called for the liquidation of the *bagnes* and their replacement by closed prisons with facilities for hard labor. Although Duchâtel as minister presented the bill, he left it to Tocqueville to carry the main burden of its advocacy: Tocqueville was seconded by Beaumont (who had also become a deputy) and received a passionate but somewhat ambiguous assist from the Chamber's most flamboyant orator, Alphonse de Lamartine. It was the "extraordinary and alarming" rise in the crime rate since 1830, Tocqueville argued, that made the need for action imperative; and it was the "deplorable" state of French prisons that contributed heavily to criminality.[78] Once again he and Beaumont rehearsed in detail the cluster of reasons for preferring the Philadelphia to the Auburn model. Duchâtel reinforced the argument by citing the latest statistics on recidivism, which showed that the proportion of repeaters in the *maisons centrales* had risen in 1844 to 45 per cent.[79] The prison experience, he observed, was obviously failing either to intimidate or to rehabilitate; a new system was desperately needed.

But it was the opponents of the proposed reform who monopolized most of the Chamber's time during the debate. The pro-Auburn disciples of Charles Lucas fought back with charges that the day-and-night cell system was barbarous, ineffective, illegal, anti-religious, and anti-social. Even some staunch government supporters like Frédéric La Coudrais denounced solitary confinement as un-French: "We are not a people of silent habits like the Americans, whose character is, so to speak, cellular."[80] The marquis de Rochefoucauld-Liancourt took a different line, arguing that the reform was completely unnecessary. Liancourt attempted to demonstrate, through manipulating the official statistics, that both the crime rate and the proportion of recidivists had actually declined since 1830, thus proving that the traditional common prison was working well.[81] Adolphe Crémieux, lawyer and stellar orator of the dynastic opposition, chimed in with an outraged denial that criminality was unduly high in France; in fact, he contended (though without offering evidence) the French rate was the world's lowest, for "in what other country can you find a people more easily led to good conduct and diverted from evil?"[82] From the far right wing the law-and-order magistrate André Duléry de Peyramont launched a long and impassioned attack on the very idea of rehabilitation. It was the philanthropists, he charged, who were responsible for the rise of crime; their humanitarian illusions, culminating in the relaxation of the criminal code in 1832, had opened the floodgates. The hard fact was that crime could never be extinguished: "It is a necessary evil. Providence has seen to it that evil exists in this world, so that man may draw on his courage and his energy in the struggle against it." Men guilty of major crimes were simply beyond redemption; the sole purpose of punishment must be to intimidate them and others, as the galleys and the *bagnes* had traditionally served to do. The reformers' real purpose, Peyramont charged, was to transform public mores by destroying the healthy repulsion toward crime and criminals. Once that goal was accomplished, society would disintegrate.[83] Another hardliner, Armand Lherbette of the dynastic left, denounced the "blind *philanthropomanie*" that had empowered juries to consider extenuating circumstances; these days, he declared ironically, one may expect juries to propose leniency for parricides on the ground that they had refrained from hacking their parents into small pieces. A few wild beasts were susceptible to taming, Lherbette cried, but it was futile to try taming tigers or rattlesnakes; in the end, the moralizers would be devoured by the moralized.[84]

As the debate progressed, more and more deputies turned to what seemed to be an easy alternative: namely, the transportation of major offenders to a distant penal colony. Transportation was one of the penalties listed in Napoleon's penal code, but it had remained a dead letter; those few persons sentenced to transportation after the British blockade ended in 1814 had been sent to the state prison of Mont-Saint-Michel pending the establishment of a penal colony. Proposals had been made from time to time either to eliminate the penalty from the code or to make it operative; there had been a rash of agitation in its favor in 1818–19 and again in 1828–29, but no decision had been taken.[85] The idea emerged more or less spontaneously during the 1844 debate, and was advocated by a number of speakers—including, notably, Lamartine, whose purple oratory electrified the Chamber. All nations throughout history, Lamartine cried, had "felt the need to disgorge their scum (if I may use the phrase) on some distant shore, to ostracize the scoundrels in order to ensure the security of good citizens." Rome had done so: England, Russia, and now even the United States, which was creating its own penal colony in Liberia (!). The English experiment in Australia, despite allegations to the contrary, had been "a magnificent success." France must follow that example, for "our civil society at this moment is replete with horror, terror, danger. . . .; honest folk are truly intimidated by the scoundrels. . . . Who can deny that crime is submerging us?"[86]

So lengthy a debate was likely to transcend the well-worn standard arguments on both sides and to probe into some new aspects of the crime problem. So it was that a number of deputies went beyond the issues of control and punishment to make brief excursions into the causes of crime. Heretofore, that question had not drawn much attention; Frenchmen had assumed either that men were rational beings who chose freely between good and evil or that they were weak, corruptible sinners who could be kept honest only by intimidation. Occasionally there had been passing suggestions that crime might have social roots in misery or ignorance, but few reformers had seen fit to develop these ideas in any depth. Those who had done so—notably some of the early socialists—were regarded as cranks and were not taken very seriously by either the politicians or the reformers. The 1844 debate, if it revealed little sophisticated thinking about the causes of crime, did at least show some awareness that the question existed. Joseph Cordier of the extreme left, for example, traced the rise of crime to lack of education and employment, low wages, and an excessive tax burden; he sought to demonstrate a perfect correlation between the curves of rising crime and rising taxes since 1830. Public funds, he contended, should be spent on prevention rather than punishment; no more palatial prisons, but schools for the young, homes for the aged, agricultural colonies for juvenile offenders.[87] For another republican, Hippolyte Carnot, the fault lay with "that exaggerated tendency toward material pleasures" which was fostered by the monarchy in order to divert men's minds from politics; he too stressed popular education as central in reducing crime.[88] Speaking for the right wing, Peyramont argued that the rise in property crimes was an inevitable by-product of increasing prosperity; natural depravity leads men to steal when they are surrounded by worldly goods.[89] Pierre-François de Saint-Priest (of the dynastic opposition) blamed moral decay caused by the licentious press, the theater, and published accounts of criminal trials; he called for rigorous censorship.[90] And the Legitimist lawyer Jean-Jacques Béchard found the decline in religious belief to be the real source of immoral conduct.[91] Variety rather than depth of analysis thus marked this aspect of the debate.

In the end, these numerous and vocal critics were overwhelmed by a largely silent majority of deputies who supported the government; the measure was approved on May 19 by a vote of 231 to 128. Dozens of amendments were rejected; a few were accepted by the bill's sponsors. The most notable change reduced the maximum period of solitary confinement from twelve to ten years and provided that long-termers would be deported after ten years to an overseas penal colony rather than transferred to an Auburn-type prison.[92] Both Duchâtel and Tocqueville reluctantly accepted this modification on the ground that only a few prisoners would be involved; Duchâtel assured the Chamber that given ten years to search the world, a proper penal colony could surely be found.[93]

But if the proponents of the cell-type penitentiary seemed to have won at last, their rejoicing was premature. When the bill went up to the Chamber of Peers, it encountered a new difficulty; some peers had become such enthusiastic converts to the virtues of solitary confinement that they saw no reason to restrict its blessings to a ten-year maximum or to dilute it by introducing the principle of transportation. The Peers requested, therefore, that further evidence and expert opinion be gathered and that the bill be re-examined by a special commission of legislators and outside experts. This diversion consumed two more years; reports were solicited from prefects and magistrates, and the commission set to work early in 1846.[94] Chaired by Minister of Interior Duchâtel, it included the inevitable Tocqueville and Beaumont along with a number of eminent magistrates, penal authorities, and one medical expert. After four months of deliberation (February–June 1846), a large majority of the commission agreed on changes that amounted to total victory for the extreme proponents of solitary confinement. The commission recommended that all prisoners, from those awaiting trial to those serving life sentences, be placed in solitary for the full duration of their prison stay. The *bagnes* would be replaced by cellular prisons, which would be built in newly conquered Algeria. Political prisoners alone would be exempted from solitary confinement; currently there were only nineteen such prisoners in France, the commission was told.

During the commission's deliberations, both Tocqueville and Beaumont put up a vigorous fight for restricting the time in solitary to twelve years. A lifetime in isolation, they contended, would be too much to bear; and besides, the Chamber of Deputies would probably balk at the idea of solitary confinement for life. But they were heavily outvoted in the commission; their long campaign for cellular imprisonment had ended by outrunning their intentions. They also opposed unsuccessfully the proposal to build the new prisons for ex-*bagnards* in Algeria: cellular imprisonment far from family and friends, Tocqueville argued, would be unduly severe. But the Algerian mirage, which emerged spontaneously during the commission's debates, was too tempting to resist; it seemed a happy compromise between the advocates of transportation and those who favored closed prisons at home. The commission also wrestled at length with two technical problems posed by the penal code: how could hard labor be organized within individual cells, and why should hard-labor prisoners in solitary confinement continue to be burdened with the ball-and-chain? In the end, the commission voted to enforce both provisions of the code in the cellular prisons; otherwise, it was argued, *travaux forcés* would be no different from *réclusion*, and the hierarchy of punishments would lose its logical purity.

Buoyed up by the special commission's findings, the advocates of solitary confinement now felt confident of success. They could also bring forward evidence collected from some twenty departmental cell prisons that had been functioning for several years and from cellular experiments in other parts of Europe. But the leisurely legislative process still had to spin itself out; a commission of the Chamber of Peers now had its innings. That commission, chaired by the former magistrate and penal reformer Alphonse Bérenger, brought in its report in April 1847.[95] The Bérenger commission accepted most of the recommendations of the special commission of 1846—notably the principle of solitary confiinement without limit of time, the replacement of the *bagnes* by closed prisons, and the requirement that the ex-*bagnards* continue to be subjected to hard labor in their cells. Work was essential, declared Bérenger, for its moralizing effect; and there was evidence that hard labor of eighty different sorts could be effectively organized within the cell. On a few points, however, the Peers commission diverged from the experts' commission. It proposed that the new closed prisons for hard-labor convicts need not be built in Algeria but might be located along the French coasts or on offshore islands. It recommended that the ball-and-chain be abandoned as useless in the cell, but that "a light chain" attached to the leg of *forçats* be retained as a kind of symbol. It voted that political prisoners must be subjected, like all others, to the standard solitary-confinement system. The Bérenger commission also introduced some ideas of its own into the much-amended bill. In order to standardize prison conditions, it proposed that all prisons, local as well as state, be placed henceforth under the central government's supervision, and that all costs of construction and maintenance be borne by the central government rather than the departments. It recommended that members of two religious congregations (the *Frères de la Doctrine Chrétienne* and the *Soeurs de Marie-Joseph*) be asked to serve as auxiliaries in all prisons, with a central role as educators and moral counselors. And it urged the immediate development of voluntary patronage societies to aid liberated prisoners in their reintegration into society.

One last hurdle remained: floor debate and a vote on the measure by the Chamber of Peers. But while various peers (including Victor Hugo) were polishing their orations, fate intervened; the revolution of February 1848 brought down the monarchy, and with it the plans for penal reform. So ended fifteen years of patient effort and bitter controversy over the conversion of France's prisons into penitentiaries. It was a frustrating outcome for the reformers; yet they could comfort themselves with the knowledge that much had changed during the July Monarchy. Material conditions in the prisons had continued to improve (though they remained uneven); the cellular principle was already operative (or would be shortly) in one-third of the departmental prisons; and a few privately founded experiments in dealing with juvenile delinquents were beginning to attract considerable notice. The most important of these, the farm colony of Mettray, had been established in 1840 by the magistrate Frédéric Demetz; its rigorous and austere discipline, combined with basic schooling and open-air work, was widely thought to be the most promising device yet

SCHOOLROOM IN LA PETITE ROQUETTE PRISON. To ensure total isolation of each juvenile inmate, this system of boxes was designed. The blackboard carries the moral lesson of the day: "Other people's property is sacred, and we must all respect it." The prison's outdoor exercise yard was also devised to ensure isolation. (Roger-Viollet)

tried for nipping criminality in the bud.[96] La Petite Roquette, the Parisian cell prison for juveniles, was also beginning to function effectively after some initial problems.[97] And the unexpected emergence in 1848 of a republic, many of whose leading figures were known to be sympathetic to social experiments, seemed to brighten the prospects for philanthropic action in the realm of criminal justice. The February revolution, therefore, appeared to mark not the end of an era of reform but the possible beginning of a new and creative time of change.

# IV

## Two Steps Forward, Two Steps Back
### 1848–1870

> This question of prisons and their reform was perfectly under-
> stood twenty years ago; it is almost forgotten today. . . . Yet it
> confronts us again in the most redoubtable form. The popula-
> tion of malefactors that fills the prisons and threatens society is
> again becoming a source of fear for all honest folk.
>
> GUSTAVE DE BEAUMONT (1864)

THE MEN WHO carry out successful revolutions—unless their purpose is merely to substitute themselves for the old ruling elite
(*"Ôte-toi, que je m'y mette,"* as the cynical French phrase goes) —
usually have in mind some fundamental change in the institutions
and values of their society. The leaders of France's revolution of
1848, even though they had not been complete outsiders in the
fallen regime, clearly aimed at creating a new political order and
some social change as well. They put it grandiloquently in the
preamble to one of the new government's first decrees: ". . . Greatness of soul is the highest form of policy; . . . each revolution carried
out by the French people owes to the world the consecration of a
new philosophical truth."[1] The area of proposed experimentation
and change included the system of crime control; so the leaders
of the new republic proclaimed a number of reforms that had been
talked about for some years past. But the provisional government's
attack on the problem was piecemeal rather than systematic, and
most of its actions (like the regime itself) proved to be ephemeral.

The most important and durable innovation was to come as a kind of aftershock, when the Second Republic had given way to Napoleon III's Second Empire: namely, the decision to close the *bagnes* and to export long-term convicts to penal colonies overseas.

The men of 1848, with few exceptions, had not been directly involved in the long debate over prison reform that had obsessed so many of the July Monarchy's politicians and ideologues for the past fifteen years. Most of them had not taken sides in the controversy over the penitentiary concept or over the rival systems of prison organization. That issue faded out of public attention; the great reform bill that had been on the verge of consummation at the end of 1847 simply slipped into oblivion. The new government turned instead to a series of immediate but limited reforms. But first it sought to avert the danger that the revolution might cause repercussions in the prisons. Moved apparently by a combination of humanitarian and law-and-order concerns, the government on its very first day in office entrusted a doctor named Leroy-d'Etoilles with a special mission to "supervise the conditions of the prisoners, to see to their subsistence, and to repress any attempts at rebellion."[2] It also requested an immediate report on prison conditions in Paris and ordered its agents in the provinces to improve the quality of prison food.[3] There was some reason for the government's worry: news of the revolution seeped into the Paris prisons and produced a surge of hope that liberation might be at hand. The government, however, had no intention of opening the prison doors; it confined its favor to those few prisoners who had been condemned for political, press, or religious offenses and who were promptly freed. Nor did the Paris crowd show much interest in opening the jails; it was content merely to liberate the inmates of the women's prison and of a suburban military prison, who were apparently regarded by the revolutionary crowd as special victims of an oppressive system.[4] Some agitation within the prisons of both Paris and the provinces occurred throughout 1848, but most of these disorders were provoked by local grievances rather than by any illusion of general amnesty, and they aroused more popular fear than sympathy in the cities where they occurred.[5]

Meanwhile the provisional government had been issuing a series of reform decrees, though always with the proviso that they would require later confirmation by an elected assembly. The earliest of these actions, adopted only forty-eight hours after the revolution, was to abolish the death penalty for political offenses and to order a temporary suspension of executions for all other crimes as well.[6] This was the decree that was declared to embody "a new philosophical truth"—namely, the sanctity of human life. It was eventually confirmed by the Constituent Assembly elected in April, but that body refused to broaden the abolition decree to include other than political offenses.[7]

The government moved next to eliminate imprisonment for debt in civil and commercial matters—a practice (known in France as *contrainte par corps*) that dated far back into the *ancien régime* and that was in general use in most countries at the time. Reformers had long denounced such imprisonment as a relic of the dark ages; it was most often used, they said, by usurers who had lent money to spendthrift sons of prosperous families. The practice allowed creditors to get a court order for the detention of a debtor for a maximum period of five years or until the debtor's friends or family came up with the money; during detention, the creditor was required to pay a small sum for the debtor's subsistence. Imprisonment for debt was not considered to be punishment, since there had been no trial or conviction; it was simply a device to enforce payment. Debtors' prisons had been briefly abolished during the Great Revolution, and the practice had been restricted since 1831 to debts of more than 200 francs. During the four years prior to 1848, an average of about 400 debtors per year had served an average of less than sixty days each; only three had spent the full five years in detention.[8] The abolition of the practice in March 1848 was to have a short life, however. Bankers and chambers of commerce immediately mounted an emotional campaign for repeal of the reform decree; they alleged that shady operators were now free to victimize honest businessmen and that the severe business slump of 1848 was traceable in large part to the reform.[9] A legislative commission in August reported in favor of annulling the decree; the threat of detention, it declared, was the only way to strike fear into the hearts of sharpers and dishonest debtors. And it was an effective deterrent, the commission added; in Paris before 1848, 75,000 complaints were brought annually before the *tribunal de commerce*, but all except some 400 of these paid up rather than face debtors' prison.[10] In December the traditional

**LIVING IT UP IN THE PARISIAN DEBTORS' PRISON OF SAINTE-PELAGIE** (*c.* 1830). This wildly exaggerated caricature reflected the popular idea of high life among debtors who could draw on concealed assets. (Roger-Viollet)

system was restored; it was to survive for another twenty years, until the Second Empire accomplished its abolition.[11]

Of all the revolutionary government's reforms, the most drastic and controversial was its decree of March 24 suspending all penal labor (except, of course, for inmates of the *bagnes*, whose sentences included hard labor as part of the penalty). Ever since the revolutionaries of 1791 had adopted the prison as the standard punishment technique, the problem of providing work for the inmates had provoked sharp controversy. Both the penal code of 1791 and Napoleon's new code of 1810 had imposed on all convicts the obligation to work; though *how* to organize prison labor was not so simple and *whether* to organize it promptly became a hot issue, as free workers and small manufacturers in prison towns complained of unfair competition. Even the purpose of prison labor was a subject of running debate. Most prison officials argued that work was necessary to maintain discipline, since idleness bred disorder. Most nineteenth-century reformers also saw it as essential, but rather as a moralizing device: idleness encouraged vice, work inculcated good habits. Many politicians and taxpayers saw it as a way to reduce the operating costs of prisons. This mixture of motives led every nineteenth-century regime to place a high priority on putting prisoners to work.

The system adopted, with rare exceptions, relied on private entrepreneurs, who bid for the right to set up prison workshops (and, until the 1890s, to supply the inmates with food and clothing and in some cases to operate a canteen). By the 1840s some 12-13,000 prisoners were thus employed, mainly in the *maisons centrales*; most departmental prisons lacked the space to set up workshops, and the inmate turnover there was too rapid to permit the training of an efficient workforce. Prison regulations set the daily wage of inmates at 80 per cent of the going rate outside; an ordinance of 1817 apportioned the earnings on a three-way basis—one-third to the prisoner for use in the canteen, one-third to a savings account payable to the inmate on liberation, and one-third to the administration to reduce operating costs.[12]

The issue of prison labor had found its way into the long debate of the 1840s over solitary confinement. Critics of the cell system had argued that it would be difficult if not impossible to organize work in the prisons if the inmates were confined to individual cells; entrepreneurs, they contended, would refuse to bid for contracts in such conditions. Proponents of solitary confinement, on the other hand, insisted that as many as eighty types of crafts could be organized efficiently in the cells. There was some talk of adopting the English device called the crank, which (like the treadwheel in English common prisons) involved onerous but usually unproductive labor). Few Frenchmen, however, were willing to speak for this "barbarous" foreign device, and it was not seriously considered.[13]

The private-enterprise system of employing prison inmates had obvious and serious flaws. Not many businessmen were eager to bid for prison contracts, since prison labor was generally inefficient and since only a few products could be turned out effectively in prison workshops. Those entrepreneurs who did seek contracts, usually for nine-year periods, were often the less reputable sort, concerned to earn a quick franc by sweating the workers, providing minimal equipment, and profiteering on the canteen and on food supplies. Conscientious prison directors in many cases carried on bitter running feuds with the entrepreneurs but had few weapons at hand to get rid of the unscrupulous ones. The most egregious case of profiteering came to light in 1847 at France's largest *maison centrale*, Clairvaux, which housed more than 2000 prisoners. An exposé by a local newspaper provoked an official investigation that revealed an appalling state of affairs. The death rate had more than doubled since a new set of entrepreneurs took over in 1844; the prefect found that the prisoners were fed bread that contained "foreign substances," meat from sick animals, dried-up or rotten vegetables, fetid and often wormy grease; clothing returned from the laundry was often vermin-infested; inmates frequently lacked shoes or stockings; and medical care for the sick was almost nonexistent. The republic in 1848 inherited this situation and eventually convicted the entrepreneurs on charges of involuntary homicide.[14] How many abuses of this sort went undetected nobody can say; perhaps Clairvaux was an exception, or at least an extreme example.

The loudest critics of prison labor from 1814 onward, and especially after 1830, were the free workers in prison towns and the chambers of commerce representing small enterprises. Tailors, cobblers, seamstresses were especially vocal in charging that prison labor (and, in the case of the seamstresses, convent labor as well) depressed the prices of their own products and drove down free workers' wages. Prison authorities and government officials sought to refute these accusations by scoffing at the idea that twelve thousand inefficient convicts could threaten the well-being of twelve million free workers.[15] In fact, the protesters presented little evidence that prison labor in that era significantly affected the market or the wage level; seamstresses were probably most directly impacted, and that competition came mainly from convents rather than prisons. But the facts were less compelling than the beliefs of those who claimed to be innocent victims of the system; and the growth of socialist and labor movements in the 1840s increased the level of protest.

The men of 1848 were naturally sensitive to these complaints. By decree of March 24 they declared that it would be "unjust and dangerous to tolerate any longer a state of affairs that engenders misery and provokes immorality." The decree suspended all work in the prisons, ordered the termination of all existing contracts with entrepreneurs, and declared that if and when a new system of work in prisons, convents, and charitable institutions were to be developed, it must end all "troublesome" competition with free enterprise outside.[16] Overnight, virtually all prison workshops ceased to operate.

Now it was the turn of prison officials and moralizers to protest. They complained that prison discipline was disintegrating as inmates lazed about and grumbled that their only source of pocket money had been cut off. "The *maisons centrales*," declared one critic, "have again become the scene of all sorts of disorders and of incessant rebellions."[17] Some serious disorders did occur during the summer of 1848, though their connection with the closing of the workshops seems to have been marginal.[18] In any case, the government began to backtrack almost at once; in April the minister of interior declared that "public opinion" had probably been wrong in exaggerating the evils of prison labor and appointed a commission to plan its restoration without threatening the well-being of free workers.[19] The commission reported in August that the March 24 decree had been a serious mistake, leading to bloody prison revolts and "the most shameful immorality and disorganization." Prison labor, it asserted, had not been a serious threat to free enterprise; it was merely "a grain of sand in the ocean of national production," as Minister of Interior Antoine Sénard put it. For example, said Sénard, in Normandy only 400 prisoners had engaged in textile production; they could hardly have threatened the livelihood of Normandy's 200,000 textile workers. Besides, prison labor was too inefficient to be a serious rival; the commission calculated that the 13,000 men employed in the *maisons centrales* had produced only as much as 6000 free workers could turn out.[20]

On the basis of this report, parliament in January 1849 ordered the reinstitution of prison labor, with the proviso that local chambers of commerce be consulted in advance and that the products of prison labor be used only to supply state agencies.[21] Two years later this last restriction was removed; a new minister of interior (Persigny) complained in 1851 that it dissuaded entrepreneurs from bidding for prison contracts. It was "a veritable scandal," he declared, "that condemned men lie about in demoralizing indolence while being provided with the necessities of life—necessities that honest artisans earn only by unremitting toil."[22] In 1852, shortly after Louis-Napoleon's coup d'état, the government restored the pre-1848 system, adding only that some prisoners might be used in work gangs outside prison walls, along with the pious admonition that the products of prison labor be used "whenever possible" by governmental agencies.[23] Thus ended the last of the 1848 experiments. But the prison labor issue itself was far from dead; it was to remain a chronic problem throughout the century and even beyond.

Although most of the Second Republic's reforms were fleeting, one piece of durable legislation did emerge: the law of August 5, 1850, concerning the treatment of juvenile offenders. In this case, the initiative did not come from the idealists of 1848 but from the more conservative leadership that moved into control of the legislature in 1849; and the drafters drew primarily on the ideas of certain *philanthropes* of pre-1848 days—notably Charles Lucas and Frédéric Demetz.

Concern about the problem of juvenile crime had been growing for a generation. Prison officials and reformers kept hammering away at the corrupting effects of the common prison, where adolescent first offenders were exposed to the dubious tutelage of hardened criminals. This concern had inspired Rochefoucauld-Liancourt's abortive plan for a model prison in 1814; it had led Inspector Moreau-Christophe in 1831 to segregate juveniles in the jails of Paris, and Prefect of Police Gabriel Delessert in 1837 to set aside the new "prison-palace" of La Petite Roquette for juveniles.[24] It had inspired reformers like Demetz and Bérenger to found in 1833 the first Patronage Society for Young Prisoners and Ex-Prisoners; and it had impelled Demetz in 1840 to create the agricultural colony of Mettray, near Tours, as an open-air rehabilitative center for errant youngsters. Mettray's success inspired the establishment of some fifty other privately sponsored agricultural colonies during the 1840s including one set up and directed by Charles Lucas, the pioneer crusader for such institutions.[25]

Frédéric Demetz was a young Parisian magistrate who during the 1830s had been drawn into an active role as penal reformer. In 1840 he resigned his judicial post and established, on a thousand-acre estate near Tours donated by a philanthropic aristocrat, the rehabilitative center of Mettray. He recruited as aides a friend and twenty young volunteers; the enterprise began with nine juvenile offenders and grew to an eventual size of 600. The inmates were boys acquitted by the courts as being below the age of discretion (sixteen), plus some who were sent there as incorrigibles by their parents. Hard work, rigorous discipline, and moralizing instruction formed the basis of Mettray's program; religious instruction was secondary. Most of the children worked in the fields, the rest in shops, where they learned a trade. A ship was installed on dry land to give youngsters practice in setting sails and learning navigation; a swimming pool was provided for recreation. Mettray was the largest and most durable of France's agricultural colonies for juveniles; it lasted until 1939, and at one time (during the 1870s) it received half of the total state subsidies granted to private colonies of the sort.[26] Demetz's supporters boasted that only 14 per cent of Mettray's "graduates" again ran afoul of the law, whereas the proportion had previously been about 75 per cent for such juvenile delinquents.[27] Mettray's success, however, depended heavily on Demetz's personal leadership; after his death in 1873 its regime became increasingly repressive, and anti-clericals denounced it as "a den of clericals and reactionaries." A new campaign of denunciation in the 1930s succeeded finally in closing it down.[28]

Mettray in its heyday nevertheless helped to inspire the law of 1850, which was intended to be a kind of basic charter covering all aspects of the problem of juvenile delinquency; it was to remain France's fundamental legislation on the subject for 101 years.[29] It provided for "moral, religious, and professional" education for all juveniles under detention, and it ordered the separation of juveniles from adults in all prisons. It authorized the creation of both public and private *"colonies pénitentiaires"* of the Mettray sort and laid down rules for their administration. It also provided for the establishment of *"colonies correctionnelles"* for juveniles sentenced to long terms or deemed incorrigible. Although the law of 1850 was hailed at the time as a progressive milestone and has been described in retrospect as "a model for all of Europe,"[30] it was in reality applied in only piecemeal fashion and for the most part in a repressive spirit. Discipline in the various *colonies pénitentiaires* became increasingly severe in the decades that followed, and

BIRD'S-EYE VIEW OF METTRAY. Frédéric Demetz's agricultural colony for juvenile delinquents was France's largest and best known. One building housed rebellious boys sent there by their parents for a taste of discipline. (From Gaillac, *Les Maisons de correction 1830–1945*)

the segregation of juveniles in the short-term prisons remained the exception rather than the rule.[31]

The rapid withering of most of the 1848 reforms left France's pre-revolutionary crime control system largely intact. The great debate of the 1840s had ended in frustration for the reformers—especially those who had crusaded for solitary confinement, and who had been on the verge of success when the July Monarchy fell. For a time, however, it seemed that the cellular idea had rooted itself so deeply in the minds of concerned Frenchmen that it would survive after all. A directive from the republic's minister of interior Armand Dufaure in 1849 ordered that all new or reconstructed departmental prisons continue to be designed on the cellular principle, in accordance with ministerial instructions in effect before 1848.[32] But this reaffirmation of the cell system was soon to be challenged—first by a strong resurgence of interest in the idea of transportation and then by the Second Empire's repudiation of the cellular principle itself. Advocates of transportation had been active in France ever since the Great Revolution (and even before) . The upheaval of 1848 revived the idea, through what seemed the force of necessity. The bloody episode in Paris called the June Days left the republic with almost 12,000 arrested insurgents on its hands, crowded into inadequate places of detention. An emergency decree ordered that they be transported to French overseas possessions "other than those of the Mediterranean."[33] Algeria and Corsica being thus ruled out, the choice of a destination became a pressing problem. Pending that choice, those insurgents regarded as most dangerous were interned on Belle-Ile off the Breton coast and were later (January 1850) transferred to Algeria until a long-term decision could be taken. Parliament legalized these actions in June 1850, ordering that political offenders be confined "within a fortified enclosure" outside continental France.[34] During the debate a lengthy list of possible destinations was mentioned: Madagascar, Désirade (in the West Indies) , Senegal, even the bleak uninhabited Kerguelen Islands near the Antarctic Circle. The government opted for the newly annexed Marquesas Islands in the south Pacific and got parliament's approval despite some strong opposition. A few offenders were shipped off to the Marquesas in 1850, but the islands were too small for more than a handful of detainees, so the search went on.

At this point a new voice entered the debate. The president of the republic, Louis-Napoleon Bonaparte, proposed in his annual message to parliament (November 1850) a number of changes in the nation's crime-control system, designed, he said, to reassure good citizens that the government was taking the crime problem seriously. As one such change, he advocated that major criminals as well as political dissidents be transported and that the *bagnes* in French seaport cities be liquidated. It was high time, he declared, to purge France of the costly and corrupting *bagnes* and to employ their six thousand inmates on the more civilized and constructive task of developing France's colonial empire.[35] The prince-president's message gave a strong fillip to the campaign for transportation; parliament set up a commission chaired by Adolphe Thiers that reported in favor of shipping the *bagnards* to Africa and eventually transporting all offenders sentenced to terms of more than two years.[36]

Before parliament got round to acting on this proposal, a new crisis intervened. Louis-Napoleon's coup d'état of December 1851 was met by widespread resistance; this time almost 27,000 insurgents were arrested, which posed a jail-crowding problem even worse than that of June 1848. During the next few weeks special tribunals ordered the deportation of almost ten thousand of the insurgents to Algeria (half of them to a kind of concentration camp, the rest left to choose their own place of residence), while 239 others, regarded as more dangerous, were shipped to Guiana.[37]

More sweeping decisions quickly followed. Late in 1851 a commission made up of naval officers and chaired by Admiral Mackau brought in a report that echoed Louis-Napoleon's message of 1850; it recommended that the *bagnes* be closed and that their inmates be transported to Guiana.[38] Minister of Marine Théodore Ducos, endorsing the Mackau report, hailed the proposal as "one of the most generous ideas of our century." The worst abuses of the *bagnes*, he declared, would come to an end; convicts would no longer be weighed down by chains and would henceforth bask in the pleasant and "salubrious" climate of the Iles du Salut off the Guiana coast.[39] Pending action by parliament, Ducos and the emperor announced a transitional experiment: inmates of the *bagnes* were authorized to volunteer for immediate transfer to Guiana. The offer, Ducos proudly reported to Napoleon, was greeted with enthusiasm; within the first few hours, 3000 *bagnards* applied for transfer to this tropical paradise.[40] The authorities managed to ship out 2000 of the applicants during 1852 and the rest during the next couple of years.

Meanwhile the parliamentary process ground onward; in 1854 still another parliamentary commission, chaired this time by Rudel du Miral, recommended the formal liquidation of the seaport *bagnes* and suggested Guiana as an ideal substitute. The commission ruled out Algeria because it was held to be too close to France and therefore not sufficiently intimidating; Guiana was distant enough to frighten malefactors yet blessed with a "particularly salubrious" climate. The debate in parliament brought a parade of deputies to the rostrum, most of them harping on the need to inspire "salutary terror" among wrong-doers and complaining of what they called the excesses of humanitarianism and philanthropy that had marked recent decades. Some passing mention was made of the idea that transportation might "moralize" offenders, but this purpose was clearly marginal in the minds of the politicians. Only one deputy, Dr. Louis-François Lelut, spoke against the measure, and he did so on the ground that Guiana would not really intimidate. To deter malefactors, he asserted, a return to the rigorous spirit of the 1810 Code was called for; and to that end, the existing *bagnes* were both cheaper and more effective, provided that chaining convicts in pairs was strictly enforced and the work imposed was heavy. In the end, the du Miral proposal was adopted by an overwhelming vote of 225 to 3.[41] The *bagnes* of Brest and Rochefort were soon emptied; Toulon survived until 1870, but only as a transit camp for prisoners awaiting transportation. Thus vanished at last an ancient institution which, first as the galleys and then as the *bagnes*, had so fascinated and repelled Frenchmen as to become part of the national folklore. The word *bagne*, however, was to survive in popular usage to describe the new penal colonies in Guiana and, later, in New Caledonia.

The vaunted attractions of Guiana soon turned out to be a tropical mirage; as one hostile publicist had predicted, it became a *colonie mortuaire*.[42] At first the prisoners were installed on two clusters of islands off the coast, but these were too small for the flood of arrivals who soon poured in, and most of the prisoners were transferred to camps on the mainland, where facilities had to be carved out of the *brousse*. To the harsh climate were soon added the scourges of malaria and yellow fever, which decimated the camps. Of the 8000 men sent to Guiana from 1852 to 1856, half were dead at the end of five years.[43] Yet the influx of new *bagnards* continued inexorably at a rate of more than a thousand a year; and beginning in 1859 a few volunteers from women's prisons were added. The authorities nursed illusions about potential marriages of liberated convicts who would, it was hoped, help to develop and populate the colony. This hope was still another tropical mirage; such marriages were few in number, and most were unsuccessful.[44]

The grim mortality figures in the new penal colony should

have been no surprise, given the record of earlier colonization fiascos in Guiana. By 1857 even Emperor Napoleon III was forced to take note of conditions; he spoke cautiously of seeking out a more propitious location for his great experiment. A French naval expedition had annexed New Caledonia in 1853, and attention naturally turned to that territory, not far from Britain's penal colony in Australia. A trial shipload of 300 *bagnards* was sent there in 1857; the experiment seemed favorable, so more were added in 1864, and three years later the government decreed that henceforth New Caledonia would replace Guiana for all hard-labor convicts from continental France.[45] During the next two decades (1867–87), the Guiana *bagne* was reserved for convicts from various French colonies—mainly Algeria and Indochina—whose populations were supposedly better able to cope with the tropical climate. The first chapter in the history of the Guiana *bagne* thus came to a virtual end after only fifteen years. During those years (1852–67), 16,805 men and 212 women were sent there; in 1867 only about 7000 of them remained alive in the colony, and only a few hundred had returned to France or would ever manage to make that return trip.[46] Yet in spite of that dismal record, the Guiana *bagne* was to experience a second and much longer chapter under the professedly humanitarian Third Republic.

One declared purpose of transportation advanced by its proponents had been its anticipated effect on the crime rate in France. Not only was it supposed to intimidate potential offenders, but it would also purge the country of its most hardened criminals. To ensure that this purge would be effective, the law of 1854 required that long-term convicts (sentenced to eight years or more) must remain permanently in the colony after completion of sentence and that shorter-term convicts must remain there for an additional period equal to the length of their sentences. This provision, known as *doublage*, rested on the dubious assumption that liberated convicts would have a chance to make a new life in the colony and would contribute to the development of the empire. This goal was to prove still another mirage. Most liberated convicts were far from being ideal pioneers; they were usually in poor health and were treated as pariahs by both free colonists and natives;

they survived as drifters, spongers, or petty racketeers. Still, the advocates of transportation were not primarily philanthropists; their central purpose was to rid France of its most dangerous criminals and thus to reduce the incidence of crime. Was this basic purpose accomplished? Official spokesmen for the Second Empire answered in the affirmative and pointed to statistics indicating a decline in the overall crime rate during the decade 1855–65. They of course had an axe to grind; but criminologists at the end of the nineteenth century, looking back at the century's long-term trends, were inclined to confirm the claim. One of them described the period from 1853 to 1865 as "the oasis of criminality"; it appears to have been the only sustained interruption (except for a brief break in the late 1890s) in the irregular but continuous upward trend of crime during the nineteenth century.[47] If the statistics are dependable, it would seem that the transporters did achieve one of their goals.

Raising the question forces one to confront a central problem in the history of crime: namely, is there any dependable measure of the crime rate, anywhere and at any time? Criminal statistics are notoriously complicated, faulty, and subject to manipulation.[48] Comparisons over time and space are risky, since definitions of crime vary from one culture to another and from one era to another; old offenses are dropped from the list and new ones added; some felonies are reclassified as misdemeanors, some misdemeanors as felonies. Furthermore, the effectiveness of repression varies; sometimes policing is more rigorous or more efficient, so that more offenders are caught; sometimes the courts become clogged and function less efficiently. Changing mores affect the outlook of magistrates as well as that of lawmakers and citizens; they become more or less tolerant toward certain types of deviance. In addition, the base for calculating  the crime rate varies: should it be the number of crimes reported, or the number of alleged offenders arrested, or the number tried, or the number convicted? Should it also include the so-called "dark figure"—the estimated number of crimes that go unreported to the police? Should crime against persons and against property be lumped together, and likewise, misdemeanors and felonies?

Despite these complications, Frenchmen in the nineteenth century did possess one of the world's best statistical records of that era for making educated guesses about trends in crime. Beginning in 1826, the ministry of justice published an annual *Compte générale de l'administration de la justice criminelle,* which provided an unrivalled and unbroken statistical record from that day to our own. In addition, the police after 1850 were required to establish a *casier judiciaire* or "rap sheet" recording each offender's arrests and convictions. Some humanitarians objected (and continue to object today) that this record hung albatross-like around the neck of each offender, making it doubly difficult for him to go straight after serving sentence. But such records did make possible a more accurate study of the incidence of recidivism—a problem that had already begun to engage public attention from the 1820s onward. By mid-century recidivism had become one of the most passionately debated aspects of the crime problem, and it was to remain so for years to come. It had been woven into the debate of the 1840s on penal reform, and it intensified the red scare that was provoked by the upheaval of 1848 and the persistence of left-wing agitation during the next few years. Many conservatives believed, without visible evidence, that the ranks of the insurgents and the social protesters contained vast numbers of chronic criminals.

In 1851 the august Académie des Sciences Morales et Politiques, "preoccupied by the continual increase in crime, misdemeanors, and recidivism," sent some of its members on a study mission to French and English prisons and devoted fifteen sessions to discussing their report.[49] The venerable reformer Alphonse Bérenger, who headed the mission, told the Académie that since the annual *Compte* began to appear in 1826, the number of crimes in France had tripled and the number of misdemeanors had quadrupled. Beginning in 1855, however, the statistics revealed a modest decline in both categories, and in 1865 Minister of Justice Baroche proudly reported that the decline had continued. During the years 1861–65 the number of cases brought before the criminal and correctional courts had declined by 12 and 16 per cent respectively, as compared to the five years 1856–60 (which in turn had recorded a decline from the early 1850s).[50] Partisans of the Empire naturally attributed at least part of the improvement to the healthy effects of transportation. Common sense suggested, after all, that the enforced exile of some 1200 major criminals annually—many of them actual or potential recidivists—would automatically reduce the crime rate.

But how dependable were the statistics, and what other factors may have contributed to the decline in crime? Retrospective studies of crime trends throughout the nineteenth century do tend to confirm the decline in the overall crime rate from 1855 to 1865, but they place this decline in a more complicated context. They suggest that the overall increase from 1826 to the mid-1850s concealed a patchwork variety of trends: some offenses declined sharply, while others increased or remained stable.[51] Either the pattern of crime or the pattern of repression was evidently changing. Moreover, the decline of 1855–66 also concealed some unexplained variations; not all types of crime went down during that decade.[52] Even more relevant for the question of the alleged benefits of transportation was the fact that the overall crime rate began to edge upward again after 1865, and with it the level of recidivism—even though the flow of convicts to the penal colonies continued. Officials of the Second Empire were bothered by this reversal but could not agree on an explanation; in October 1869 the emperor set up a commission to study the problem.[53] But the Empire fell before the commission could finish its work, and the problem was deferred for action by the new generation of republicans.

Even if transportation had indeed helped to reduce the crime rate for a decade (inexplicably losing its magic thereafter), there were other factors that probably contributed to the so-called "oasis of criminality" from 1855 to 1865. One such factor may have been an increase in the severity of police repression; Napoleon III followed a hard-line policy at first and increased the size of both the rural gendarmerie and the urban police force.[54] That policy, however, might just as logically have increased rather than reduced the number of arrests and convictions. A more persuasive argument can be made for the tendency of magistrates and the imperial regime to "correctionalize" certain offenses—that is, to reduce them from crimes to misdemeanors, or to reduce misdemeanors to mere *contraventions* handled by local police courts or by justices of the peace. In 1859 most forest offenses, which had long cluttered the correctional courts, were downgraded in this fashion, thus reducing the number of misdemeanors (*délits*).[55] And in 1863 the government pushed through parliament a number of amendments to the Penal Code which "correctionalized" a considerable number of crimes.[56] Hard-liners complained that this reform would have dangerous consequences; they reminded the government of the first Napoleon's dictum that "weakness toward malefactors means cruelty toward everybody else," and they took an I-told-you-so attitude when crime again began to rise.[57]

The era of the Second Empire, for students of attitudes toward crime, is often seen as a kind of interlude in a century of steady humanitarian progress—a reversal in the direction of reaction, repression, and neglect. To some degree that view is justified. In contrast to the period of the July Monarchy, when crime and punishment held center stage, the Empire does seem not only repressive but also quiescent. Yet more was happening than one might think in light of the reduced level of public debate about the crime problem. No single theme stands out; it was a time of varied initiatives, of continuing but more restrained discussion of old issues and of the emergence of some new ones as well.

Pre-eminent among the old issues was the controversy over the penitentiary idea in its alternative forms. The Philadelphia system had won out by 1848; but that which its enemies had been unable to do was accomplished by the February revolution. From the first days of that revolution, declared a leading jurist of the period, "the idea of the cell began to lose ground."[58] The leading advocates of solitary confinement had belonged to the power elite of the fallen monarchy, and its fall dislodged them from positions of influence. The new elite was not inclined to give the issue high priority. Besides, many Frenchmen were no doubt tired of hearing the old arguments hashed and rehashed. In any case, except for Minister of Interior Dufaure's circular in 1849 ordering that new or rebuilt departmental prisons be constructed on the cellular model, no one talked very much about the techniques and purposes of imprisonment. On the other hand, few people expected a brusque change of direction; yet that is what France got in August 1853, shortly after the establishment of the Second Empire.

The emperor's minister of interior and confidant, Fialin de Persigny, startled the informed public by ordering an end to the building of cell-type prisons and a return to the common-prison model with "separation by quarters," as it was then called. That system was based on the segregation of inmates by categories

within each prison: men from women, adults from juveniles, indicted persons from those serving sentences, and so on. Persigny's
circular (described by one critic as marked by "a truly oriental
laconicism") avoided all theoretical arguments; he justified the
action on the purely pragmatic ground that cellular prisons cost too
much to build and that this cost factor had prevented the upgrading of the departmental prisons, which were still in lamentable
condition.[59]

Partisans of the new Empire were quickly mobilized, or came
forward voluntarily, to praise Persigny's move as the voice of
wisdom and humanitarian concern. The most resounding voice was
that of Dr. Prosper de Pietra Santa, whose pamphlet published in
1853 was a ringing endorsement of the new policy line.[60] Pietra
Santa could claim special expertise on the sharply debated question of the physical and mental effects of solitary confinement. He
had served as a doctor in the newest Paris prison (Mazas, built
during the 1840s as the largest cellular prison in France) and had
then been transferred at his own request to an old-style common
prison. The contrast, he claimed, had been striking and had
cured him of his former allegiance to the cellular system. Madness
and suicide at Mazas, he asserted, had been abnormally high; young
prisoners were especially likely to become unhinged when isolated
in separate cells. Pietra Santa poured lavish praise on Persigny
and on the emperor (to whom his pamphlet was dedicated) for
acting vigorously rather than wasting further time on empty debate. There had been too much of this already, he declared; *la
réforme pénitentiaire* was "a phrase filled with illusions born of
the philosophical imagination." Worse still, the whole idea of penal
reform had come from the United States, *"cette patrie des ex-
centricités"*; during the past generation, many ambitious opportunists seized upon it as "a stepladder to honors." Pietra Santa's
thesis was picked up at once by the pro-governmental press and
was echoed enthusiastically by the anti-cell faction of the medical
profession.

A few of the surviving *philanthropes*, still bitterly regretting
"the February catastrophe" that had derailed their great reform bill
and stung by Pietra Santa's aspersions on their motives, struck back
as best they could. The doctor's own motives, they suggested, were
a bit suspect; he belonged to the imperial entourage and was out

to curry favor. The anti-cell campaign, they alleged, was mainly political in inspiration; it was merely an excuse for violent attacks on the parliamentary system of Louis-Philippe and on its leading figures, whom the new elite was trying to brand as "passionate admirers of the inventions of the Anglo-Saxon race."[61] "Certain doctors," the critics added, "can see only the medical aspect of a social question." In fact, they argued, Pietra Santa's evidence was shaky; it was drawn from the single example of Mazas, which was in no way typical. One unrepentant advocate of the cell put his case more bluntly: "A few extra cases of dementia may not be too high a price to pay for a great decline in cases of corruption."[62] But the times, and the repressive nature of the Empire in its early years, discouraged a vigorous pursuit of the old cellular debate; the issue was to be raised only at intervals so long as Napoleon ruled.[63]

Although Persigny had justified his U-turn by the need to improve the disgracefully inadequate departmental prisons, one result seems to have been a marked slowdown in prison-building and renovation. During the July Monarchy forty-seven cellular prisons had been built, fifteen were begun, and six more were planned. But of the 396 departmental and local prisons in France, only sixty (plus the new cellular prisons) were even able to segregate different categories of prisoners as required by the new instructions.[64] Most of the departmental authorities seized upon the Persigny circular to avoid costly modernization. The Empire did follow up with a cautious step toward standardizing conditions in the departmental prisons; a law of 1855 shifted the burden of "ordinary operating expenses" from the departments to the central government. But the cost of construction and building maintenance was left to the local authorities, who preferred to spend their money elsewhere.[65] Defenders of the regime boasted that the law of 1855 lowered the costs of operating the prison system, improved food and health conditions, and led to the introduction of work programs in most departmental prisons.[66] Léon Vidal, an official spokesman for the Empire, claimed in 1869 that the mortality rate among prisoners had been reduced from 8–10 percent to 2–3 per cent, that overcrowding had been corrected, that the sexes had at last been effectively separated everywhere, and that more religious influence had been introduced into the prisons.

He even argued that "penitentiary science" had at last become a true science; all of its essential principles were now known and agreed upon, and all that was needed was to apply them.[67] Vidal's confidence that all penal problems were at last on the verge of solution seems, in retrospect, a trifle premature.

Napoleon III's turn from authoritarian to more liberal practices during the 1860s rekindled the hopes of the surviving prison reformers. "The long interlude of torpor and inertia" was ending, declared the jurist and former deputy Raymond Aylies; Frenchmen were becoming aware that many penal problems still had to be confronted.[68] But his prediction of a vast surge of interest matching that of the years before 1848 was to be disappointed. Never again, indeed, was the crime problem to become the major focus of French attention; the years of the July Monarchy had been the all-time peak. True, there was a considerable burst of interest during the 1860s in the issue of capital punishment, which provoked a freshet of brochures pro and con and, in 1870, a proposal by the republican minority in parliament to abolish the death penalty.[69] There was also a resurgence of argument about the crime rate and the level of recidivism; critics of the Empire pointed out that both curves were rising again from the mid-1860s, while the government's spokesmen retaliated that better records and more efficient policing tended to inflate the figures.[70]

Although the Empire's turn toward liberalism introduced some cautious reforms in other spheres, it brought few changes in the area of crime control and penal policy. The revision of the Penal Code in 1863 (the first such reform since 1832, and the last during the nineteenth century) embodied an odd mixture of relaxed and increased repression; it reduced some crimes to misdemeanors but also narrowed the authority of judges to consider extenuating circumstances.[71] Two years later, in 1865, the government embarked on what seemed to be a more progressive action: it introduced a bill to abolish the ancient practice of imprisonment for debt. The project aroused sharp debate in the *Corps législatif*, reflecting the tensions between the liberal and the authoritarian factions in the Bonapartist camp. One skeptical deputy complained that the government was stirring up needless trouble, since there had been no public agitation in favor of this reform—to which Minister of Justice Baroche replied that a liberal

PRISON OF LA SANTÉ, PARIS. Built in the 1860s and still in use to-day as a short-term prison, this barracks-like structure was described by an official in 1872 as a "model prison." In its early years it was partly cellular, partly common prison. (Roger-Viollet)

regime ought sometimes to lead rather than merely follow public opinion.[72] In the end the bill was adopted by a narrow margin (112 to 95); it was, in the retrospective view of one hard-line critic, "one of the most remarkable manifestations of that vague humanitarianism that makes us forget the victim and sympathize with the debtor."[73] The reform was partially undone by the conservative National Assembly in 1871, which restored the right of the state to imprison offenders for failure to pay a fine or court costs.[74] Still, the Empire did put a permanent end to one vestige of the past: no debtor would henceforth be imprisoned at a creditor's request, but only after formal condemnation by the courts.

One other action of the imperial government is of interest not because it embodied some basic principle of penal policy but simply because it concerned one of France's best-known historical monuments, the ancient abbey of Mont-Saint-Michel. That remote and spectacular structure, on a small rocky island at the point where Normandy and Brittany meet, had served as an occasional prison since the late middle ages. At first there were merely a few cells for offenders from the vicinity or for erring monks; then Louis XI during the fifteenth century began to use it occasionally for political prisoners. It was Louis XI who was supposed to have installed the iron cage which, according to dubious legend, was suspended by ropes in mid-air and was used to confine victims of royal displeasure.[75] Louis XIV and Louis XV put the abbey to increasing use, mainly for *lettre de cachet* cases. According to the most careful calculation, only 147 prisoners were incarcerated there during the century from 1685 to 1789; more than half of these were locked away at the request of the prisoner's family.[76]

Mont-Saint-Michel's conversion to a full-time prison came in 1792, when the revolutionary government sent some three hundred non-juring priests there pending eventual deportation to Guiana. They were joined after 1796 by a scattering of common criminals and royalist partisans.[77] In 1811 Napoleon gave the Mont regular prison status and added some prisoners of war to the other categories. By 1817, when the restored monarchy rebaptized it as a *maison de force* (i.e., a prison for hard-labor convicts), it held almost 400 inmates, and that figure soon rose to a maximum of almost 600.[78] For some years the prison housed men, women, and children down to the age of ten, with little segregation by sex or age. During the seventy years from 1793 to 1863, 14,000 prisoners served sentences at the Mont—among them a number of noted political dissenters such as Auguste Blanqui and Armand Barbès.[79]

Such prison records as have survived suggest that Mont-Saint-Michel was a grim place, ill-suited to its penal function (though probably no worse than most French prisons of the time). True, the prison director from 1817 to 1827, one Duruisseau, praised the ex-abbey as "excellent for both safety and salubrity"; but the archives contain a prisoner's letter that sounded a quite different note. He described it as *"la plus vil maison de l'Europe,"* complained of *"barbarie tyrannier"* on the part of the entrepreneur who supplied food and work, hinted at goings-on in the sleeping quarters that were *"horribles et peu délicats,"* and begged the Paris authorities to transfer him, no matter where.[80] The prefect, after a visit in 1818, reported that the prisoners were miserably ill clothed; inmates arrived with only the rags on their backs and were provided with nothing by the state. Some prisoners had to go shirtless despite the raw Breton climate.[81] The prefect praised Duruisseau for his energetic efforts to improve conditions, but it was obviously an uphill battle. The director was chronically short of funds for the essential task of converting the abbey into a prison, and he had to put up with an entrepreneur named Vidal who was evidently one of the worst of his breed. In 1826 Duruisseau urged the ministry not to renew Vidal's nine-year contract; Vidal had, he declared, let the place fall into "a disgustingly dirty state"; the prisoners were eaten by vermin, and work was provided for only two hundred of them. Vidal was indifferent to the inmates' welfare, said Duruisseau, and cared about nothing but money.[82] The director did manage to get most of the female prisoners transferred elsewhere in 1821 (over Vidal's strong protest), but his efforts to move the considerable number of young boys out of this corrupting day-and-night association with adult offenders were fruitless.[83] Exhausted by his ten-year effort to solve such severe problems, Duruisseau sought retirement in 1827 after what he called "ten years of exile."

Conditions improved very little under the July Monarchy, and in some ways they seem to have gotten worse. In 1843–44 Mont-Saint-Michel came into the public eye through allegations of scandalous abuses there, especially affecting political prisoners. Marquis Gaetan La Rochefoucauld-Liancourt, son of the famous *philanthrope*, charged in a pamphlet that brutal disciplinary measures in certain prisons, notably the Mont, had caused a wave of suicides and madness.[84] Opposition newspapers seized upon the charges to lambaste the government and, incidentally, to denounce the advocates of cellular prisons; it was solitary confinement, these critics alleged, that had driven so many inmates to despair. The issue soon reached the floor of parliament; in April 1844 several deputies interrupted official spokesmen to demand an accounting, and at last Alexis de Tocqueville took it upon himself to respond.[85] Admittedly, he declared, Mont-Saint-Michel was not the ideal prison of the reformers' dreams, but it was not so bad as the critics believed. During his visits there he had found the political prisoners enjoying large and airy quarters; food, heat, and light were sufficient, even abundant; unlike common criminals, the "politicals" were not required to work and were allowed a daily two-hour walk in the courtyard with other prisoners of their choice. Tocqueville granted that some years earlier there had indeed been disciplinary excesses. Prisoners guilty of serious misconduct had been incarcerated in frightful medieval *cachots*—in extreme cases for as long as sixty-six days. (Alphonse Bérenger later recalled seeing one convict who had spent eleven months in such a *cachot*, for the attempted murder of another prisoner.[86]) Certain troublemakers, said Tocqueville, had been put on bread and water for as long as twenty-eight days, impairing both health and reason. But these excesses, he concluded, belonged to the past; in 1842 the minister had ordered reforms, ruling out the use of *cachots* save in extreme cases. Tocqueville charged that the current outcry was inspired by the opponents of the cellular principle, who had dredged up past abuses to justify their own prejudices.

Some critics were still not satisfied. Deputy Lherbette hinted at a governmental cover-up and demanded official answers: was it true that prisoners were denied the right to complain to the ministry of justice? Had the cell system been illegally installed at Mont-Saint-Michel? Were political prisoners victims of governmental vengeance? Was it true that of twenty political prisoners at the Mont, four had gone mad and three had committed suicide?[87]

The minister was at last provoked to respond. Of course prisoners had the right to complain to the ministry, he declared; but as in all prisons, such complaints had to be routed through the prison administration. Besides, all prisons were open to the visits of any member of parliament: they could see for themselves if they wished. Solitary confinement was not practiced at the Mont; political prisoners were allowed to walk in pairs during their free time. Larger groups could not be allowed out together, since the republican inmates were split into four or five factions and would "tear one another apart" if allowed to associate. Even in pairs, said the minister, fights sometimes occurred, and misconduct among these hotheads was common. The disciplinary cells were neither cramped nor unlighted—they measured $2\frac{1}{2}$ by 3 by 3 meters. The cases of madness or suicide stemmed from personal or family problems that predated imprisonment. Furthermore, since the change of rules in 1842, there had been no prisoner complaints or disorders. In fact, the minister declared, Mont-Saint-Michel was one of France's most salubrious prisons, with a mortality rate of only one in twenty-three as compared with the general rate of one in thirteen. The complaints of the political prisoners, he concluded, were completely unjustified; indeed, no past government had been so fair and generous toward its opponents.[88] His peroration drew vigorous applause from the Chamber, and criticism of abuses at the Mont promptly died down. But the government chose to blunt further attacks by transferring the remaining political prisoners (there were only twenty-three of them at the Mont) to Doullens in northern France.

Prison records reveal a curious interlude in 1846–50, when a reform-minded director attempted to carry out drastic changes. Léon Régley, a career bureaucrat, had no past experience in prison administration, and he seems to have been shocked by his first inside look at a French prison. He moved at once to soften disciplinary rules at the Mont and steadily bombarded the ministry with proposals for change. Frustrated by the indifference of his superiors, he welcomed the revolution of 1848 as opening the way for his experiments. But his appeals to Paris brought only counsels of patience; the problem, said the new minister, was "under study," and besides, the government had to be careful not to treat prisoners better than free citizens. Régley also failed in his effort to get rid of the entrepreneur at the Mont, who, he alleged, was guilty of flagrant graft and mistreatment of prisoners. After four fruitless years, the authorities in Paris lost patience and replaced Régley. Good will and energy on the part of a director were evidently not enough to transform a flawed institution.[89]

The final chapter came in 1863, when Napoleon's government, acting (it said) at the request of the *conseil-général* of the Manche department, ordered the liquidation of the prison at Mont-Saint-Michel. For some years, admirers of historical buildings had been complaining that the venerable abbey was being "mutilated" by its inmates and by reconstruction measures to convert it to prison use. The vast chapel, for instance, had been made into a series of workshops by building in several levels, one transept was used as a kitchen, and the magnificent cloister had become the prison's exercise yard.[90] There were complaints too that the prison's remoteness made it difficult to supply and that security was inadequate.

The government's decision brought an immediate outcry from the residents of the tiny village at the foot of the Mont; many of the eighty families there had made their living by providing services for the prison officials and guards. The town council protested vigorously at this "unexpected and terrible blow"; one innkeeper claimed that the small contingent of soldiers who had served as guards had been insatiable customers, consuming annually fifty 1500-liter barrels of cider, plus uncalculated quantities of wine and spirits. The local priest joined the chorus; if the government did not reverse its decision, he warned, all but ten or fifteen families would be forced to migrate elsewhere. He urged that the abbey be converted into a penitentiary for juveniles. When the residents' protests proved ineffective, they turned to demanding an indemnity for the loss of their livelihood. The government, after emptying the prison in 1864, did pay indemnities to forty-three families, but those who were overlooked complained bitterly, and most of the favored ones protested that they had been underpaid. The authorities rode out the storm; after granting a few supplementary indemnities, the complaints tapered off.[91] Several difficult years followed before the abbey was reoccupied by a monastic order, the Pères de Saint-Edmé. Gradually, the monument was cleared of its prison impediments and restored to something like its former state. Only a few dark *cachots*, little more than caves cut into the rock wall of a corridor, remained as grim reminders of the distant past. And the villagers were soon compensated for the loss of their thirsty customers; a trickle of equally hungry and thirsty tourists grew steadily into a stream and then a flood.

# V

## Theory and Practice: From the Classical to the Positivist Era

1814–1914

> We are suddenly aware that reason, education, mores are under-
> going a profound revolution. . . . The moral sciences are being
> swept along by one of these currents of ideas. . . . Everywhere
> one sees a positive tendency to view the soul as a branch of physi-
> ology. . . . The chimera of free will is vanishing, replaced by
> what is called determinism. . . . One is driven to ask—what, then,
> becomes of the right to punish?
>
> E. M. CARO (1873)

IN ANY AGE, in any realm of human action, the relation between
theory and practice is problematic. Sometimes practice is built on
a base of theory; sometimes the two develop simultaneously; sometimes the theorists follow along, like an army's baggage-train. In
the absence of developed theory, practitioners are likely to fall back
on the society's mores or values—a set of beliefs and attitudes that
are widely accepted but often remain largely unexamined and
undiscussed.

One might expect, in a nation like France where deductive
logic is inculcated from childhood, that criminological theory
would have anticipated penal practice at every stage of history.
In fact, the two aspects seem rather to have evolved in parallel
fashion, sometimes affecting each other, at other times following
independent channels. It is clear, however, that theorizing about

crime and punishment loomed larger in France (and on the Continent generally) than in the Anglo-Saxon countries, where inductive reasoning was more highly honored and where problems were normally attacked by pragmatic experimentation. The history of crime-control efforts in Britain or the United States can probably be written without much reference to theoretical disputes (though not without reference to mores and values). France is a quite different case. Theorizing about crime was taken seriously, and it evolved over time.

In the beginning was the Enlightenment. Until then, France of course had its share of crime, but did not yet have a "crime problem" in the modern sense of the term: that is, it was not a highly controversial issue. Until the mid-eighteenth century, such questions as the causes and the nature of crime and the purpose of punishment inspired little debate, since these were taken to be self-evident matters. Frenchmen, like most Europeans, assumed that those who violated royal statutes or religious taboos or social norms acted out of free choice—a choice that might be influenced by some moral defect or by urgent material need, but that involved individual moral responsibility. Punishment in turn was commonly seen as embodying either social vengeance, enforced expiation, or deterrence through intimidation, and sometimes as a mixture of all three. Rehabilitation, except in the restricted form of expiation through suffering, remained an almost unknown concept until the nineteenth century. Eliminating wrongdoers seemed in those days to be simpler and more effective than trying to reform them. Even that great sixteenth-century humanist Michel de Montaigne declared bluntly, "You don't improve a man by hanging him, but you improve others through his example."[1]

The Enlightenment thinkers took the first long step toward making crime and punishment a matter for controversy when they challenged the traditional methods of punishment. Beccaria and his disciples in France and elsewhere were moved by a blend of humanitarian and practical considerations: excessive and brutal penalties, they believed, were unworthy of civilized nations, and in addition they served no useful end. The essential purpose of punishment was utilitarian rather than vengeful: each penalty should be precisely calculated so that the pain imposed would barely outweigh the pleasure of successful wrongdoing. The influence of Jeremy Bentham, whose utilitarian theory was even more starkly stated, further reinforced that of Beccaria for the Revolutionary generation and its immediate nineteenth-century successors.

But Beccaria and his French followers mixed their utilitarianism with a continuing element of retributionism. If the chief purpose of punishment was to deter future transgressions by the offender and others, the wrongdoer should also be made aware that he had violated the social contract. Each punishment should therefore bear some analogy to the crime committed, and penalties should involve suffering and, if possible, a feeling of remorse. This combination of the utilitarian outlook and the older spirit of social vengeance marked the thinking of the men of 1789, and suffused the reforms of the Great Revolution. Napoleon's penal codes also, though they were more severely repressive, continued the heritage of the Enlightenment thinkers. To that heritage the next generation of penal reformers added another strain, deriving from the teachings of Immanuel Kant. Kant bluntly challenged the utilitarian doctrine of crime control; for him, there existed moral absolutes which must not be infringed. His celebrated illustration of this principle presumed an island society in the final stage of dissolution; as the inhabitants prepare to abandon the island, one resident commits a murder. Should the murderer be left free on the island, where he could no longer injure society, or should he be executed as the last act before departure? For Kant, there could be no doubt: justice had to be done. Retribution could not be evaded by resorting to the utilitarian argument.[2]

Although not all of the *philanthropes* of the early nineteenth century adopted the pure Kantian position, it did enter into the blend of utilitarianism and retributionism that came eventually to be known as "classical" theory. Until mid-century and even beyond, most Frenchmen who were concerned with the crime problem, either practically or theoretically, shared that classical view. Every offender, in this view, was a rational and morally responsible individual who had made a conscious choice in violating the law (or had acted irrationally, which did not relieve him of moral responsibility unless he was clearly deranged). Penalties should be related to the crime, and should be precisely defined in advance, with no flexibility to fit the individual criminal or circumstance. For the purists of this school, Beccaria was right in rejecting the idea of an effort to reform offenders against their will; at most, isolation should be allowed to exert its beneficent influence on those wrongdoers whose consciences were still alive, and who could seek redemption through introspection and prayer.

In England, the movement for penal reform inaugurated by John Howard and others had been powerfully influenced by evangelical Christianity.[3] The evangelical movement had no exact equivalent in France, but in some Catholic circles and among the small Protestant minority there was the same moral urge impelling some of the reformers of the early nineteenth century. This religious impulse was, however, less marked than in England; alongside it ran a strong secular reform current, the product of the humanist spirit that had emerged during the Renaissance era and had culminated in the Enlightenment. But both the secular and the religious reformers went beyond the Beccarias and the Benthams by introducing the idea of rehabilitation as an important (though usually secondary) purpose of punishment. Perhaps they had ulterior motives. It is reasonable to suppose, as social-control theorists believe, that there was a strain of self-serving hypocrisy in their enterprise; as members of the political and social elite, they had a stake in keeping the society stable and persuading rebellious elements to accept it.[4] Yet human motivations are complex. If the class-bound interest in social control is a reasonable hypothesis, so is the belief that an altruistic impulse can move men— a few men at all times, a considerable number of men at certain times.

Theorists and practitioners who shared the classical outlook did not always agree on the right techniques for reintegrating offenders into "honest" society. The broadest consensus was on the virtues of prison work as a way to inculcate disciplined habits and to teach inmates a useful trade. There was more controversy over the value of providing illiterate prisoners with some elementary education, and even over the idea that mass education of the young would reduce the level of crime. Victor Hugo's dictum— "Open a school, close a prison"—was often quoted, but many classical theorists and penalists voiced serious doubts, and even suggested that schooling—especially the wrong kind—might actually increase crime. Prison Inspector Moreau-Christophe, for example, complained that although ignorance was a cause of crime, statistics showed that the incidence of crime was actually highest in those parts of France where education was most general. Indeed, he declared, the worst inmates of prisons were those whose minds had been sharpened by education. He accused the schools of having concentrated too much on improving body and mind rather than nourishing "the virtues of the heart."[5] Likewise the ex-deputy and Academician J.-J. Baude suggested that schooling bred crime by producing "those masses of *déclassés*, needy place-hunters, whose education deprives them of an attainable goal."[6]

Most classically oriented jurists and penologists gave at least lip service to the idea of rehabilitating offenders through a nurturing of the religious sense. Many of them, however, were skeptical about its potential effectiveness in France. Beaumont and Tocqueville had found most prisoners at Cherry Hill reading the Bible, but prison inspector La Ville de Mirmont called this inconceivable in France, where "religious sentiments scarcely exist."[7] The journalist Léon Faucher shared these doubts, except for offenders of rural origin. In the United States, the Bible might be "the most indispensable furniture of the cell," but France was different: neither cell nor Bible would suit this "most sociable and least religious nation of the two continents."[8] *Bagne* official Vénuste Gleizes reported that efforts to revive the religious sentiments of *bagnards* had failed utterly.[9] Both Charles Lucas and prison doctor Vingtrinier, on the other hand, urged strongly that members of religious orders be placed in charge of internal administration in all prisons. But religious instruction there, Vingtrinier added, must be "freed of that mysticism, of those exaggerated practices and ulterior motives which, in former times, may have given it a dangerous slant."[10] The experiment was tried during the 1840s: the *Frères de la Doctrine Chrétienne* took over the task of prison surveillance in a few men's prisons, and the *Soeurs de Marie-Joseph* in all women's prisons. But Minister of Interior Duchâtel remained skeptical; in 1847 he ordered the corps of inspectors to check carefully on this new venture. Were the Frères efficient, and did they accept administrative authority? More serious still, had the nuns abused their power? Duchâtel noted that the death rate in women's prisons had risen sharply since the order had taken over in 1841, and he suggested the possibility that "an excess of religious observances, a too continuous moral constraint, an overemphasis on exclusively mystical readings and teachings, may have penetrated the souls of many of these women so violently as to weaken the body's resistance."[11] For the governing elite of the July Monarchy, the rehabilitation of offenders via religion had not only attractions but also risks.

Classical theory in criminology soon came under challenge from certain reformers and jurists who found it unduly rigid and narrow. The principle of fixed penalties for each crime, leaving no leeway for adapting punishment to individual offenders and cases, seemed much too arbitrary. Not only did it offend the senses of fairness, but it led in practice to frequent acquittals by magistrates and juries who preferred to acquit rather than impose harsh sentences. In addition, the emergence of a primitive form of psychiatry within the medical profession began to cast some doubt on the classical belief that crime represented a rational choice (or a briefly irrational aberration) by morally responsible individuals. By the 1830s the sharp edges of classical theory began to be softened somewhat; the revision of the penal code in 1832 reflected this change by authorizing judges and juries to reduce charges and penalties on the basis of extenuating circumstances. The courts also began to hear expert testimony from doctors specializing in mental disorders (though such testimony was given at the court's option, and could be ignored). Those students of crime who advocated these changes in classical theory came to be labelled, in later retrospect, the neo-classical school.[12] Its adherents clung to the concept of individual moral responsibility and to punishments that combined utility and retribution, but they introduced some flexibility, shifted the focus in part from the crime to the criminal, and opened the door slightly to what later came to be called "individualized punishment." Throughout the rest of the nineteenth century, the neo-classical school was to dominate criminological theory in France, and it would retain a strong influence among jurists and penal authorities down to the present day. A smaller faction of "pure" classicists resisted the trend, complaining bitterly that the neo-classical heretics had opened the floodgates of crime. But a far more serious challenge to the neo-classical doctrine was to emerge after mid-century, in the form of the so-called positivist school of criminology.

Jurists of the neo-classical school—magistrates and the law

school professors who trained them—were fascinated by one theoretical issue: the basis for society's right to punish. Was that right
based on moral or utilitarian considerations? The moralists looked
to Kant for the clearest and most forthright expression of their
views; the utilitarians preferred Beccaria and Bentham. By mid-
century most neo-classicists had arrived at a kind of eclectic position
that brought the two viewpoints into uneasy balance. The most
authoritative expression of this eclecticism came from Joseph Ortolan, professor of penal law at the Paris law faculty. Ortolan began
by identifying a series of rival conceptions of the basis for punishment. These included social vengeance (a substitute for the private
vengeance of an earlier age); violation of some sort of social contract; reparation to the victim or to society; protection of the
society against those who would undermine it; and straightforward
utility. None of these, according to Ortolan, was satisfactory if
taken alone. Only a combination of theories could satisfy what
Ortolan saw as two natural urges in man: a deep sense of what is
just, and a conception of what is useful. Actions ought to be
punished if they injured both of these sentiments; but punishment
ought never to exceed the lower limit of what was required to
satisfy the impulse for either justice or utility. Ortolan admitted
that measuring the just and the useful was not easy; as the major
test, he fell back on what he took to be an innate sense of right
and wrong shared by most men.[13] A similar eclecticism marked the
teaching of another eminent mid-century jurist, Adolphe Franck,
of the *Collège de France*. After listing and rejecting most standard
theories of the basis for punishing (and adding one more to Ortolan's list—the idea that punishment should be seen as the cure for
a disease harmful to individuals and to the society), Franck concluded in favor of what later came to be called the theory of social
defense—the right of a society (as of an individual) to self-pre-
servation, and the duty of men in that society to protect it in order
to ensure "moral order."[14]

Although the jurists (along with some penal authorities and
reformers) dominated the theoretical discussion of the crime problem until mid-century, a segment of the medical profession was
gradually drawn into the debate as time went by. Many of the

doctors confined themselves to practical issues, notably the controversy over the physical and mental effects of solitary confinement; but some of them also became involved in attempts to explain the causes of crime and the nature of criminals. Characteristically, medical men were attracted to the idea that criminal behavior might have physiological roots. Some of the earliest pioneers were forerunners of the psychiatrists, and came to the subject through an interest in insanity. Since criminals and madmen were commonly confined in local prisons, often without effective segregation, prison doctors were called upon to treat both categories. They pressed for, and eventually achieved, the establishment of separate asylums for mental cases; but in the process, they began to reflect on a possible link between crime and madness. Their ideas posed a potential challenge to the classical view of individual moral responsibility and, by extension, of society's right to punish.

The earliest of these pioneers, Dr. Georges Cabanis, rose to prominence as a politician and writer as well as a physician during the Revolutionary years. His *Traité du physique et du moral de l'homme* (1802) was an uncompromising manifesto of Enlightenment materialism. But unlike the followers of Beccaria, he challenged the view that criminals act through rational choice. Speaking in the parliament of the Directory, Cabanis declared:

> You are surely aware that certain types of prison, by their very nature, are much like hospitals: for example, the so-called houses of correction, where an attempt was made to treat systematically the vicious tendencies of youth. Some day the same will be true of the prisons for persons condemned by the courts to long or short periods of detention. Indeed, these prisons might easily become veritable infirmaries of crime; they will treat that kind of illness with the same precision of method and the same hope of success as the other derangements of the mind.[15]

Cabanis furthered the career of that remarkable reformer Dr. Philippe Pinel, who served as chief of medical services at Bicêtre prison just outside Paris, and then at La Salpêtrière hospital in Paris itself. Pinel started the process of moving insane persons from prisons to asylums, and inaugurated dramatic changes in the treatment of mental patients.[16] But in addition, he advanced the theory of "moral insanity" as an explanation of some criminal behavior, implying that crime as well as mental illness might be traceable to physiological defects, and that such criminals should be treated rather than punished. Pinel's disciple Jean Esquirol carried on his work, and added the concept of "monomania" as a behavioral aberration that led to crime.[17] The idea of moral insanity persisted for decades among the early psychiatrists; it was to turn up in 1868, for example, in Dr. Prosper Despine's *Psychologie naturelle*. Despine advocated the treatment in special asylums of criminals who lacked "moral sense," and even proposed the indefinite internment and treatment of those who had committed no crime but were likely to do so.[18]

Meanwhile another set of pioneers was investigating the anatomy of the brain, and suggesting a connection between its structure and deviant behavior. Dr. Franz Josef Gall and his associate Johann Spurzheim developed the dubious science of phrenology, which was widely accepted until mid-century. Gall was a German who settled in Paris in 1807; the term "phrenology" was Spurzheim's brainchild, but the idea was Gall's. He contended that the brain could be mapped to show the sources of certain traits and abilities, and that abnormal development of certain segments of the brain could be detected by external characteristics such as the shape of the skull.[19] Gall has been described as partially right for the wrong reasons; in the end his "science" came to be discredited and ridiculed. But its widespread acceptance until the 1850s (phrenologists were sometimes called to testify in criminal trials) reinforced the growing belief that criminal deviance might be physiological in origin. It anticipated the work of the later positivist school led by the Italian doctor Cesare Lombroso.[20]

Still another current of thought within the medical profession emerged from the study of heredity, and suggested the possible inheritance of pathological tendencies. Dr. Prosper Lucas, younger brother of the penal reformer Charles Lucas, produced a massive tome in 1847 arguing that "heredity is the predisposing cause, the basic cause, of crime."[21] There were social causes as well—bad companions, lack of education—but they were strictly secondary. This did not mean, according to Lucas, that criminals were innocent because they were fatally driven to rob or kill; except for the insane, they had a choice. They inherited a propensity, not an irresistible urge. Nevertheless, crime should be studied in the same manner as disease.[22]

Of greater impact was the work of Dr. Benedict Morel, who put forward in 1857 the concept of degeneracy. Both crime and madness, wrote Morel, were growing in epidemic fashion. "The constant increase in suicides, misdemeanors, crimes against property if not against persons, the monstrous precocity of young criminals, the bastardizing of the race . . . are undeniable facts."[23] These aberrations were traceable to a process of physical and moral decay, brought on among the working classes by disease, unwholesome living quarters, alcohol, drugs, and adulterated foods; the consequent degeneracy was transmitted to the children, and grew progressively worse. Nevertheless, criminals were different from insane persons, since they still had a choice; they should not be treated for a form of illness. What was needed was "moral hygiene" to "moralize the masses."[24]

Degeneracy theory had an immediate and lasting impact. Not only did it shape Emile Zola's series of Rougon-Macquart novels, but it was widely accepted by the public and by writers on crime well into the twentieth century. Specialists like Dr. Charles Féré, a psychiatrist at Bicêtre, lent their authority to degeneracy theory but drew conclusions somewhat different from Morel's. No line could be drawn between crime and madness, said Féré; both should be treated as forms of illness.[25] Likewise Dr. Eugène Dally, an early member of the Société d'Anthropologie and the translator of Huxley's works, flatly rejected the idea that either criminals or insane persons could be considered morally responsible. To speak of the need for expiation or of society's "right to punish" was, he declared, "a relic of the middle ages." Both sorts of deviance sprang from the same source: organic flaws, caused in part by illness and misery. Criminals as well as madmen should therefore be considered sick rather than guilty, and the purpose of treating them should be social utility, not punishment. Some of them might have to be confined or deported, but only in order to protect society; punishment for its own sake was simply "barbarous."[26] Dr. Valentin Magnan, on the other hand, kept Morel's doctrine intact until the end of the century: crime and insanity were quite different products of degeneracy. "We do not know," he wrote in 1895, "what crime is, or what human responsibility is; we are sure about only one thing—that there are harmful beings who are called criminals, and who are degenerates." They should be jailed, said Magnan, without fixed sentences, simply as threats to society.[27]

Some doctors, and virtually all jurists and penal specialists of classical and neo-classical outlook, were disturbed or outraged by the new medical theories—especially by the idea that crime was a form of illness. This heresy, they declared, was tainted with "materialism" and "socialism."[28] They clung stubbornly to the traditional belief in individual moral responsibility, without which, they insisted, society's right to punish lost its foundation, and society itself might disintegrate. But the trend after mid-century was strongly against the traditionalists; positivism, with its worship of science and its rejection of "superstition," was emerging as the dominant temper of the new age. A confrontation between "spiritualists" and positivists over the nature of the crime problem was unavoidable. But it was deflected somewhat by the eruption of an extreme version of positivism beyond the Alps. As Beccaria's ideas a century earlier had prodded Frenchmen into rethinking their views about crime, so Dr. Cesare Lombroso's startling book L'uomo delinquente (1876) forced them to grapple with his unorthodox doctrine. Lombroso, remarks one French scholar of our day, "sowed the seeds of a veritable revolution in current conceptions of penal justice. Positivism had the great merit of shaking up the jurists, by showing them that crime was something more than a set of legal definitions . . . in the penal code."[29]

Lombroso was a young army doctor who based his initial work on a study of army recruits. He claimed to have identified a category of "born criminals," easily recognizable by certain physical traits, and destined by their innate qualities to a life of crime.[30] In his subsequent work, broadened to include studies of several thousand prison inmates, Lombroso described these "born criminals" as cases of atavism—throwbacks to an earlier stage of primitive human development. Their identifying traits, according to Lombroso, included such physical characteristics as a low sloping forehead, a heavy lower jaw, prominent ears, abnormally long arms, and insensibility to pain or pity. He later added such social traits as a penchant for tattooing and for the use of argot, and suggested a frequent connection with left-handedness. Lombroso's work, based on what seemed to be scientific observation, was a forthright manifesto of the new positivist spirit, and the group of disciples that clustered about him soon began to call itself the school of criminal anthropology, or the Italian positivist school of criminology.[31]

Few books in the history of criminological theory have created such a stir, though the full impact in France did not come until the 1880s, and the French translation of Lombroso's work until 1887. The starkness of his "born criminal" concept was made to order for quick popularization, and journalists everywhere seized upon it. But serious students of the crime problem were attracted as well, since Lombroso's thesis not only harmonized with the new scientistic spirit of the age but also seemed to open a new and clearly marked path toward the effective control of crime. Indeed, it promised to add an entirely new dimension to crime control by making possible the prevention rather than merely the ex post facto punishment of crime; for if potential criminals could be so accurately identified, their crimes might be averted by surveillance or internment. Furthermore, if Lombroso was right the idea of individual moral responsibility suddenly seemed irrelevant, and the idea of punishment outmoded. For if offenders were predestined to a life of crime, it would be meaningless to speak of punishment; the new alternatives would be either curative treatment or elimination for the good of society. The social theorist Gustave Le Bon put the matter succinctly when he wrote in 1881: "When a mad dog bites me, I don't ask whether he is responsible."[32] The "born criminal" was presumably the hominoid equivalent of the mad dog; both had to be controlled as a measure of social defense.

The Lombrosian bombshell might have been expected to provoke an immediate showdown in France between the traditionalists and the positivists. French doctors from Cabanis to Morel had already anticipated Lombroso's position in their theories of moral insanity, degeneracy, and the inheritance of pathological tendencies; their theories had prepared the way for acceptance of the Lombrosian doctrine. Most French jurists and penalists, however, were appalled at the new heresy, and were further outraged when the Italians scornfully dismissed them as outmoded "spiritualists," whose idea of moral responsibility based on free will was merely "a hypothesis accredited by priests and despots."[33] Yet the repercussions of the Lombrosian theory in France proved to be much more complex. It was not the "spiritualists" of the classical and neo-classical tradition who led the counterattack, but rather a group of French positivists who mobilized in opposition to the Italians, and who in the end developed a rival French school that shifted the central emphasis from biological to social factors and that edged the Lombrosians into the discard. At times, the contest between them took on the appearance of what might be called criminological Olympic Games, with the French and the Italians pitted against each other for world supremacy.[34]

The initial encounter in this open contest came in 1885, when the Italians convened the first international Congress of Criminal Anthropology in Rome. It met, symbolically and no doubt intentionally, at the same time and in the same city as the Third International Penitentiary Congress, which brought together the more traditionalist jurists and penal officials. The new congress was attended mainly by Italian and French delegates, but the Lombrosians hoped that its success would consecrate their theories as the new orthodoxy, recognized as such throughout Europe. Instead, they met vigorous contradiction from some of the French delegates, notably Dr. Alexandre Lacassagne, a professor of legal medicine from Lyon. Lacassagne challenged the basic assumptions of the Lombroso school and charged that its practical consequences would be devastating; it would leave societies, he said, with no choice but to keep all deviants locked up in prisons or asylums. Lacassagne then put forward the basic premise of what was to emerge as the rival French school of criminal sociology: namely, that crime was the product mainly of social causes. In the course of his argument, Lacassagne coined two epigrams that were to be quoted almost *ad nauseam* over the decades that followed. "The social milieu," he declared, "is the mother culture of criminality; the microbe is the criminal, an element which gains significance only at the moment when it finds the broth which makes it ferment." And in concluding his challenge he added: "Societies have the criminals they deserve."[35]

The Italians, who dominated the Rome Congress by their numbers and their militancy, overrode this French objection. But their dogmatism and combativeness won them more enemies than friends; they claimed that science had led them to a new absolute truth, and they ridiculed the "spiritualists" as "a cult [which is] ready to fall." Lombroso's disciple Raffaele Garofalo added a confident prediction: "Moral responsibility and punishment proportional to the crime—these two pivots of penal law are disappearing from our system, and one can truly say that penal science has been renewed from top to bottom." "Moral monstrousness," Garofalo declared, was something that could be detected in infancy; it could not be altered by education or social reform.[36] The theory seemed to imply the systematic elimination of "born criminals" from society.

Perhaps the Italians savored their Roman victory too much, or exaggerated its proportions. Their contemptuous dismissal of the idea of moral responsibility infuriated the jurists and penalists who, whether outmoded or not, still dominated the official crime-control establishment in most of Europe, and certainly in France. But the Italians' claim to total truth also offended most of the French medical fraternity and the new specialists in criminology (as it was beginning to be called). National pride was no doubt another factor in mobilizing the French positivists against the Italians. When the second Congress of Criminal Anthropology met in Paris in 1889, the Lombrosians found themselves a beleaguered minority. Lacassagne's criticisms were reinforced this time by a whole cluster of French experts: the criminal anthropologists Léonce Manouvrier and Paul Topinard, the professor of legal medicine Paul Brouardel, the magistrate-turned-sociologist Gabriel Tarde, the psychiatrist Valentin Magnan. From various angles they challenged the Lombrosians' methodology as well as the conclusions that emerged from their data. French speakers insisted that criminal behavior was mainly of social rather than hereditary origin; it stemmed from poverty, alcoholism, ignorance, evil companions, a bad home environment. They warned that the Lombrosians' extreme determinism was likely to produce bad side-effects; it would alienate the general public and would breed despair among those children identified as criminally inclined. Gabriel Tarde added the stinging suggestion that Lombroso's theory was "merely a new phrenology, unaware of its identity."[37] The so-called criminal type, Tarde later added, "emerged from the Paris Congress "badly crippled, or rather reduced to the condition of a fading phantom."[38]

The Congress of 1889 successfully blunted the Lombrosians' drive to be recognized as the new orthodoxy, and it speeded the emergence of the French school of criminal sociology. The French rather than the Italians were to take the lead in Europe during the next couple of decades. Their victory was accomplished, Robert A. Nye has persuasively argued, in part by a shrewd strategy of avoiding an open challenge to the jurists and penalists who clung to the old orthodoxy of individual moral responsibility.[39] Leaders of the new French school concentrated their fire on the Italians, and managed to leave space for the idea of free will; they ensured a tacit truce between traditionalists and positivists in France, joined in a common front against the Italians.

This is not to say that the feud with the Italians had wiped out the differences between "spiritualists" and positivists in France and had brought a condition of euphoric harmony. Some French positivists continued to be impressed by Lombroso's work, and thought that he had merely pushed his conclusions too far. Thus Dr. Charles Letourneau, president of the *Société d'Anthropologie* of Paris, wrote a laudatory introduction to the first French edition of *L'uomo delinquente* in which he endorsed the concept of atavism and joined the Italians in consigning to the junkheap such "metaphysical ideas" as free will and moral responsibility. In the age of science, he concluded, such ideas had come to seem "merely pitiable."[40] The second French edition was prefaced by an enthusiastic letter to Lombroso from the eminent literary critic and historian Hippolyte Taine: "You have shown us libidinous, ferocious orangoutans with human faces; certainly, being such, they cannot act otherwise than the way they do; if they rape, rob, and kill, it is no doubt by virtue of their nature and their past. All the more reason to destroy them as soon as one is sure that they are and will always remain orang-outans."[41] The eccentric anthropologist Georges Vacher de Lapouge, known for his racist version of Social Darwinism, drew on both Lombroso and the degeneracy theorists to advocate an extreme form of social selection and drastic methods of crime control. Able-bodied criminals, he declared, should be employed at hard labor, but society should waste no resources on imprisoning or transporting the others: "the question calls for only one solution that is sure, economical, energetically selective: death!" And since criminal tendencies were inherited, the offspring of delinquents must be denied the right to procreate.[42] His views were echoed as late as 1912 by the Paris prosecutor Joseph Maxwell, who continued to use the terms "atavism" and "born criminal," and who advocated the castration of criminals in order to prevent "*procréations malsaines.*"[43]

The persistence of a small faction of super-Lombrosians in France was more than counterbalanced on the opposite extreme by a vigorous reassertion of the pure classical doctrine by the so-called "spiritualists." The issue on which they took their stand was the existence of free will which, they held, was essential to the very concepts of crime and punishment. If an offender's actions were beyond his control, they asked—if they were determined by biological or social factors, or both—how could society presume to punish him? But the alternatives to punishment, they held, were unworkable or unthinkable. Curative therapy had proved to be flabby and ineffective; social defense through elimination of deviants would open the way to the worst extremes of tyranny and injustice.

In 1886 the *Académie des Sciences Morales et Politiques*, which had once been a leading forum for discussion of the crime problem, undertook to stimulate reflection on the matter. The Academy announced a prize competition for the best manuscript on penal philosophy—specifically, on modern ideas about the principles underlying punishment. Only two mediocre entries were received, so the Academy tried again in 1888, this time with better luck. Six manuscripts were entered, and two of them were declared joint winners.[44] Both authors were jurists: Louis Proal was a magistrate, Georges Vidal a professor of law. Both, not surprisingly, presented vigorous defenses of the free-will thesis, rebutting the arguments of both the French and the Italian positivists.

Criminals, declared Proal, are not abnormal beings or "moral monsters" fatally destined for a life of crime. They are like the rest of us, and we have no right to exclude them from the human race. Crime springs from the weakness of human nature; all of us are exposed to temptations and passions, and some of us fail to resist. "No matter what efforts are made to reduce crime, there will always be criminals among us." The defense of society is one valid purpose of punishment, but it is not enough; if separated from the idea of justice, it becomes arbitrary. The individual's moral responsibility is central; society itself rests on the rock of free will. "If criminals were treated as merely sick, if there were no shame attached to crime, if prisons were to become hospitals and jailers no more than nurses, honest folk would be reduced to asking for a place in these refuges, for society would no longer be secure." Proal accepted the idea that social flaws contributed to crime and should be corrected but the fundamental sources of criminality, he insisted, were the human passions, and only the threat of punishment could deter those persons too weak to resist.[45]

A long and repetitious debate ensued—a debate that was ultimately recognized as futile, since neither side could offer convincing proof that free will did or did not exist. For the "spiritualists," the concept of free will was absolutely central; it was "the most noble attribute, the most sacred right of the human soul." Abandoning it, cried the magistrate Camoen de Vence, would "free men to indulge their most perverse instincts," and would lead to "a struggle among savages loosed against one another."[46] Crime, added Judge Adolphe Guillot, was the product of "successive abdications of the human will."[47] Why, in the eyes of the "spiritualists," had crime risen so alarmingly during the nineteenth century? Judge Guillot's diagnosis was simple: "women and racetracks—these are the main sources of crime . . . in Paris."[48]

But other jurists and criminologists of the classical outlook offered more varied and perhaps more sophisticated explanations. France, they believed, had entered upon an era of profound moral crisis, perhaps the most severe crisis since the sixteenth century.[49] This state of "moral decomposition" had been brought on by the disintegration of traditional values, by the perverted effects of public secular education, by the ravages of alcohol and a licentious press, and by the abusive results of the jury system which undermined respect for the law. The broadened base of education, they said, had done nothing to reduce crime; it had merely produced more literate criminals.[50] The schools had become sterile; they had abandoned moral training in favor of factual head-stuffing; they disordered "the weak brains of simple peasants, adding thus to the throng of failures and déclassés of all sorts."[51] Alcohol abuse was a spreading plague since the law of 1880 had eased the rules on opening bistrots; consumption had risen threefold, fourfold, sixfold (depending on the observer) since then.[52] A corrupt popular press glorified criminals and aroused evil passions through its "sensuous" appeal.[53] Prosperity had bred a desire for luxury among the lower classes; they had lost their religious faith, which had formerly shown them the necessity of "certain social inequalities."[54] (As Judge Louis Proal put it: "Why are the great majority of Parisian workers communists? Because . . . we have deprived them of heaven without giving them earth; let us give heaven back to them."[55]) As for the jury, the capriciousness and ignorance of jurors and their susceptibility to emotional appeals had made the public cynical about the system of justice.[56]

These views, widely shared by conservative jurists, penologists, and politicians at the end of the century, were of course rejected by most Frenchmen of the left. Leaders of the growing Socialist movement adopted the standard Marxist view that most crime was the product of an acquisitive and unjust social system that virtually drove many oppressed citizens to a life of crime. The Socialists in France paid only marginal attention, however, to either the theory or the reality of crime in their capitalist society. Some Radical politicians, moved by their fervent anti-clericalism, spent a good deal of energy in a campaign to "laicize" the prisons by restricting or eliminating the use of chaplains in men's prisons and of the Soeurs de Marie-Joseph in women's prisons.[57] In the realm of theory, the eminent sociologist Emile Durkheim (a Socialist in his politics) stirred up a furious conservative reaction by his unorthodox ideas about the nature of crime and criminals. Crime, he suggested, was a normal phenomenon in any society; it occurred universally, and could not be eradicated. Nor should it be: its presence had some useful social functions, provided that it did not exceed certain undefined limits. It enabled a society to set clear boundary lines between acceptable and outlawed behavior, thus reinforcing social values. And (as in the example of Socrates) it sometimes reflected a healthy challenge to existing mores, opening the way to changes in the society's value-system. Without crime, Durkheim suggested, a society would be likely to grow rigid and stagnant; without crime, it would lose part of the cement that makes the society cohere, as its members join in rejecting aberrant behavior.[58] Conservative critics were outraged by these ideas, and accused Durkheim of encouraging crime; Durkheim retorted that his ideas were being distorted and travestied. Their practical effect on criminal policy seems to have been slight or non-existent.

Although the more fervent believers in free will and determinism continued their polemics into the twentieth century, an eclectic blend of the two positions was already emerging during the 1890s. On the "spiritualist" side, the eminent literary critic Fernand Brunetière, the moralist Alfred Fouillée, the criminologist Gabriel Tarde all sought to mediate the dispute in various ways.[59] On the determinist side, many positivists who clung to degeneracy theory (which continued to enjoy a great vogue in France and elsewhere) focused their attention on degeneracy's supposed weakening of the human will, which decreased the individual's resistance to debauchery and crime.[60] By retaining this emphasis on the will, the positivists made it easier to find common ground with the "spiritualists" of the classical school. In any event, by 1900 the argument over free will was beginning to seem both stale and futile; many of the contestants asked themselves whether it was really central to the practical problems of understanding and controlling crime. The tacit agreement that had brought together most of the French jurists and doctors to block the challenge of the Italian school was maintained, but crystallized into a more doctrinal form. The new eclecticism rested primarily on the theories of the French school of criminal sociology and the idea of social defense, yet it preserved a place for the concept of individual moral responsibility as well. The leading proponents of the new consensus were two well-known professors of criminal law, Raymond Saleilles and Paul Cuche.

Saleilles, a disciple of Gabriel Tarde, put forward his ideas in an influential book called *L'Individualisation de la peine* (1898). He pleased the neo-classical jurists by arguing that the general public still believed in free will, moral responsibility, and retribution, so that penal sanctions must satisfy that sentiment. Methods of dealing with offenders, on the other hand, should be based on positivist ideas; punishment, through scientific analysis, should be adapted to the special circumstances and needs of the individual offender. "If the criminal is not fundamentally a pervert," he wrote, "the punishment should not contribute to his further perversion. It should serve for his regeneration and his rehabilitation. If the criminal is an incorrigible, the interests of society demand his

punishment as a measure of protection and of radical prevention."[61] Saleilles's thesis of "individualized punishment" opened
the way to a wide variety of experiments in the treatment of
offenders, with the emphasis on preparing them to re-enter society.
It was to remain for almost a half century the classic statement of
the French criminological consensus.

Paul Cuche, professor at Grenoble in the newly created field
of "penitentiary science," was likewise an eclectic whose influence
was felt throughout his long career. In his standard textbook
(1905), Cuche bluntly declared that since the rival schools of
criminology could not agree, it was useless to go on arguing
about the right to punish or the causes of crime; rather, the
focus should be on the purpose of punishment. Moralists and
utilitarians, he contended, would never see eye to eye on that
purpose. In practice, utility was the only workable test. Nevertheless, nothing should be done to diminish the moral coloration of
punishment; "no positivist should forget that the crowd sees it as
expiatory—and it is useful that this should be so."[62] Earlier in his
career, Cuche had expressed serious concern at what he called "the
decadence of punishment" in France; the nineteenth century, he
held, had brought an almost unbroken softening of penalties as the
idea of intimidation had lost its hold. If the trend continued, society
would end with nothing more than a system of "moral hygiene,"
which would not be enough to deter potential lawbreakers.[63] He
continued to sound this note in the years that followed, and to
insist that even though the classical idea of moral responsibility
was impossible to measure, punishment must retain a moral dimension. For the general public, punishment must appear to satisfy
both justice and utility; in France, "where repression fails either
to eliminate or to correct, punishments are primarily useful for
comforting honest folk."[64] Cuche's peculiar doctrine of utilitarian
social defense with a frosting of moral retribution to suit the public taste seems to have represented the consensus view of French
criminologists and penologists on the eve of World War I.

# VI

## Incarcerators versus Transporters
### 1871–1914

> Arguments about the Auburn or Pennsylvania-style cell are nothing more than an old outmoded song. . . . The less we imprison, the better. The more we transport, the better.
>
> JULES LEVEILLÉ (1893)

> For a time, it was fashionable in certain circles to go about repeating: "Prison is the punishment of the past." Meaningless words: prison can be the punishment of the past only if there's something to replace it in the future.
>
> HENRI JOLY (1910)

FOR FRENCHMEN attracted by theoretical questions—philosophers, jurists, moralists, certain doctors—the heart of the crime problem during the later nineteenth century was the controversy over the sources of criminal behavior, the purpose of punishment, and the basic nature of man. Was the primary goal of the crime-control system intimidation and deterrence, or retribution, or rehabilitation? Should repression be based on social vengeance, on the defense of social order and prevailing values, or on some principle of abstract justice? Should the idea of punishment give way to the concept of treatment, analogous to that provided for the physically or mentally ill? Was a flawed society responsible for the offender's misdeeds? Was the criminal an ordinary man gone wrong, or did he belong to a different breed, quite distinct from honest folk through physical inheritance or sociocultural conditioning?

These questions were not considered irrelevant by those more pragmatically minded Frenchmen—magistrates, prison officials, charitable souls—who had to cope with the steady flow of some 200,000 accused or convicted persons who passed through the French prisons each year. They too were drawn into the debate over the causes of crime and the nature of the criminal, over the basis for punishment and its essential purposes. But the practical necessity of dealing with the crime problem in its daily reality led them to concentrate mainly on techniques of crime control and prevention, on ways to protect honest folk from malefactors. In retrospect, the second half of the nineteenth century can be seen as a protracted debate between the advocates of cellular imprisonment and the proponents of penal transportation.

The cellular school had enjoyed its greatest prestige during the generation before 1848; but the revolution of that year had broken the impetus of the movement and had opened the way to the Second Empire's rejection of the cellular principle and its decision to experiment with penal transportation. By the time the Empire fell, the practice of shipping long-term convicts overseas no longer seemed experimental; it was widely accepted by Frenchmen as a natural response to the crime problem. True, the initial phase in Guiana had hardly been auspicious, but the recently opened penal colony in New Caledonia gave the transporters hope that they had found a workable solution. Furthermore, the leaders of the new Third Republic found themselves burdened at the very outset with a massive practical problem: what to do with the 36,000 ex-Communards who had been rounded up after the crushing of the Paris Commune? To the men in power, New Caledonia seemed the obvious solution. During the next two years, between four and five thousand Communards were deported to the penal colony.[1]

It might seem, therefore, that the transporters had won the battle even before the incarcerators had regrouped their forces to fight. Yet the advocates of cellular imprisonment had not given up hope, even though they had experienced nothing but frustration since 1848. Some of the leading activists from the 1840s—Tocqueville and Beaumont, for example—had left the scene, but others were still on hand, ready to renew their crusade when the opportunity might offer. Some newcomers were also recruited to the cause dur-

ing the years that followed, as they became persuaded that the
existing common prisons and overseas *bagnes* were either brutal
survivals of a past age or breeding places of additional crime. So
there was a resurgence of the old debate about the cell during the
next couple of decades.

The issue emerged, though in somewhat muted form, during
the new republic's formative years. Late in 1871 an Orleanist peer
and deputy, Comte Othenin d'Haussonville, proposed that the National Assembly establish a commission to study the state of
France's prison system and to recommend needed reforms. The
Second Empire, he declared, had evaded the problem by transporting its worst offenders; but by 1869 even Napoleon III (according to Haussonville) had been forced to recognize the failure of
that policy, and had set up an investigating committee to look into
the reasons for resurgent crime. The fall of the Empire had left that
committee's work incomplete. The problem, Haussonville asserted,
was still unsolved; crime was dangerously on the rise, and France's
prisons were in more deplorable condition than ever after a generation of neglect.[2] The Assembly agreed; a commission of inquiry
was named, and met, with some interruptions, for more than three
years (March 1872 to July 1875). Its membership included eighteen
deputies (among them Haussonville as secretary and, eventually,
rapporteur) and nineteen experts (including such eminent figures
as the ubiquitous Charles Lucas, the aging *philanthrope* Frédéric
Demetz, the magistrate and penal theorist Arnould Bonneville de
Marsangy, and the lawyer Fernand Desportes, soon to become secretary-general of a new *Société Générale des Prisons*).[3] Other deputies who played active roles were René Bérenger, son of the noted
penal reformer Alphonse, and Dr. Félix Voisin, magistrate and
deputy of the left-center. The commission heard extensive testimony, collected a small library of factual data, and sent its members
on study tours of French and foreign prisons. Not much in the
way of formal legislation came out of its work: a single law of
limited scope, affecting the short-term departmental prisons alone.
But if the mountain produced a rather small mouse, the commission did leave for historians a mass of evidence bearing on the
condition of the prisons in that era and on the issues that divided
the governing elite of the new republic.[4] At the time, its apparently
slim achievement was taken to be a sign of greater victories to

come—the full-scale triumph, sooner or later, of the cellular idea.

The commission's early months were devoted to accumulating a factual base for action. Lengthy testimony from top prison officials, doctors, and chaplains gave clear proof that the prisons had improved somewhat since the Royal Prison Society had made its survey just fifty years earlier. In the 1820s Charles Lucas had bluntly asserted that France had no prison system worthy of the name; in the 1870s there was at least a system, whatever its remaining defects. The Director-General of Prisons, Jaillaut, reported that all prisoners in both *maisons centrales* and departmental prisons were now adequately fed and clothed, either by the state or by private entrepreneurs. Iron cots had replaced the old piles of straw on the floor; inmates were provided with a clean shirt weekly, a bath every two weeks, a change of sheets monthly. Those in the *maisons centrales* received bread and soup twice a day and meat twice weekly; they could supplement this diet by buying vegetables (up to fifteen centimes' worth a day) at the canteen. These long-term prisoners had access to elementary instruction, religious services, and rudimentary libraries; one director had even organized a prisoners' chorus which was said to be a great success.[5] Indeed, the director of the *maison centrale* at Melun told the commission that material reform had reached its outer limit; it could go no further without making the prisons "an object of attraction for unemployed workers."[6]

But when the testimony turned from the twenty-two *maisons centrales* to the almost four hundred departmental prisons, the contrast was glaring. The short-term prisons housed 20,000 of the total prison population of 38,000—those awaiting trial, and those serving sentence of a year or less. Half of these institutions, Inspector Watteville reported, simply disregarded the regulation that called for separation of inmates by categories. Not only were condemned prisoners mixed pell-mell with those awaiting trial, but there was often little effective segregation of children from adults or, in some cases, of men from women. Most of the buildings were former convents, dismally ill-suited to their current use; the local authorities had been unable or unwilling to remodel them. Even in the 150 prisons that had managed to separate inmates by categories, and in the sixty-eight cellular prisons that had been built or reconstructed since 1838, the regulations were often evaded

DEPARTMENTAL PRISON AT MOULINS IN CENTRAL FRANCE. The tower, built in the 14th century, is the remnant of an old chateau. It holds about forty prisoners, most of them awaiting trial. In 1979 the Penal Administration described it as "the most insalubrious prison in France," and proposed that it be replaced. (Roger-Viollet)

because of overcrowding or inadequate supervision.[7] The food provided in the short-term prisons, Jaillaut admitted, was skimpier; medical services were meager; religious rites were minimal, primary education almost nonexistent, facilities for work often lacking.

Discipline in each prison was in the hands of the head jailer, who in some cases managed a bit of profiteering on the side and often exercised ruthless control. Jaillaut reported that in the course of his recent campaign to control disciplinary abuses, he had "collected a real museum of irons," including some that a robust man could not lift. Jaillaut's conception of reform suggested, however, that his humanitarian impulse had its limits. In place of irons and pitch-dark *cachots*, he proposed an unheated *salle de discipline* in which violators of rules would sit silent and immobile on narrow stone benches, under constant surveillance by a guard.[8]

Although the long-term prisons shone by contrast with the makeshift departmental prisons, Inspector de Watteville was frank to admit their flaws as well. Four-fifths of them, he declared, desperately needed to be rebuilt, for they too were in most cases converted convents or chateaux, overcrowded, inefficient, and expensive to maintain. A shortage of guards (Jaillaut declared that he really needed to triple or quadruple the existing force of 2500 in the *maisons centrales*) led to the use of trusties for surveillance; some of them were petty racketeers, men of "detestable morals." Religious counselling, though formally provided, was minimal; the chaplains were ill-paid, and contented themselves with quick visits to say mass.[9] Although Jaillaut contended that workshops in the *maisons centrales* were now well organized and that the gouging entrepreneurs of earlier times had been replaced, Watteville was more critical; some entrepreneurs, he complained, still enjoyed such authority that they overshadowed the prison director, and they sometimes short-changed the inmates on food.[10]

The commission, staggering under the weight of four months of such testimony, scattered during the summer holiday to take a first-hand look at some of the departmental prisons. What they saw shocked them deeply. Deputy Edmond de Pressensé, reporting on his visits to Orléans, Bourg, and Le Hâvre, declared himself "filled with stupor and horror" at the sight of these "crime factories." At Mortagne, Dr. Félix Voisin found "total promiscuity"; the prisoners were provided with no work, no education, and virtually no religious counselling. At Argentière—one of the few new cellular prisons—inmates had to double up in the cells, and were turned out into the courtyard during the day to idle away their time. At Besançon, things were in a "deplorable and revolting state"; the prison was "a filthy cellar without light or air, into which thirty or forty prisoners were crowded." And at Belleveau, criminals, beggars, invalids were confined pell-mell; "it's a museum of all the human infirmities."[11]

But the commonest flaw, to which the commissioners kept returning, was the failure to segregate prisoners awaiting trial from those already condemned, thus corrupting young inmates who were often first offenders or who might even be judged innocent. This was a refrain that had been voiced by almost every reformer from the early nineteenth century onward, and that would continue to be heard well into the twentieth. During the commission's second year of sessions in 1873–74, there was almost interminable discussion of this problem, and of the most obvious solution—to transfer ownership and maintenance of the short-term prisons from the departments to the central administration.[12] Everyone favored such action in principle, but most commissioners predicted insoluble tangles over property rights and renovation costs. A complex cost-sharing scheme was finally worked out, but it never came up for discussion on the floor of the National Assembly. Legislation on the matter was deferred for another twenty years; and when a bill authorizing transfer of the departmental prisons to the central government was finally adopted in 1893, it remained a dead letter for technical reasons. Not until 1946 did the transfer finally take place.

The commission meanwhile had made a brave effort to broaden its inquiry into all aspects of the penal system. It heard lengthy reports on the overseas penal colonies, on agricultural colonies for juveniles, on patronage societies for liberated convicts and young offenders, and on the surviving remnants of the first Napoleon's *dépôts de mendicité*. But a growing awareness that it would take years to grapple with all of these issues forced a choice of priorities; and the top priority clearly seemed to be a thorough reform of the short-term prisons. It was here that the cellular crusaders saw their chance to seize the initiative.

Commission members who returned from summer visits to foreign prisons were especially struck by two alternative models: the Belgian system of day-and-night solitary confinement, with its rigors somewhat softened by frequent visits, instruction, access to reading matter, and work in the cell; and the so-called Irish or "progressive" system involving a short initial period of rigorous solitary confinement designed quite frankly to intimidate, followed by transfer to a common prison in which good conduct would earn progressively more generous treatment.[13] Both models thus utilized the cellular principle, though in different ways; they offered the advocates of isolation a chance to push for their solution.

Among those advocates there were some—like the magistrate Raymond Aylies and the founder of Mettray, Frédéric Demetz— who were holdovers from the reform commissions of the 1840s, and who had lost nothing of their old convictions. The cell, Demetz insisted, was the best way to moralize the offender, and it was even the best base on which to organize prison work. Many prisoners, Aylies added, grew so attached to their cells that they would resist having to leave them. One prison chaplain in his testimony chimed in with a further argument: the cell, he said, isolated young offenders against the use of argot—"and when one speaks argot, he is enlisted in the army of malefactors."[14] Commissioners and witnesses who opposed the cellular system no longer sought to argue that it was a threat to health and reason, but rather that it was inhumane, costly, and profoundly unpopular among the general public.[15] The moderates who supported the use of the cell— notably Haussonville and Bérenger—responded with a more cautious line than that used during the 1840s. They readily agreed that public repugnance toward the cell was widespread, and that this unpopularity might stampede parliament into rejecting any reform based on that system. They proposed, therefore, to limit its initial use to short-term convicts and to persons awaiting trial. They added also a bit of semantic sleight-of-hand; instead of *"régime cellulaire,"* their report would speak of *"séparation individuelle."*[16]

Since even the anti-cell faction saw some merit in isolating young first offenders against the moral contamination of the common prison, the commission reached consensus on this point without much debate. But the pro-cell leaders now faced a more serious problem: how to restrain the enthusiasm of a number of commissioners who were recent converts to their doctrine. These enthusiasts now insisted that since cellular imprisonment was good for short-termers, and since it had a healthy intimidating effect as well, there was no reason to deny its benefits to long-termers also. Let us not be over-cautious, argued commissioner (and Protestant pastor) Edmond de Pressensé; our discussions here have completely overcome my old prejudice against the cell, and a bit of education will convert parliament likewise. Neither parliament nor the country would understand, declared commissioner Tailhand, if we were to propose the cell for short-termers only. You don't succeed by starting small, added commissioner Bonnat.[17] The moderates barely managed to beat off this zealous pressure for total victory. It was lack of moderation, Bérenger warned, that had done in the cellular forces in 1844. With a little more restraint at that time, parliament and the nation would have adopted the system, and by now it would be deeply rooted in French mores. Let us adopt the principle, he argued; it will quickly prove itself, and can then be extended.[18]

The strategy succeeded; the commission's bill was approved by the National Assembly in July 1875 as one of that Assembly's last acts. The law ordered that all departmental prisons be converted to the cellular model, and that all sentences of a year or less, and all commitments to detention pending trial, be served in such prisons. It was the commission's only palpable achievement for its three years of labor. Nevertheless, it was hailed by the cellular forces as a major breakthrough on the road to further triumphs. For the first time in France, Haussonville exulted, "a legislative act has placed prisoners under a regime inspired by theoretical and rational considerations."[19] Several leading members of the commission, led by Fernand Desportes, moved promptly to organize a society of jurists and penalists for the study and discussion of penal questions. But their central purpose (though undeclared) was to use the society as a pressure group for the cellular idea. The *Société Générale des Prisons* met for the first time in 1877, with a membership of about four hundred; Desportes was elected secretary-general. He and the *Société*'s first president, Jules Dufaure, deplored the public's "passive and indolent" attitude toward penal problems, and proposed to conduct *"une véritable agitation salutaire et féconde."*[20] For the next several decades the *Société des Prisons* was to become one of France's most important forums for the discussion of criminological and penological issues; and its periodical, called at first the *Bulletin* and then the *Revue Pénitentiaire*, remains even today a mine of information on many aspects of the crime problem as viewed by Frenchmen.

But the hopes of the cellular enthusiasts were quickly frustrated. Most of the departments found excuses for evading and postponing the costly task of converting their prisons, and successive parliaments of the Third Republic balked at voting subsidies for the purpose. In 1890 the criminologist Henri Joly declared gloomily that not more than twenty prisons in France were in compliance with the law of 1875; in 1905 the number had risen only to forty-one.[21] Cellular crusaders complained constantly that public money was available but was being diverted to other penal purposes (notably to maintenance of the overseas penal colonies). Their complaints had no effect. Few short-term prisons were converted; none of the long-term prisons operated on the cellular system. Instead, they retained a modified form of the Auburn plan, with daytime work in common, and with dormitory accommodations rather than individual cells at night. It was perhaps symbolic that in 1898 the authorities in Paris ordered the demolition of Mazas prison, built during the 1840s as the largest and most modern cellular prison in France. The cellular enthusiasts were still not ready to capitulate, but their time of greatest influence was clearly over.

In a sense, the cellular forces' victory in 1875 had been illusory from the start. The fact was that the penal transporters had already dug themselves into a strong defensive position; their formula had become an integral part of France's penal system, and they would not soon be dislodged. Long after most other European nations abandoned the practice of shipping criminals overseas, the Third Republic continued to do so. There was vigorous opposition from the outset, building up at last to a climax in the 1930s; but until then, there was enough official and public support to insulate penal transportation against its detractors.

The Second Empire had sent a total of 19,069 hard-labor convicts to Guiana and 2,883 to New Caledonia.[22] Since 1867 the main destination had shifted to New Caledonia; for the next two decades, Guiana received only offenders from the African and Asian colonies, who were believed to be better able to cope with the humid tropical climate. The new penal colony in the South Pacific was reputed to be working well; officials of the Second Empire and the naval administrators who ran both penal colonies boasted of its success, in the hope no doubt that it would make France's critics forget the Guiana fiasco. Most of the convicts sent to New Caledonia were clustered in a penal reserve at the southeastern end of the island, where they were segregated from the native Melanesians. Some were assigned to build roads and docks; a few were hired out to free colonists.

The natural impulse of the Third Republic's governing elite was to reverse whatever the Empire had done. But the aftermath of the Paris Commune made it difficult to abandon the New Caledonia experiment. The throng of arrested dissidents was even greater than it had been in June 1848 or December 1851; detention facilities in France were totally inadequate. It is hardly surprising that the government of Adolphe Thiers took the easy way out by deporting between 4000 and 5000 Communards to New Caledonia.[23] Most of them, as political offenders, were segregated from the hard-labor convicts; they were crowded onto a small and unproductive offshore island, the Ile des Pins, where room was made for them by displacing some natives to the main island.[24] Some of the most prominent Communard leaders were confined in a disciplinary enclosure near Noumea; a small number got hard-labor sentences, and were merged with the other convicts.

Meanwhile a steady flow of several hundred hard-labor convicts each year continued to arrive in New Caledonia; by the end of the 1870s the number of *bagnards* there outnumbered those in Guiana.[25] Some Frenchmen complained about the cost of shipping prisoners so far, but for some years there was no serious pressure to abolish the system. The Haussonville commission did hear testimony from various officials, including a former governor of Guiana, Admiral Fourichon, who opposed transportation because it interfered with colonization by free settlers. Besides, he added, it was inhumane to send offenders to an island whose natives were "the dregs of humanity," a threat to life and limb. Were they cannibals?, asked one commissioner. Indeed they were, replied the admiral; at the outset of the French occupation they had eaten three petty officers and sixteen sailors from one landing party.[26] But the commission was more impressed by a detailed and generally favorable report from a high official of the colonial ministry, Hubert Michaux. Locating a penitentiary in Guiana, Michaux admitted, had been "an unhappy thought," but New Caledonia was quite different. In this "land of eternal springtime," convicts were better off than they had been in France. The solution was a temporary one, Michaux believed; for eventually an influx of free settlers would, as in Australia, create pressure to liquidate the *bagne*. But meanwhile convict labor would have been useful in developing the colony's resources, and the penitentiary could eventually be shifted to an unpopulated colony elsewhere.[27] Michaux followed up his testimony with a well-documented book in defense of penal transportation; critics of the system complained testily that he had dazzled the public by his persuasiveness, so that no one would listen to negative arguments. (Perhaps Michaux won his audience by his disarming preface; he apologized in advance for any boredom his readers might suffer, since his boredom in writing the book had been far greater.[28]) In fact, the glamor of "la Nouvelle" took on such proportions that inmates of French prisons began to assault or murder guards or fellow prisoners in an effort to gain transfer to the island paradise. The Director of Prison Administration reported a hundred such crimes between 1873 and 1877—which led parliament in 1878 to adopt a law ruling out transfers to the colony for crimes committed in prison.[29]

By the late 1870s, however, a contrary current was setting in; the critics of transportation finally began to get a hearing. Their campaign was fed by a steady drumfire of complaints from the exiled Communards and their sympathizers, who alleged a wide variety of abuses and mistreatment; there were ugly rumors about the treatment of ordinary *bagnards* as well. Parliament in 1879 finally voted an amnesty for the Communards, almost all of whom left New Caledonia at once. But protest continued; the crusading Senator Victor Schoelcher, who had won fame as the man who had ended slavery in the French West Indies in 1848, chimed in with accusations of brutality in the Guiana *bagne* as well.[30] Parliament set up a commission of inquiry, focused on New Caledonia; it held extensive hearings in 1880–81 and brought in a report confirming many charges of serious abuses by a few guards, administrators, and trusties.[31] Some ex-Communards, captured after attempting to escape, claimed to have been confined to punishment cells for thirty-three days, legs bound to the so-called "bar of justice," hands tied behind their backs; and a lengthy list of reputable witnesses testified to a variety of refined tortures for obstreperous *bagnards*, along with accounts of graft and drunkenness among trusties and guards. Trials of the accused guards followed, but all except one were acquitted; the lone exception was fined one hundred francs. But the scandal did lead to drastic reform of the displinary code in both penal colonies, including the substitution of cellular detention for the whip.[32]

The reforms of 1880–81 introduced an unusual period of change and experiment in the penal colonies—the humanitarian decade, some later called it. Severe discipline gave way to more relaxed methods, and a few abortive attempts at innovation occurred. The results were intensely controversial at the time, and have remained so in retrospect. Viewed by critics, the effect was growing disorder that built up to chaos and near-anarchy; viewed by sympathizers, it was a noble effort that failed—in part because of sabotage by doubters, in part through the naïveté of some of its sponsors, and in part because it may have been chimerical to try generous penal experiments in such a place as the *bagne*.

The most intriguing figure in this thwarted experiment was naval captain Pallu de la Barrière, whose stormy career as governor of New Caledonia lasted only from 1882 to 1884.[33] Pallu was a flamboyant and strong-willed character, filled with an urge to transform both the penitentiary and the colony as a whole. Shortly after his arrival, he wrote to the director of the penal colony outlining the goals he had in mind. The *bagnards*, now about 7000 in number, were no longer to be confined to the penitentiary compound, but would be dispatched throughout the island in work gangs that would build an elaborate network of roads. As rapidly as possible, they would then be assigned to work for free colonists, who would train them as farmers, fishermen, or artisans. The final step would be grants of agricultural, mining, or fishing concessions to convicts who had proved themselves, whether or not they had served out their sentences. Thus the island's resources would be opened to thousands of free colonists, and alongside them thousands of ex-convicts would take their place as free and equal citizens.[34] The governor's letter, reported one journalist, caused "a profound sensation." "What outbursts of enthusiasm in Noumea! In every letter and newspaper there is only one cry, a cry of sympathy and gratitude toward this intelligent and just man."[35]

Buoyed by this reception, Pallu appointed a large commission of local notables to study his plans. It would take seven thousand convicts six years to complete the road network, he told the commission; then France would have to find another location for the penitentiary. Seven thousand concessions would be required for the rehabilitated *bagnards*; five thousand women should be brought from France to enable them to found families. For this purpose, he was asking Paris to set aside 110,000 hectares of good land on the island. Within a few years, he predicted, the penal origin of these men would be forgotten; they would be respected as pioneers and solid citizens.[36] While the commission debated these grandiose plans, Pallu moved into action. Road-work gangs moved out to all parts of the island; several hundred agricultural concessions were granted, mainly at Bourail in the central part of the island. In 1884, the authorities in Paris approved the request to add 110,000 hectares to the penal reserve.[37] Utopia, it appeared, was moving from dream to reality.

Instead, the dream was quickly shattered. Pallu's experiment, described by his bitterest critic as the product of "a great heart or a disordered brain," ran into immediate difficulties.[38] At the outset, this critic admitted, there had indeed been enormous enthusiasm; convicts wrote poems in honor of the governor, or had his portrait tattooed on their arms. But relaxed discipline brought its toll; the number of severe punishment cases doubled in a year, and most of the first batch of convict concessionaires failed miserably as farmers. Still more serious was the outrage voiced by many free colonists, who were outnumbered three to one by the convicts. They complained that the work gangs were spreading terror throughout the island, that the native population was threatening to revolt because its lands had been expropriated, and that the *bagnards* were being given more privileges than the free colonists. Critics warned too that as reports of utopia in "la Nouvelle" spread to France, the crime rate there would rise dramatically, since crime, even when offenders were caught, obviously did pay. The only solution, wrote Pallu's chief opponent, was to make the *bagne* once again what it had formerly been—"the most feared penalty in our code."[39]

By midsummer 1884 the critics had won the ear of the Minister of Navy and Colonies. Pallu, who had been a headstrong and difficult subordinate for the minister, was abruptly ordered home to explain his actions, and he was replaced by a civilian administrator who had served under his orders. En route home, Pallu fired off a series of long and plaintive letters protesting to the minister at his unceremonious dismissal and enclosing several testimonials signed by some three hundred free colonists in Noumea, praising his efforts and regretting his departure.[40] The captain then vanished into the obscurity from which he had so recently emerged, leaving behind only a dusty file in the colonial archives. For many years, nevertheless, he was to be a kind of whipping-boy for advocates of hard-line penal methods in the *bagnes*.[41] His reforms were quickly undone, and a few years later a new administrative commission in Paris put an end to the "humanitarian decade" by drafting a set of tough disciplinary rules for both New Caledonia and Guiana.[42] Once again, the good intentions of a single administrator had proved insufficient to transform a penal institution into a place for rehabilitation. Perhaps the effort itself was futile; or perhaps it was a case of the wrong man in the wrong place at the wrong time.

Meanwhile, in 1885, the overseas penal colonies were assigned an additional burden; parliament voted to transport not only hard-labor convicts and political offenders but also habitual criminals—recidivists found guilty of several less serious offenses. From the late 1870s, pressures had been building up in France for such a solution to the problem of recidivism. The agitation was fed by a widespread belief that recidivism was getting worse, that the existing prison system had failed either to deter or to rehabilitate, and that "professional criminals" simply had to be removed from the society of honest folk. For the first time, official crime statistics were now being widely publicized in the popular press, and they helped to fuel public passions. Most major crimes, it was argued, were committed by persons who had begun as vagrants, beggars, or petty thieves; therefore serious crime as well as minor offenses could be reduced by ridding France of petty recidivists.[43] Parliament was bombarded with petitions from local councils and citizens' groups; in 1880 the Freemasons of France submitted a monster petition carrying 60,000 signatures.[44]

The politicians quickly responded to the pressure; during the election campaign of 1881, a number of candidates came out for the transportation of recidivists—among them the republicans' chief spokesman Léon Gambetta.[45] After Gambetta's sudden death in 1882, his disciples took up the crusade. Joseph Reinach, in an impassioned brochure, reminded his readers that there was worthy precedent: the men of the Great Revolution had decreed that second offenders should be transported for life. The heroic leaders of that era, wrote Reinach, had not suffered from "the imprudent compassion and sickly sympathy that has misled our generation." Unfortunately, the first Napoleon had undone their work, and had condemned France to "the most extensive spread of criminal gangrene ever recorded in statistical history." Now at last the public was awakening to the facts; a cry of alarm was arising from the best republicans; tomorrow would be too late to act against the "compact army" of professional criminals.[46] Another Gambettist deputy, René Waldeck-Rousseau, introduced a bill resurrecting the law of 1791; the government then countered with its own bill.

Three years of parliamentary haggling and bitter controversy preceded the adoption of the bill in 1885. Critics of the proposal, outside as well as within parliament, branded it as unworkable, inhumane, costly, juridically flawed, a craven concession to public pressure—in short, a "bizarre" proposal that would punish petty offenders more severely than many major criminals.[47] If adopted, warned Fernand Desportes of the *Société des Prisons*, it might require the transportation of 11,000 offenders annually, or 100,000 in ten years; the only practical way to handle such crowds would be to dump them in some desert continent where they might compete for survival with the wild beasts and cannibals.[48] Deputy Edmond de Pressensé protested, "You can't clean up a whole society the way you clean up the streets of a big city"; and Deputy Georges Périn warned of disastrous results for colonial development: "The penal element is like manure; in small amounts it fertilizes the soil; in large quantities it burns and renders sterile."[49] Many of the bill's opponents were dedicated advocates of cellular imprisonment; they insisted that public funds should not be diverted from upgrading the short-term prisons, as required by the law of 1875. And they expressed quite reasonable doubts about the bill's philanthropic façade—the argument that it would offer habitual offenders a chance to remake their lives in "a new French motherland" and to serve the nation by developing the colonies.[50]

The bill's proponents, however, were just as strident. Since 1854 the transportation of hard-labor convicts, cried one magistrate, had done wonders in purging France of major criminals and even moralizing a few. But now more of the same was needed: "We have reached a time when crime is rising to the point of overflow"; only drastic action could save society.[51] And Senator Verninac, taking a different tack, claimed that Australia provided a dazzling example: convict labor had converted it from "a seemingly useless continent" into "one of the most prosperous countries in the world."[52]

During the long parliamentary process, the bill underwent several important changes. The term "transportation" was replaced by "relegation" on the dubious ground that this was not technically a punishment (the offenders in question had already served out their sentences in French prisons), but was merely a matter of social hygiene designed to eliminate such offenders from honest society.[53] Another amendment excluded ordinary vagrancy and begging from the list of offenses that might lead to relegation, even though paranoia about vagrancy had done much to fire up the public agitation that produced the bill.[54] Still another amendment provided that *rélégués* without financial resources (which meant, in practice, all of them) would not be set free to work or starve in the colony (as originally intended), but would be kept under penal supervision and put to work as though they were *bagnards*.[55] There were lengthy arguments over where to send the *rélégués*; a short list of possible destinations was drawn up, but in the end parliament ruled out all of them.[56] The decision was left to the penal administration, which fell back on the easiest solution—using the existing facilities in Guiana and New Caledonia.

In the end, both houses of parliament adopted the measure by a wide margin. If "bizarre" was the right word for this law, one of its stranger aspects was the source of its main support. Its most committed backers were the bourgeois republican politicians, the Opportunists and some of the Radicals, while the opposition was led by members of the monarchist right and the socialist left.[57] This was a law-and-order measure designed to purge the country of incorrigibles; it responded to the panicky fears of "honest folk," ordinary citizens of modest position who had been persuaded that "the army of crime" was at their doorsteps. It was the work, cried one conservative, of Gambetta's disciples—"the heirs of the dictator"—determined to carry out their idol's demagogic promise.[58] The final vote in parliament came just before the general election of 1885, and the opposition charged that fear of the voters explained the wide margin of approval.[59] Perhaps so; at any rate, the episode suggests that it is not only the rich and powerful who can be swept along by a wave of social fear and can resort to harshly repressive measures to protect the lives and property of *les honnêtes gens*.

In practice, relegation satisfied almost no one, though opinions differed as to the reasons for its ineffectiveness. For the first few years after 1885, most *relégués* were shipped to Guiana; a minority —those who were judged to be most capable of rehabilitation— went to New Caledonia. Despite the law's distinction between *relégués* and *bagnards*, almost all of them were kept under penal supervision (though in separate camps).[60] Very few were set free to "make a new life"; a story circulated that the first *relégué* granted this privilege died of emotion on hearing the news.[61] For a time, between one and two thousand *relégués* were transported annually, but the flow soon slackened and levelled off at between four and five hundred.[62] The partisans of relegation complained that French magistrates were at fault; they were reluctant to impose exile for life on petty offenders, and found ways to reduce the charges against them.[63] Opponents of relegation continued to argue that the cost of exporting *relégués* diverted funds from the upkeep and improvement of prisons.[64] Socialist Alexandre Millerand, who had observed a load of *relégués* about to be shipped out, told the Chamber of Deputies that "if those pimps and prostitutes can be transformed into working colonists just by an ocean voyage, M. Freppel [a deputy who was also a Catholic bishop] can point to at least one real miracle."[65] The controversy was renewed when, for a few years after 1896, the crime rate declined for the first time since the Second Empire. The defenders of relegation took this to be a delayed result of the 1885 law; the critics replied that it was traceable rather to the so-called Bérenger laws of 1885 and 1891, which had introduced the practice of early conditional release from prison for good behavior, and had authorized judges to hand down sus-

**CELL-BLOCK OF THE BAGNE IN NEW CALEDONIA.** During the later 19th century thousands of major offenders served time in these barracks. (Roger-Viollet)

pended sentences for first offenders.[66] In fact, conditional release (an unsupervised form of parole) was not widely used in France until the 1960s; but suspended sentences undoubtedly did prevent some recidivism and contributed to the drop in the crime rate.

While Frenchmen argued over the merits of relegation, the *bagne* in New Caledonia was the target of criticism both from the slowly growing population of free colonists and from French and foreign visitors to the island. The return to more severe disciplinary rules after 1890, and a policy of hiring out large batches of *bagnards* to mining and sugar-refining entrepreneurs, led to accusations of renewed brutality and of a "white slave traffic."[67] During the fifth International Penal Congress in Paris in 1895, the French and Russian delegates barely managed to defeat a resolution calling for an end to all penal transportation. One French delegate scornfully dismissed these foreign critics as "theoretical extremists" who prided themselves on acting "in the name of alleged higher principles."[68] But it was not the humanitarians who put an end to the New Caledonia *bagne*. Rather, it was accusations that the island was too attractive, a tropical paradise for rascals maintained at public expense. By comparison, complained one visiting journalist, the beach resorts of the Riviera and Greece seemed second-rate.[69] There were even rumors in France that some *rélégués* had free colonists at their service.[70] Three deputies, in an effort to make transportation more intimidating, proposed in 1898 to move all the *bagnards* and *rélégués* from both New Caledonia and Guiana to the icy wastes of the Kerguelen Islands, near Antarctica.[71]

In 1897 the authorities in Paris quietly suspended further convoys of either convicts or *rélégués* to New Caledonia, and the suspension proved to be permanent. Yet the remnants of the *bagne* in the Pacific were not liquidated for another thirty years, and controversy about it continued for a decade. Several thousand *bagnards* and *rélégués* remained on the island after 1897, without the right to return to France after completing their sentences. Local councils representing the free colonists petitioned Paris repeatedly to repatriate the *libérés*, while a minority of colonists argued for resuming shipments in order to provide cheap labor.[72] These differences were echoed in France, where all of the old arguments continued to be repeated *ad nauseam*. But the issue gradually faded as the number of convicts and *libérés* declined. By 1913 the penal population had shrunk to a thousand *bagnards* still under sentence, two thousand *libérés*, and a thousand *rélégués*.[73] Most of these were gradually concentrated in a single detention center near Noumea, pending a firm decision on the destiny of the *bagne*.

In Guiana, on the other hand, the *bagne* was thriving—if that is the appropriate word. From 1867 to 1887, when it had been reserved for convicts from the African and Asian colonies, the penal population had declined from 5500 to 3500, or one-third of the New Caledonia figure.[74] The Penal Administration's policies in Guiana had followed a haphazard, zigzag path; a long series of experiments in housing and employing the prisoners was tried, abandoned, sometimes resumed and abandoned again.[75] Durable accomplishments, except for the construction of penitentiary headquarters at Saint-Laurent-du-Maroni, were meager; the jungle quickly swallowed up most roads and experimental farms. The death rate, after the first disastrous years, fluctuated around an annual average of about 6 per cent, but malaria and anemia remained common, and the hospitals were always crowded.[76]

In 1884, while parliament was considering the relegation bill, the Ministry of Marine dispatched a Parisian professor of criminal law, Jules Leveillé, to report on Guiana's suitability for *rélégués*. Leveillé, who prided himself on being a tough law-and-order man and was to become a vigorous advocate of transportation, returned with an enthusiastically affirmative report. Guiana, he declared, was eminently suitable for white colonization if supported by penal labor; its past difficulties were traceable to excessive administrative turnover and lax discipline. Convicts there, he alleged, lounged about and worked little; guards let them have their way. Leveillé urged a return to severe discipline; *bagnards* should be provided with bread and water and should earn anything more by hard work. Guiana could absorb not only hard-labor convicts from France but all the *rélégués* as well, provided that they were kept under penal control. In order to speed colonization, Leveillé recommended what he called *"métissage méthodique,"* by which he meant arranged marriages of liberated convicts with native Indian girls. Experience to date, he concluded, fully justified the policy of transportation; it could be compared to channelling the sewage of Paris onto a sandy suburban plain, which was enriched by this effluvium.[77]

Leveillé's report had multiple consequences. It encouraged the authorities in Paris to assign most of the *rélégués* to Guiana, and (in 1887) to resume sending some French hard-labor convicts there as well. It led the government in 1890–91 to end the "humanitarian decade" and to restore severe disciplinary rules. And it impelled Leveillé to stand successfully for the Chamber of Deputies (in 1893) where he became for a time the most vocal advocate of transportation and of severe anti-crime policies generally. After the convoys to New Caledonia were cut off in 1897, the flow to Guiana increased even more. Thereafter, almost a thousand convicts arrived each year, along with four to five hundred *rélégués*. There was also one celebrated political prisoner: Captain Alfred Dreyfus, convicted by a military court of selling secrets to the Germans. Although New Caledonia had been the legal place of detention for political offenders, it was regarded by Dreyfus's enemies as insufficiently rigorous; they pushed a law through parliament designating the Iles du Salut for this purpose.[78] Dreyfus was confined alone on the smallest of these, called Devil's Island, which had formerly been used for a variety of purposes, including the housing of lepers. A visitor to Guiana in 1897 (a former colonial governor) complained that "this monster" was the most coddled prisoner in the *bagne*; he sat alone on Devil's Island with nothing to do but "polish his lorgnon."[79]

By 1910 the penal population in Guiana had risen to about 8,500.[80] Most Frenchmen knew little about the *bagne*, but were content to see so many malefactors shipped off to permanent oblivion; honest folk could sleep more soundly. True, occasional reports by returned visitors portrayed the *bagne* there in idyllic terms, much as earlier visitors had done in the case of New Caledonia. "More and more," complained the noted criminologist Henri Joly, "newspapers and reviews tell us of the peaceful existence of the so-called workers of Cayenne and Maroni. . .; each convict is shown as living the life of Riley [*comme un 'coq en pâte'*]."[81] Some Frenchmen, however, had a clearer idea of what went on in the *bagne*, and its existence was an increasing embarrassment to them. The Minister of Colonies in 1895 expressed his personal repugnance at the system and declared his hope that it could be ended soon. A learned professor reminded his readers that "the practice of transportation led to England's loss of the United States," and warned that France's colonies might likewise be lost.[82] A former colonial governor who favored preserving the *bagne* admitted nevertheless that he had never seen a convict rehabilitated by the experience; when their terms ended, he said, they were all even more *gangréné* than on their arrival.[83] If the purpose of transportation was simply to purge France of major criminals and habitual petty offenders, it was obviously a success—though its effects on reducing the rate of recidivism had not been clearly demonstrated.[84] But if it was really meant to be constructive and humanitarian as well, by contributing to colonial development and by offering offenders "a new life under new skies," even its defenders had trouble making a persuasive case.

And yet it survived. When Senator Emile Chautemps, a former Minister of Colonies, set out in 1908 on a campaign to end transportation, the evidence that he presented seemed overwhelming. France's reputation in the world, he argued, was becoming tarnished by the *bagnes*; only Portugal, Spain, and Russia still clung to similar policies. All attempts to use convicts as colonists had failed miserably; very few had made good as farmers, despite government aid. Penal labor had done little to develop colonial resources, or even to provide an infrastructure of public works. And to speak of rehabilitating malefactors in these cesspools of humanity was at best a bad joke. "As for the nature of the *bagne*," he wrote, "our pen hesitates to continue. We would blush if forced to speak of it before an international congress. . . . The convicts are left to themselves throughout the night; they are free to strangle one another or to indulge in other foul practices according to their taste." The *rélégués* were no better off; those who had been sent to a temporary "transit camp" on the Ile des Pins (off New Caledonia) were still there twenty years later, completely idle and under penal detention. Besides, argued Chautemps, the cost of maintaining a transported convict was eight times as great as it had been in the old French seaport *bagnes*.[85]

While Chautemps's bill was making its way through a Senate committee, it inspired a long and emotional debate between transporters and incarcerators in the *Société des Prisons*.[86] Although that society had long been the stronghold of the cellular crusaders, it was the defenders of transportation who seized the initiative and dominated this debate. Jules Leveillé warned of the dangers of liquidating the *bagnes*; the sudden repatriation of "fifteen thousand elite malefactors" would, he said, bring on a crime wave of appalling proportions. Former colonial governor La Loyère insisted once more on the need for penal labor to develop colonial resources. But it was the eminent professor of criminal law Emile Garçon who aroused his colleagues to frenzied applause by his stirring protest against "this new effort to disarm society." "I prefer to see these malefactors slaughter each other in Cayenne rather than in Paris," he cried. Critics tell us that the French bourgeoisie, in its policies of crime control, is "pitiless." How unjust! "If there exists anywhere a sentimentalist in matters of repression, it is surely the French bourgeois. This bourgeoisie, to its honor, has inspired all the laws of indulgence, of mercy, and pardon that mark our entire penal legislation. If I were to offer any reproach, it would be that this bourgeoisie has had too many generous illusions about regenerating the hardened professional criminal and . . . has shown excessive indulgence toward certain misdeeds that profoundly trouble the social order." The common people, Garçon continued, were much tougher-minded when it came to repression. Besides, transportation was in fact a humane penalty; and other nations actually envied France for its convenient solution for the crime problem. Of course convicts had not succeeded as colonizers; it had been a complete illusion that such "vicious bandits, the sweepings of society" might achieve anything constructive. The point was that although the crime rate in France remained high, it would have been far higher without the *bagnes*. As for the critics of transportation, they were in many cases unrepentant partisans of the cell, still seeking revenge for their defeat in 1854. "The elimination of malefactors is the most effective means of repression at hand to combat the rising flood of dangerous crime. Take care! If you disarm society, beware of the excesses of a violent reaction! (Prolonged applause) ."[87]

Thanks to such spirited defenders, the *bagne* in Guiana survived, if it did not exactly prosper. Chautemps's bill remained stalled in a Senate committee, in part because he offered no easy substitute for the *bagne*. It would be the task for the next generation to grapple once more with the problem—and, eventually, to solve it by a final act of liquidation.

# VII

## Vagrants, Workers, Executioners
### 1880–1914

> There are no "facts of crime" as such, only a judgmental process that institutes crimes by designating as criminal both certain acts and their perpetrators. In other words, there is a discourse of crime that reveals the obsessions of a society.
>
> MICHELLE PERROT (1975)

THE MANNER in which the members of any society think and talk about crime is likely to reflect its values, its concerns, and at times its obsessions. Surely there is a solid core of truth in Michelle Perrot's shrewd observation. It is also true that obsessions can sometimes be based on fact; as the popular saying goes, paranoids *can* have real enemies. Threats to public order and personal security are not always merely imaginary, nor are these concerns inspired solely by the narrow self-interest of a privileged elite. Yet the obsessional side does enter in, for criminal behavior and its repression are matters laden with emotion, easily colored by irrational factors. From the early nineteenth century to our own day, one can cite an unbroken series of rhetorical outbursts by Frenchmen who indulged in panicky predictions about "the rising flood of dangerous criminality," a torrent that threatened to "burst the floodgates" and inundate the country; about "the army of crime," "the horde of barbarians," poised to sweep down upon the unprotected honest folk of France. The regularity of this repetitive drumbeat through successive generations, no matter what the current level of crime happened to be, does suggest its obsessive nature.

Three special aspects of the "crime problem" were chronic sources of worry and debate in France throughout the nineteenth century, and lapped over into the twentieth as well. These were the problems of vagrancy, of prison labor, and of capital punishment. Though all three were persistent enough to justify the adjective "chronic," they reached a climax of special intensity during the golden years of the Third Republic—the years that nostalgic Frenchmen call *la belle époque*. Concern about vagrancy rose to such a peak in the 1880s, and remained intense until the Great War; contentious argument about prison labor came next, during the 1890s; and capital punishment became the burning issue during the decade after 1900. While the theorists and the politicians continued to joust over free will and determinism, and to debate the respective merits of solitary confinement and penal transportation, ordinary Frenchmen felt more strongly about the specific issues that form the subject of this chapter. Those issues seemed to impinge more directly on everyday life; they affected the average citizen's sense of security and, in the case of the death penalty, touched his ethical beliefs and his deeper emotions.

If the term "obsessive" is appropriate for any of the three issues in question, it would surely be the problem of vagrancy as a presumed threat to public order and a source of serious crime. In both the learned and the popular writings of the nineteenth century, the phrase *vagabonds et mendiants* recurs with tiresome frequency, the two terms almost always linked together as a single locution. The law made some effort to distinguish between them, and most commentators agreed that roving vagrants were far more dangerous than the relatively harmless local beggars. Most Frenchmen, however, lumped the two categories together and viewed them both with deep suspicion. They were seen as an ominous threat to personal security and as natural recruits for "the army of crime." "In principle," declared one police official, "every vagrant is a potential malefactor, and becomes one sooner or later."[1] It is true that a subordinate current of sympathy for the suffering poor, seen as innocent victims of social injustice, also persisted throughout the century and nourished efforts at private charity; but that current was clearly weaker than the sentiment of hostility and fear. It was com-

mon practice to express compassion for the "deserving poor" and
to distinguish them from the incorrigibly lazy and vicious types.
But those who made such distinctions usually limited themselves
to a ritual bow in the direction of innocent misery before focusing
their attention on the threat to honest folk.[2]

The problem of vagrancy was of course not new in the nineteenth century, nor was it confined to France. For centuries all
European societies had been afflicted by this "plague" (as it was
most commonly described) ; and the French monarchy, like others,
had groped for remedies that had been consistent in only one
sense: they had always failed. From the time of Francis I in the
sixteenth century, able-bodied beggars had been subject to whipping or the galleys. Louis XIV in 1656 had tried the experiment
sometimes called *le grand renfermement* (roughly, "the great lock-
up") , compelling indigents to enter a branch of the so-called *Hôpi-
tal Général,* and assessing fines against well-meaning citizens
caught in the act of giving alms to a beggar.[3] This grandiose
scheme of creating a *"Versailles de la misère* (as one sardonic critic
later described it) soon broke down; toward the end of the Sun
King's reign, Marshal Vauban estimated that one Frenchman in ten
survived by begging.[4] In 1718 a brief venture into transporting vagrants and beggars was tried; several hundred were rounded up by
agents of John Law's Mississippi Company and shipped to Louisiana, but protests both in France and in the colony quickly ended
the practice.[5] Louis XV's government in 1724 tried unsuccessfully
to employ able-bodied beggars on road-building gangs. By mid-
century, the number of vagrants and beggars was estimated at
nearly 200,000, and they were said to be terrorizing the peasantry
in many rural areas.[6] Besides, declared the magistrate Le Trosne,
they constituted "the seed-bed of thieves and assassins."[7] The government in 1764 ordered a severe crackdown: three years in the
galleys for first offenders, a life sentence on the third arrest. Three
years later it substituted a new version of the great lock-up: *dépôts
de mendicité* were to be established throughout the country, in
which able-bodied indigents would be confined and forced to work.[8]
Some of these *dépôts* survived until the Great Revolution, but they
were miserably inadequate institutions that became little more than
dumping-grounds for unfortunates of all kinds, halfway houses between prisons and asylums.[9]

The Revolution of 1789 seemed to portend a real new era; its leaders believed (as a later politician described it) that "misery is sacred."[10] One of the first acts of the National Assembly was to establish a Committee on the Extinction of Mendicity; if it succeeded in its task, one member predicted, the nation's crime problem would be three-quarters solved.[11] But in the end the committee's report bore a surprising resemblance to the policies of the *ancien régime*; it proposed to replace the *dépôts de mendicité* by *maisons de répression* for first and second offenders, and to punish a third arrest by transportation for life to a penal colony.[12] The Convention in 1793 wrote these recommendations into law, and revived Louis XIV's order that citizens caught in the act of giving alms should be fined. Madagascar was designated as the site for transported beggars.[13] But the revolutionary upheaval pushed the new law into the discard; vagrants continued to be dealt with in the traditional haphazard way.

Napoleon, whose tolerance for disorder was low, decided in 1808 that begging must be extirpated once and for all. He ordered that the moribund *dépôts de mendicité* be generalized throughout France, and that they be reorganized so as to give vagrants and beggars a taste for hard work and regular habits. Beggars who sought to evade these philanthropic institutions were to be jailed.[14] In fact, only thirty-seven departments got around to establishing *dépôts* before Napoleon fell, and once again they quickly became nothing more than dumping-grounds for the sick, the aged, and the insane.[15] The restored Bourbon monarchy knocked the props from under the *dépôts* by freeing the local authorities of any obligation to establish and finance them. It is hardly surprising that only six *dépôts* remained in operation when the Bourbons fell in 1830.[16]

Private charity, with some support from Louis-Philippe's government and from municipal authorities, was left with the task of trying to cope with the flood of drifters, misfits, and unfortunates that seemed to be rising again. The new ruling elite of the bourgeois era took the problem seriously—some of them for genuinely philanthropic reasons, some out of fear that property and public order might be threatened. Both motives are clearly reflected in administrative reports of the time. In 1831 the prefect of police in Paris made a fervent plea for governmental funds to provide work relief; "the extreme and desperate misery of the working class," he declared, was swelling the number of beggars and vagrants to dangerous proportions. Of the 100,000 workingmen in Paris, two-fifths had been unemployed for a year; they had sold their meager possessions and were forced to steal or starve. What they really wanted, the prefect insisted, was jobs, not a life of crime.[17] Both the city and the central government subsidized *ateliers de secours,* and the return of better times alleviated the problem somewhat. Both the government and private bodies undertook elaborate surveys of the condition of the poor, but officials admitted that they simply did not know how serious the problem was.[18] A socialist of the time, Pierre Leroux, alleged that the government itself estimated the number of beggars in France at four million—a figure that was picked up and repeated by Karl Marx.[19] In fact, no government authority had suggested such an inflated figure, and private estimates by specialists ranged from 75,000 to 200,000.[20] But prison inspector Moreau-Christophe judged that two million citizens were living below what was officially considered the poverty line, and that the figure would be closer to six million if the marginally poor were added.[21] At one point the government made a hesitant move toward reviving the *dépôts de mendicité,* but their evil reputation was such that the idea was quickly dropped.[22]

The men of 1848, like those of 1789, made a brief but dramatic effort to grapple with the problem of rootless and indigent citizens. They proclaimed the right to work, and for a few months provided state-financed jobs through a system that in our time might be called workfare. The abolition of these so-called National Workshops and the bloody conflict that followed in June 1848 left much of the bourgeois elite traumatized;[23] for a generation, there were no serious efforts to deal with the problem of vagrancy and begging. The booming prosperity of the 1850s also reduced the pressure for controls or concessions. The issue receded into the background during the Second Empire, even though the number of wandering beggars seems to have remained fairly stable. When a magistrate in 1862 published a monograph on vagrancy, it went almost unnoticed. Twenty years later, issued in a second edition, it was to find a considerable public.[24] The country's mood had obviously changed in the course of that twenty-year period.

Why the mood of indifference in the 1860s gave way to a surge of interest and even panic in the 1880s is not easy to discover, even in retrospect. Logic would suggest that there must have been a dangerous rise in the number of rootless wanderers, and an increased brazenness as they exacted tribute from honest folk in the cities and in the countryside. Many Frenchmen at the time believed this to be the case, even though the evidence for it was slight. From the late 1870s onward, petitions flowed into Paris from provincial authorities, calling on the government to take drastic emergency action. Vagrants, it was alleged, were terrorizing and victimizing the peasantry; they stole whatever was not nailed down, attacked women working in the fields, exacted tribute by threats to burn barns or haystacks.[25] These exactions, one jurist declared, cost the peasants more than did the property tax.[26] Town and city dwellers soon joined the chorus; the Freemasons in 1880 collected 60,000 signatures calling for severe repression. The "resurgent plague" of vagrants and beggars—described by one magistrate as "the most dangerous enemies of society, and the most miserable of human creatures"[27]—seized the interest of officials and criminologists; impressive statistics were assembled to prove that matters had reached a crisis stage, threatening not only property but life and limb. The politicians were prompt to respond to this surge of emotion by adopting the relegation law of 1885, designed to purge France of habitual offenders by transportation for life. Ironically, however, the clause providing for enforced exile of ordinary vagrants and beggars was removed from the law before its adoption; only "aggravated vagrancy" (i.e., involving threat or disguise) would be counted in sentencing to relegation.[28] The original impulse behind the law thus remained partially unsatisfied.

There are times when popular beliefs outrun facts, and this was probably the case with respect to the vagrancy panic of the 1880s. It is true that there is no way to measure accurately the real gravity of the threat to lives and property at that time. The statistics used by contemporaries were drawn from the Ministry of Justice's *Compte général* for 1880, which analyzed trends since 1826. These figures seemed to justify the nation's fears, since they suggested that convictions for vagrancy and begging had risen from an annual average of 2,910 in 1826–30 to 10,429 in 1876–80 (far exceeding the rate of increase for any other offense), and that recidivism among vagrants and beggars was higher than for any other category of offenders.[29] The widely accepted estimate that the vagrant population had reached 400,000 was, however, no more than a guess; and the repeated assertion by politicians and publicists that vagrancy was the first step toward major crime rested on equally shaky assumptions. The venerable Charles Lucas, after studying the official statistics, contended that the common pattern of recidivism was not from petty offense to major crime, but downward from crime to misdemeanor or horizontally from one misdemeanor to another.[30] The deputy and ex-magistrate Alexandre Bérard admitted that there were no statistics on the number of crimes and misdemeanors committed by vagrants, but insisted nevertheless that all magistrates believed the figure to be "enormous."[31] No doubt there was reason for Frenchmen to be concerned about vagrancy as a reflection of the broader problem of poverty within an affluent society; but the facts hardly justified the intensity of the social fear that marked the 1880s.

That fear was only temporarily allayed by the relegation law of 1885. For a few years, convictions for vagrancy and begging fell slightly, but the number rose again in the early 1890s to a new high of 19,723.[32] Once again, complaints from the provinces began to pour in upon the central authorities.[33] The intensely cold winter of 1890–91 brought the problem home to Parisians; indigents flooded into the city, swamping the private and city-owned shelters. Public sympathy was briefly aroused; the President of the Republic and other notables visited the shelters, and newspapers took up collections. But with the return of spring the drifters stayed on, and were joined by employed workers who found the shelters cheaper than rooming houses. Eventually the authorities evicted all but the sick and infirm. Too much indulgence, complained one penal official, had created the problem, and had turned Paris into a dangerous city for honest folk. "We must resign ourselves," he told the *Société des Prisons*, "to a return to penal repression [for vagrants], which was abandoned too soon."[34]

Throughout the 1890s, a rash of books and press articles kept public attention fixed on the vagrancy problem. One enthusiast studied the issue at first hand by posing for a time as a street beggar; the Paris deputy Georges Berry recruited a police agent to guide him to a beggars' auction where a valuable place at a church entrance was sold to the highest bidder. Berry was told that lists containing names and addresses of generous givers were also on sale (at prices varying with the level of generosity), and that young mothers rented out their babies to beggars for evening use (especially on Christmas Eve).[35] Learned authorities wrote theses on the social and psychological roots of vagrancy, debating its relation to degeneracy and suggesting that vagrants might be primitive nomadic types, descendants of those ancient hordes that had once migrated en masse and peopled the world, but who now had become useless and dangerous.[36] Deputy Alexandre Bérard branded them as "victims of atavism," "true wild beasts gone astray in a civilized world."[37] One criminologist, however, suggested that the roving spirit was not all that abnormal; consider, he said, the number of honest folk who in August feel an irresistible urge to leave home for the mountains, the seashore, or simply to wander aimlessly through the countryside.[38]

Beginning in the mid-1890s, convictions for vagrancy and begging suddenly dipped sharply, falling from 19,000 to 12,000.[39] Crime specialists argued over the reasons for the drop, some attributing it to the delayed results of the relegation law, others to the use of suspended sentences since 1891. Hard-liners complained, however, that the real cause was excessive indulgence on the part of the authorities. Magistrates, they claimed, were evading the relegation law, and municipal authorities in Socialist-controlled towns were refusing to crack down on vagrants and beggars.[40] There was some truth in both charges; judges were sending fewer *relégués* to the penal colonies, and Socialist mayors and councils did order more lenient policing.[41] From 1900 onward, however, arrests and convictions for vagrancy and begging again rose sharply, and so did demands for increased repression. A number of deputies, responding to pressures from their constituents, introduced bills designed to deal with the problem in a variety of ways. In 1910 the Chamber named a special commission to study and report on these accumulated proposals. Rapporteur Marc Réville, a Radical deputy, summed up the committee's conclusions thus:

> Over the past twenty years, vagrancy and begging have increased in the countryside and the cities of France to the point that a remedy is urgently needed. . . . Honest citizens are pressing for action. For the farmer, the *rouleur* . . . is an object of real terror. The honest citizen's generosity, born of fear, further increases the social parasitism of these 400,000 Frenchmen who have sworn undying hatred for steady or even occasional work.[42]

The cities, Réville continued, were likewise infested by these parasites whose goal was to live at society's expense; they would refuse
work even if it were offered. Current laws were obviously inadequate, since only 20,000 of the 400,000 vagrants were convicted
each year, and since short prison terms were obviously no deterrent.
This "veritable social malaise that strikes fear into city and country-
dwellers alike," Réville declared, called for both tougher penalties
and an adaptation of the law to the vagrants' special mentality. A
first or second offense should be punished by one or two years in
prison; a third should call for several years of forced labor in special work camps, where offenders would be taught a trade and
might possibly overcome their native aversion for work. Such a system, he argued, would actually save the taxpayers money; only
twenty million francs would be needed to set up the work camps,
whereas 400,000 beggars averaging alms of one franc a day were
costing the nation 146 million francs a year. The camps must be
Spartan in nature: "for these professional parasites and loafers, we
must not imitate the costly follies that have marked the construction of certain prisons where thieves and assassins enjoy greater
comfort than they could earn through honest labor." Réville admitted that few of these miscreants would be reformed by such
treatment, but at least they would be out of circulation for a while.
The commission brushed aside a substitute bill offered by one of its
members, Fernand Dubief, which was based on the idea that vagrants were degenerates who needed help, rather than delinquents
who deserved punishment. The plague would continue to spread,
said Réville, unless repression were given a penal character.[43]

   Although the commission's bill had strong support in the
Chamber, its critics (mainly on the left) threatened a hard fight
on the floor, so the commission chose to postpone public debate.
But the advocates of a crackdown were untiring, and in July 1914
they again persuaded the Chamber to name a high-level commission
of inquiry "to study measures for the repression of begging and vagrancy." It was hardly a propitious moment; the commission had
time for only one organizing session before Europe exploded into
war.[44] Although no one could anticipate the future, the Great War
marked the end of the persistent French obsession with the issue of
vagrancy. There would still be vagrants and beggars after the war,
and in scarcely diminished numbers; but their activities would no
longer provoke chronic debate and generalized social fear. And

with the adoption of a social security system after World War II, indigent Frenchmen at last had an alternative to their traditional choice—beg, steal, or starve.

It was during the 1890s that the issue of prison labor reached its climactic intensity; for a time it rivalled the question of vagrancy for popular and parliamentary attention. This issue too had been around for a long time—indeed, ever since an organized system of prison workshops had been installed in the *maisons centrales* after 1815. Complaints from artisans and small businessmen in prison towns had led to the Second Republic's brief and unhappy experiment of 1848, when all prison work was abruptly suppressed. That experiment had brought even sharper protests, and the gradual return to the traditional system in 1849–52 was welcomed in almost all quarters. Scarcely anyone henceforth ventured to suggest the elimination of prison labor. When one deputy proposed in 1878 to replace work in the short-term prisons by "elementary education and gymnastics," the Chamber's spontaneous response (as recorded in the official record of debates) was "*hilarité.*"[45] Work, a prison official told the *Société des Prisons* in 1901, was man's natural destiny: "Free or imprisoned, man must work: it is his lot, his distinctive quality, the mark of his nobility and his greatness." The august assemblage responded with warm applause.[46] Karl Marx himself in 1875 lent the weight of his authority to those who defended the dignity of prison labor.[47]

But if the basic principle was now pretty much beyond controversy, sharp differences persisted about the purpose and the proper organization of work in prisons. From the late 1870s onward, the annual discussion of the Prison Administration's budget in parliament brought a surge of complaints by deputies on behalf of their constituents, who with tedious regularity claimed that they were gravely threatened by unfair competition from prison-made goods. As in the 1840s, spokesmen for the growing labor movement added their own protests about the depressant effect of cheap prison labor on wages outside, and about the unemployment that allegedly resulted. Martin Nadaud, the self-educated mason whose election to the Chamber in 1876 made him the chief spokesman for his own artisan class, led the campaign in parliament for basic changes.[48] His goal was not to abolish prison work but to end the entrepreneurial system traditionally used in France, whereby individual enterprisers contracted with the state to supply prisoners with food, clothing, and medical care and to employ convicts in prison workshops. Under this system, the state normally paid the entrepreneur a fixed sum per prisoner for basic supplies, while profits from the sale of prison-made goods were apportioned among the three parties concerned—the entrepreneur, the convicts, and the prison administration. Nadaud and his associates of the left accused the entrepreneurs of mercilessly exploiting the convicts, of driving down the wages of free workers, and of depriving the government of profit that might have been used to reduce the cost of prison operation. Their solution was to introduce direct state management of all prison production (known in France as *la régie*). A successful experiment of this sort had been in effect since the 1840s at the prison of Melun and at three smaller prisons, but the example had not spread further.[49] Some politicians and reformers of more conservative bent joined Nadaud and the left in advocating an end to the entrepreneurial system, mainly with a view to reducing prison operating costs; and some of them suggested also that prisoners should produce only for consumption by state agencies rather than for sale on the open market.[50]

Officials of the prison administration stubbornly resisted these proposals. Over and over, they cited statistics to ridicule the idea that a few dozen or a few hundred inefficient convicts could seriously threaten the welfare of tens of thousands of free workers, and they insisted that private entrepreneurs were far more skilled than prison officials at setting up and operating workshops.[51] As for the idea of producing solely for state agencies, they argued that no branch of the government had any interest in buying prison-made goods. The army and navy—the largest potential market identified by the reformers—were especially reluctant to change their habits; they had contracted for years with certain private suppliers of uniforms and equipment, and enjoyed this comfortable arrangement.[52] As for the suppliers, they had come to regard army and navy contracts as a form of vested interest that was above challenge, and they lobbied vigorously against the pressures for change. The government did make one concession when it promulgated (in 1882) more elaborate rules for setting wage scales in the prisons. Since 1844 those wages had been set at roughly 20 per cent below the going wage outside. The new rules called for calculating the cost of production for each prison product individually, and readjusting the figure annually on the basis of the cost of production of that item by free workers.[53] The system proved to be excessively complex, and quickly gave way in practice to a more empirical arrangement; but the change did something to counter the complaints about "cheap" prison labor.

Discontent nevertheless continued to build up and to become more vocal from the mid-1880s onward, as the socialist and trade union movements gained strength. In 1888 the basket-makers' union took the initiative in organizing a protest movement—the *Ligue de Protestation contre le Travail dans les Prisons et les Communautés Religieuses*. Prison-made basketware, they alleged, was produced at half the normal cost and was flooding the market. By 1891 thirty-seven craft unions plus a feminist organization (the *Ligue pour l'Émancipation de la Femme*) had adhered to the new *Ligue de Protestation*.[54] A series of emotional rallies followed at the Paris Bourse du Travail, but the protesters had trouble agreeing on goals. A minority (notably the anarchists) wanted to return to 1848 by abolishing all prison labor, while the majority favored equalizing the wages of prisoners and free workers. Some even proposed the adoption of the eight-hour day in prisons—which inspired one outraged official of the *Société des Prisons* to the caustic prediction that the protesters would soon want billiard rooms and bars for the convicts' leisure hours.[55] The *Ligue*'s nearest approach to consensus was its call for replacement of the entrepreneurial system by *la régie*. Several Socialist deputies attended the *Ligue*'s third rally in 1892, and promised vigorous action in parliament. Jean Allemane, in a long and fiery speech to the crowd, accused the government of profiteering from prison labor and thus committing "a veritable act of theft, an attack on organized labor." Besides, he added, most prisoners were not really responsible for their misdeeds and were being unjustly punished.[56]

In response to the *Ligue*'s pressure and to their own doctrinal views, Socialist deputies as well as some others bombarded the

Chamber during the early 1890s with bills calling for an end to the entrepreneurial system and for a variety of other reforms. All of these proposals remained buried in committee. Some of the pressure for change was relieved by partial concessions by the government—notably by a decision in the early 1890s to narrow the scope of the entrepreneurial system. France had been unique in Europe in the use of so-called "general entrepreneurs" to supply prisoners with food, clothing, and medical services. The practice had led to charges of profiteering and to some major scandals; it had also given the general entrepreneurs such authority that they sometimes overshadowed the prison directors and were familiarly known as "kings of the prisons."[57] The supply function was now transferred to the prison administration. Entrepreneurs remained in charge of prison labor and production, but their power was reduced and their conduct better controlled; the system thus became less vulnerable to attack.

Although the annual round of complaints at budget time continued into the new century, the focus of discontent shifted somewhat. Socialist spokesmen concentrated now on the goal of equalizing the wages of prisoners and free workers in order to end what they called unfair competition. Prison officials claimed that this was in fact a devious scheme to put all prison workershops out of business.[58] Conservative critics put their energies into an effort to keep prison-made goods off the open market. The hard-liner Jules Leveillé had persuaded the Chamber in 1895 to adopt a resolution calling on the prison administration to produce for state consumption alone, but officials continued to plead inability to persuade state agencies to buy.[59] The use of prison labor to supply the prisons themselves was expanded somewhat, but one official complained that the result was a sorcerer's apprentice phenomenon. After a workshop was set up in one large prison for this purpose, he said, the administration soon found itself with enough wooden shoes, berets, and shirts for several generations of prisoners in all of France.[60] Sporadic proposals to employ prisoners on road-work gangs, or to set up agricultural colonies for convicts of rural origin, continued to be put forward, as they had been throughout the nineteenth century; but they aroused little enthusiasm.[61] Gradually, in the years before the Great War, the prison-labor issue lost its in-

PUBLIC EXECUTION, 19TH-CENTURY STYLE. From 1851 until the end of the century, executions in Paris were carried out on the sidewalk at the entrance to the Grande Roquette prison. After 1900 the locus was shifted to the vicinity of La Santé prison, farther from the city center. (Roger-Viollet)

tensity and faded out of public notice. It was to receive some renewed attention, though briefly and much less emotionally, during the interwar era.[62]

The test of a society's level of civilization, it is sometimes said, may be found in the nature of its punishments. The perennial debate over the death penalty brings the issue into sharpest focus. For its opponents, capital punishment is a barbarous survival of a less enlightened age, a violation of the basic principle that neither an individual nor a society has the right to take human life. For its defenders, it is the essential keystone in any system of penal repression, both for its supposed deterrent effect and for its value in satisfying the public's sense of justice. France is by no means the only country that has had long experience with this debate. But it is probably unique in one paradoxical sense: for almost two centuries the abolitionist campaign enjoyed much influential and eloquent support, yet the abolitionists—until 1981—never managed to attain their goal. While most other European nations abandoned capital punishment one by one, France not only retained it but continued —until 1939—to carry out executions in public. At certain moments the abolitionist cause seemed about to triumph, notably during the Great Revolution, in 1848, and during the first decade of the twentieth century. It eventually succeeded as a by-product of the sweeping Socialist victory at the polls in 1981—and then not because the winners were given a mandate to suppress the death penalty, but because the new president, François Mitterrand, had made up his mind to act in spite of majority opinion in the country. No real debate preceded or accompanied the decision in 1981. There was such debate in the 1906–8 episode—lengthy and impassioned debate. It provides us with a clearer view of the forces in France that have been aligned (in that era at least) for and against capital punishment.

The Enlightenment reformers who followed Beccaria in opposing the death sentence took their stand on utilitarian rather than humanitarian grounds. Like Beccaria, they wanted a substitute that would be an even more effective deterrent: not "the terrible but momentary spectacle of the death of a rascal, but the torment of a man deprived of liberty and transformed into a kind of beast of burden."[63] Men like Diderot and Brissot shared this opinion; indeed, Brissot talked of lifetime "slavery" at hard labor as a proper substitute.[64] The leading reformers of the Great Revolution sought to write Beccaria's formula into the Penal Code of 1791. Le Pelletier advocated a substitute for the death penalty that would inspire even greater "salutary terror" in wrongdoers—solitude, darkness, chains, privation. A majority, however, balked at outright abolition of capital punishment, although they did confine it to fewer offenses.

The crisis of 1793–94, brought on by foreign invasion, domestic subversion, and rising fanaticism, swept away all humanitarian restraints. Sheer hysteria marked the sessions of the National Convention in March 1793; a series of citizens' deputations appeared at the rostrum to demand the death penalty for a variety of suspected compatriots, and the Convention itself quickly caught the spirit. Bertrand Barère rose to propose the death penalty for those who advocated the division of property (la loi agraire), but the assembly interrupted him by rising to a man and shouting, "La peine de mort!" The hysteria spilled over into the next day's session, when peine de mort was extended by acclamation to a considerable list of offenses.[65] The blood bath that followed sobered the politicians for a time, and inspired one of the Convention's last acts in 1795: the death penalty was abolished in principle, with the proviso that the reform would take effect only with the return of peace.[66] Instead, the war with England dragged on, and in 1801 First Consul Bonaparte annulled the decree. Capital punishment was given a prominent place in Napoleon's Penal Code of 1810, which rested on the principle of social defense through intimidation. The Code made thirty-six crimes punishable by death, and the penalty was frequently imposed by the Empire and the restored Bourbon monarchy. Although pre-1826 statistics are unreliable, executions during the later years of the Empire have been estimated at an annual average of 264. In 1826–30 death sentences averaged 111 yearly, and actual executions, 72.[67]

The abolitionist movement took on substance after Napoleon's time, fed by the philanthropes' belief in the sanctity of human life and the idea of rehabilitation of wrongdoers. Charles Lucas in 1827 was one of the first advocates, and he persisted doggedly in his campaign until his death in the 1880s. François Guizot contributed a forceful pamphlet in 1828, though he favored abolition only for political offenses. After 1830 such eminent figures as Victor Hugo and Alphonse de Lamartine spoke and wrote eloquently for the cause, and King Louis-Philippe privately expressed his sympathy. But the abolitionists met stubborn opposition not only from conservative disciples of de Maistre and believers in retributive justice, but from many philanthropes as well. For them, capital punishment was needed as a deterrent and as the essential keystone in a logical hierarchy of penalties. The reformers had to be content, therefore, with a revision of the Penal Code (1832) that reduced the number of capital offenses to twenty-two and that allowed the courts to consider extenuating circumstances. Largely because of this softening of the Code, the annual average of death sentences fell to 51 and of executions, to 32.[68]

The revolutionaries of 1848 promptly abolished the death penalty for political offenses (an action that endured until 1939), but they failed to push further. The abolitionist campaign lost momentum during the Second Empire, but it revived during the 1860s and was vigorously pushed by the republican opposition. The defenders of capital punishment found their favorite text not in de Maistre's dictum about the executioner as linchpin of society but in the witticism of the popular journalist Alphonse Karr, which they never tired of quoting. Karr had written in 1840, "Let us abolish the death penalty, but let *Messieurs les assassins* begin."[69] The phrase, like most successful *bon mots*, soon became a tired cliché used as a substitute for rational argument, yet it continued to be trotted out each time abolition was proposed during the nineteenth century.

The abolitionists of the 1860s were also confronted by a new complication that hampered their effort during the rest of the century. The Penal Code called for public executions, on the theory that their deterrent effect would be lost unless ordinary citizens were allowed to observe the grim fate of evildoers. There was a certain logic in this position, but some Frenchmen from mid-century onward began to question its validity, arguing that executions often degenerated into bacchanalian orgies that brought out the beast in men and thus provoked rather than prevented new crimes. A number of reformers therefore diverted their efforts from capital punishment itself to the practice of public executions, which (they hoped) would be a first step toward complete abolition. But some defenders of the death penalty joined this more limited crusade with a view to preserving the penalty itself; and many dedicated abolitionists warned against this partial reform on the ground that it would relieve the pressure for change by removing the most gruesome aspect of capital punishment.[70] The argument erupted in the *Corps législatif* in 1870 when a republican deputy, François Steenackers, introduced a bill to end public executions. In the debate that followed, conservatives complained that the reform would leave no place for "salutary fear and the satisfaction of the public's need for vengeance." Deputies of the left argued, on the other hand, that the public would suspect a cover-up if executions were carried out in secrecy behind prison walls; and they quoted Gambetta on the need to keep the guillotine out in the open as the best way to turn people against capital punishment. The bill's sponsors pointed out that observers drawn by lot would be present at all executions to reassure the public that justice had been done. But the legislators over-whelmingly rejected the clause that provided for observers, even though they had voted favorably on the basic principle of ending public executions; and Steenackers therefore withdrew the bill from further consideration.[71] The fall of the Empire only six weeks later ended this round in the abolitionist campaign.

By now the idea of making executions private had caught on, and most reformers from 1870 to 1900 concentrated their energies on that goal. Efforts by the penal authorities to reduce the carnival aspect of executions failed one after the other. The guillotine in Paris was moved to a less accessible place; executions were sched-uled for the crack of dawn; access streets were blocked off. Nothing worked; crowds of raucous curiosity-seekers always managed to find their way to the scene.[72] The Senate in 1885 and again in 1898 adopted bills to move the guillotine within prison walls, but the Chamber of Deputies balked, rejecting the first bill by a narrow margin and refusing to take up the second.[73] The decisive margin against the reform was provided by the opponents of capital pun-ishment (mainly Radicals and Socialists); they continued to suspect that the Senate's purpose was to blunt their drive for real abolition.

From the turn of the century, however, the abolitionists' pros-pects suddenly brightened. By now the death penalty had been abandoned in a number of countries, with no consequent rise in homicides or other capital crimes. In France itself a change was oc-curring; while executions had averaged about thirty annually from 1871 to 1895, the number plummeted to an average of five in 1896–1900, and to only two in 1901–5.[74] The principal factors in this dramatic decline were the reduction of sentences on grounds of ex-tenuating circumstances and an increased use of presidential com-mutations. But in addition, the general crime rate had shown signs of decline at the turn of the century; changing mores, it seemed, were reducing violence and lessening social fear among honest folk.[75] The new mood was reflected in parliament where, during the Chamber's annual budget debate in 1906, a proposal to delete the usual appropriation for the public executioner's salary was vig-orously advocated and barely defeated.[76]

Encouraged by their near-victory in this symbolic action, the abolitionists now mounted a major assault. In 1906 several dozen deputies from all parties, headed by Gambetta's onetime lieutenant

Joseph Reinach, brought in a bill for outright abolition of the death penalty. There was no evidence, declared Reinach, that capital punishment had ever prevented a single crime; its deterrent effect was a myth. Besides, in a system of law "oriented toward reason and pity," why should society retain a penalty that sprang from anger and fear?[77] Several conservative deputies promptly brought in rival bills designed to reaffirm capital punishment; as one of them put it, there *are* incorrigible men, "beasts with human faces," who must be eliminated.[78] But the abolitionists now had momentum; late in 1906 the cabinet headed by Georges Clemenceau announced that it was taking over sponsorship of the Reinach bill, with some modifications.[79] Its success now seemed assured; and pending its adoption, the cabinet requested the president of the republic to commute all death sentences to life imprisonment. For the next two years, for the first time since 1792, the guillotine went into storage.

What followed, however, was a violent and emotional public reaction against the impending reform. In part, this outburst was undoubtedly a spontaneous expression of deep social fear, surviving even in a time of general security. But in part it was artificially whipped up by advocates of severe repression and by certain mass-circulation newspapers, which seized upon a few dramatic and bloody crimes as evidence that the lives and property of Frenchmen were gravely threatened.[80] The press played up the new phenomena of motorized gangs of malefactors and so-called "apaches" in Paris (allegedly copied from America), and thus encouraged the sense of panic. All through 1907, juries at the quarterly sessions of the assize courts deluged Paris with resolutions of protest against the projected reform.[81] The elected councils of departments and towns joined in this pressure campaign; so did the Radical party's regional congress in Lyon.[82] The *Petit Parisien*, read mainly by the petty bourgeoisie, conducted a "referendum" in which the vote was overwhelmingly (1,083,655 to 328,692) for retaining the death penalty.[83] Juries, which had recently inclined toward leniency in their verdicts, turned tough; the number of death sentences, which had been running at about fifteen yearly since 1900, rose to 30 in 1906 and to 40 in 1907.[84] Crime statistics, which had shown a slight decline from 1898 to 1902, turned upward again thereafter, feeding popular fears.[85] Some villages, mainly in the Paris basin, began to form vigilante groups, borrowing the English term "self-defense."[86] Members of the august *Société des Prisons* warned that the assassins and bandits were growing more audacious daily, and that when they were caught and convicted, they simply lolled about in comfortable prisons while awaiting an early and sure pardon.[87]

In the face of this wave of passion, the government and the abolitionists stubbornly pushed ahead. A Chamber committee, after much hesitation and by a narrow majority, endorsed the government's bill; but before the rapporteur could present his case to the Chamber, some committee members had second thoughts. Crime, they said, was rising; public opinion was aroused; more deliberation was needed. Convened once more, the committee reversed its stance, voted to retain the death penalty, and chose a new rapporteur.[88] Minister of Justice Aristide Briand, whose talent for compromise was legendary, tried for a middle way that might satisfy the committee: why not devise a substitute for capital punishment that would be a more awesome deterrent than the one currently on the books (transportation for life)? He suggested lifetime solitary confinement with no possibility of release. The committee expressed polite interest in adding such a penalty to the Penal Code, but only if capital punishment were retained as well.[89]

A long and emotional debate followed in the Chamber, lasting from July to December 1908 (with a long break between sessions). Many of parliament's luminaries took part: Maurice Barrès and Louis Puech for the opposition, Reinach, Jean Jaurès, and Emile Deschanel for the government. As minister of justice, Briand put up a vigorous fight for the bill, denying the reality of the alleged crime wave and offering figures to show that capital crimes had been in steady decline for a generation. Homicides, he conceded, had been rising for a decade, but most of these were not of the sort that normally drew the death penalty. The bandit gangs that had won such notoriety, he pointed out, had committed their depredations while capital punishment was still being imposed, and not in response to its de facto suspension. Briand added statistics to show that countries which had abolished the death penalty had experienced no subsequent rise in crime. France's lawmakers, he pleaded, should not blindly follow public opinion, which was sometimes misled; they should provide courageous leadership.[90] The Socialist leader Jaurès drew on his oratorical skills to appeal to the humanitarian instincts of his colleagues; they were urged to seek guidance in the twin traditions of Christianity and the Great Revolution. All men, he cried, share responsibility for crime so long as their societies have not found ways to dry up crime's sources. Other Socialists, Allemane and Dejeante, spoke out more bluntly, accusing the defenders of capital punishment of succumbing to scare tactics inspired by the capitalists. Maurice Barrès, responding for the law-and-order forces, charged that the reformers were suffering from "a temporary malady of the intelligence, in the form of non-resistance to evil," and warned that the "apaches" were not "handsome barbarians challenging common morality" but were simply degenerates with no claim to sympathy. Daniel de Folleville argued that the "steadily rising tide of crime" was traceable to softened prison conditions, and begged his colleagues to "think a little less about the criminals and a little more about honest folk." Other speakers sought to refute Briand's statistics with their own, and resorted to the standard phrases about a society's right to defend itself.

When the marathon debate ended on December 9, 1908, and the votes were counted, the reformers were resoundingly beaten, 334 to 210. The *Gazette des Tribunaux*, which had originally backed the bill but had later switched, concluded that the main grave-diggers of the reform had been "those who would have profited by it"—namely, the criminals themselves. "The murderers and assassins, having responded with increased audacity and ferocity, contributed most effectively to the failure of the reform; once again, they obstinately refused to begin."[91] So ended the most sustained effort to rid France of the death penalty, with the standard ritual reference to Alphonse Karr's "let *Messieurs les assassins* begin."

Two months later, the first executions in three years were carried out; the guillotine fell on four convicted members of the "Pollot gang," a band of thirty men and women who had terrorized northeastern France during 1905–6. The execution drew thousands of spectators from all parts of France and even from Germany; army units had to be called out to maintain order, but "savage demonstrations" were reported nevertheless, and photographers abounded at the scene.[92] A kind of normalcy set in thereafter, though juries continued to recommend the death penalty more often than they had done before 1906.[93] In 1912 the press reported an execution at Riom that was strongly reminiscent of earlier centuries: ten thou-

PUBLIC EXECUTION EARLY 20TH-CENTURY STYLE. Efforts by the authorities in Paris to reduce the carnival aspect of executions and to keep the crowd at a distance from the guillotine were not very successful. (Roger-Viollet)

sand people flocked to town from the entire region, camping overnight in tents in the public square, renting window space in hotels overlooking the guillotine, conducting themselves during the grisly rite in the manner of Romans viewing the confrontations of Christians and lions.[94] Such excesses briefly revived interest in the banning of public executions, but still another bill to that effect died in committee in 1913. The Great War found the problem still unsolved, and the rival factions unreconciled. Another half-century would pass before the issue of capital punishment would once more emerge to seize the attention and rekindle the emotions of the French public.

# VIII

## Ebb Tide

## 1918–1940

> In France there has never been any durable interest in penal problems. Indifference toward such matters is an affair of national temperament. . . . I doubt that our national pride will ever seek satisfaction in the progress of our penitentiaries.
>
> PAUL CUCHE (1922 and 1936)

SHAKESPEARE REMINDS us that there are tides in the affairs of men. He might have added that floodtide inexorably gives way to slack, and slack to ebb. "Inexorable" is doubtless too strong a word to explain the shriveling of interest in criminological questions in interwar France. But whatever the reasons for the change in mood, the period appears in retrospect as a time of stagnation and drift. Contemporaries were aware of it too, and specialists like Paul Cuche complained of public indifference. Yet the specialists themselves showed signs of intellectual stagnancy, and should probably share responsibility with the public. No new crop of criminologists and penologists emerged to challenge the orthodoxy of their elders by advancing innovative theories about the causes and control of crime and the manner of handling criminals. In parliament, the politicians toyed intermittently with some of the old issues that had aroused such fervor among their predecessors, but the emotional commitment was gone; most reform proposals got perfunctory discussion and were buried in committee. Only three achievements of any importance interrupted the drift: in 1926 half of the dilapidated local prisons were closed, in 1927 the time-honored system of contracting out prison labor to private entrepreneurs was abandoned, and in 1938 the *bagne* in Guiana was finally liquidated.

Ever since 1789, the aftermath of France's wars and revolutions had brought bursts of reform talk, and even some action, in the realm of crime control. The war of 1914–18 proved to be the great exception. The strain of the long conflict left the nation with enormous problems of reconstruction and readjustment that took priority over the crime problem. And the war brought no political upheaval of the sort that had in the past brought to power new elites with new ideas. But something more seems to have been involved as well. The French neo-classical school of criminologists, penologists, and jurists had been, in a sense, too successful. In developing an eclectic doctrine that absorbed certain aspects of positivist theory, it had achieved a broad consensus in France as well as a position of leadership in Europe. That consensus was too firmly based to allow room for serious challenge within France; the French rested on their laurels and abdicated leadership to other nations, notably the United States, where new ideas emerged and new research strategies were tested. The luminaries of the prewar era— Gabriel Tarde, Raymond Saleilles, Henri Joly, Emile Garçon—had disappeared from the scene or were about to do so; but their successors clung doggedly to the tradition. Paul Cuche, dean of the Grenoble law faculty and the most articulate spokesman for orthodoxy, even retreated somewhat from the principles embodied in Saleilles's classic statement. Cuche cautioned his colleagues in the *Société des Prisons* against investing much hope in the goal of rehabilitation; the central purpose of the criminal justice system, he insisted, must be retribution and deterrence. Individualizing punishment was all very well, but it had now gone too far. "Let us keep the intimidating effect of prison and the economic yield of prison labor, and frankly admit that we can't do more for a long time to come."[1] Another leading expert from the Strasbourg law faculty, J.-A. Roux, likewise argued for retaining the neo-classical ideas of individual moral responsibility and intimidation, if only because public sentiment needed to be satisfied. The neo-classical school, he contended, had already absorbed the "useful parts" of positivist doctrine—namely, the need to protect society against habitual offenders. But the positivists, he complained, proposed to punish criminals for what they were, not for what they had done.

Such positivist devices as indeterminate sentences opened the way, said Roux, to "the arbitrary punishments of ancient law and to the restoration of the Bastille and the Inquisition."[2]

Challenges to this rigorous orthodoxy were rarely voiced during the interwar years. In the venerable *Société des Prisons*, which for a half-century had been one of the most important centers for debate about crime and penal policy, there seemed to be little left to argue about. Indeed, the *Société* itself showed signs of withering; it continued to meet and hear reports, but its sessions lacked the old verve. Its officers complained that members were reluctant to present reports or even to appear at meetings. The *Société's* bimonthly *Revue Pénitentiaire* degenerated into a dull gray compilation of factual data about penal developments around the world and summaries of the sessions at international penal congresses. The depression finally swept it away; in 1933 it ceased publication, its demise almost unnoticed. Even the official *Compte général de la justice criminelle*, which had appeared regularly from 1826 to 1913 and was the pride of French criminologists, fell on evil times; the annual volumes for 1920 to 1925 did not appear until 1926, and then only as a pale shadow of former times—a few pages tucked away in the *Journal Officiel*. There were, however, some faint signs of intellectual renewal. In 1925 a group of students and ex-students of the Institute of Criminology in Paris founded an ephemeral periodical called *Etudes Criminologiques*, with the sponsorship of two eminent jurists at the law faculty—Emile Hugueney and Henri Donnedieu de Vabres. The depression forced it to merge with the *Revue Pénitentiaire* in 1930 and to disappear along with the latter three years later; but some of its editors, again sponsored by Donnedieu de Vabres, tried again in 1936 with better luck. Their quarterly *Revue de Science Criminelle*, with the young magistrate Marc Ancel as editor, asserted in its inaugural number that criminological theory in France had been dead on its feet since the end of the nineteenth century, and declared its intention to correct this failing. It would be dishonorable, declared the editors, to let other nations seize and monopolize the true French tradition that had refused to separate penal law and morality.[3] The new *Revue* was to endure and to become, in the second postwar era, the leading French organ in the so-called "criminal sciences."[4]

Specialists in the study of crime and the administration of prisons complained frequently about the indifference of both the general public and the political elite to the knotty problems of penal justice. For most people, they grumbled, criminology was equated with lurid press accounts of the bloodiest crimes. Paul Cuche saw this as nothing new: "In France there has never been any durable interest in penal problems."[5] Such reluctance to think seriously and consistently about the crime problem has of course not been confined to the French; most citizens everywhere have preferred to ignore it except during brief interludes of concern or panic. Yet France throughout the nineteenth century had never been without a sizable and active minority of concerned citizens in search of solutions, and at times the phenomenon of crime and its control had been the liveliest and most debated of all social issues. The public's relative indifference in the interwar years, like the watchdog's silence in the Sherlock Holmes tale, calls for some attempt at explanation.

The simplest answer, and probably the best, is that the crime rate seemed to have leveled off and had even begun to decline. True, this did not happen at once; for a brief period after the war (1920–21) all types of crime rose sharply, and the courts responded with more severe penalties. This phenomenon reflected a common wartime pattern, the so-called V-curve: crime normally rose just before the outbreak of war, then fell sharply during the war years, and rose to an even higher level during the postwar period of demobilization and readjustment.[6] This postwar increase did cause some popular concern. "The public, which doesn't always reason accurately but always understands its own feelings, has become troubled," wrote J.-A. Roux in 1922. "It has no idea whether the theory of determinism is well-founded, or whether the old doctrine of free will is still preferable. It probably hasn't read the works of Lombroso. . . . It cares little whether delinquents are abnormal or are like everybody else. What it wants is protection of person, life, and possessions. . . . Well, it now feels—and the newspapers continue to demonstrate this fact—that it is not protected."[7] But the statistics were already beginning to contradict Roux's observation. Beginning in 1922 the crime rate (especially the level of violent crime) declined sharply, reaching in 1925 the lowest figure in the Third Republic's history; and while there was some fluctuation thereafter, the statistics gave no cause for serious concern.[8] There were encouraging signs too that juvenile delinquency was on the wane, and the prison population stabilized at about 24,000. Some politicians might still point with alarm to what they called "the grave problem of criminality" and "the moral crisis, fatal consequence of the war"; as Senator Henri Roy put it, "the statistics may not show it, but just look around."[9] Most Frenchmen who looked around, however, were more reassured than frightened by what they saw.

Given these trends, there was little pressure on the politicians, and no great urge among penal administrators, to carry out reforms or to inaugurate costly experiments. Prisons continued to serve mainly for warehousing offenders; efforts at rehabilitation took a strictly secondary place. Although early release for good behavior had been legalized in 1885, the necessary decree regulating its use had never been issued, so the practice received only limited use. No machinery for supervised probation was created, nor would it be until 1958— far later than in most Western countries.[10] Suspended sentences for first offenders, legalized in 1891, were by now in common use and did help in lowering the prison population and, probably, the rate of recidivism.

Many of the old issues that had provoked such controversy in the nineteenth century did flicker briefly into life during the interwar years, though little action followed. One such issue was the hoary argument over cellular imprisonment, which produced one last flurry of debate in the *Société des Prisons* in 1922. Ever since 1875, the advocates of solitary confinement had been complaining that the law of that year requiring the cellular principle in short-term prisons was not being implemented. They were right; most of the departments had evaded the conversion of their prisons on grounds of inadequate funds. The pro-cell faction had long pointed to the Belgian example as the model that proved their case; the Belgians had early adopted cellular imprisonment even for long-term convicts, and French visitors returned to sing its praises as beneficial to both society and the prisoners themselves.[11] But after the Great War, the Belgians began to question the virtues of their system, and Minister of Justice Emile Vandervelde in 1921 ordered a partial return to the common-prison model.[12]

Shaken by this unexpected heresy, French advocates of the cell reasserted their case before the *Société des Prisons*. A pro-cell report by Paul Cuche, followed by an emotional debate, revealed the shock and puzzlement of most of the *Société*'s members at the Belgians' challenge to their cherished beliefs.[13] Cuche and others blamed the Belgian reversal on certain intellectuals who had been jailed during the German occupation and had found isolation unbearable. But he and most of his colleagues held the real culprits to be the Socialists, who had allegedly embarked on a campaign against the prison itself as a bourgeois institution based on outmoded ideas of punishment and expiation. The Socialists, according to Cuche and several other participants in the *Société*'s debate, hoped that common prisons would give them a chance to spread their doctrines among the convicts. Vandervelde was a Socialist; so was the Italian criminologist Enrico Ferri, who had once called solitary confinement "the great aberration of the nineteenth century." The *Société*'s debate produced considerable passion but no practical results; it proved to be the last occasion for the cellular forces to reassert their ancient faith.

A few years later, however, something was done at last about the short-term prisons; but the stimulus was financial, not doctrinal. For many decades they had been attacked as disgraceful survivals of an unenlightened past; Paul Cuche, with some hyperbole, described them as "centuries behind the times."[14] Parliament in 1893 had authorized the departments to transfer ownership and operation to the central government, but only on condition that the department provide an annual operating subsidy. Most of the departments therefore demurred; only two prisons were transferred, and most of the others steadily deteriorated.[15] Budget rapporteurs had been recommending for forty years that the smaller prisons be closed, and their inmates grouped in one or more prisons in each department. A survey showed that half of these jails averaged fewer than ten inmates at a time; some "phantom prisons" stood empty for several months each year, and in one a single inmate was found, guarded by four jailers.[16] Cellular prisons were still the exception, so the old cry of corruption of young offenders by hardened criminals continued to be raised. In many of the departmental prisons there were no work facilities, so inmates idled away their time in a courtyard or common room. Experts estimated that closing about two hundred of the 374 short-term prisons would save money and put an end to many flagrant abuses.[17]

In 1926 a severe financial crisis brought Raymond Poincaré back into the premiership, and he was given special decree-law powers to slash governmental expenditures. As part of that pruning operation, the departments were authorized to close their smaller prisons. By 1929, the number had been reduced by more than half (from 374 to 175); many of the most dilapidated buildings were abandoned or torn down.[18] Then, by a curious parliamentary accident, this reform was partially undone. An obscure deputy attached a rider to a pending bill, ordering that the prisons closed since 1926 be reopened. The rider slipped through unnoticed, producing a period of confusion; some sixty jails were reopened before parliament in 1933 got round to reversing its 1929 action.[19] In this awkward fashion, the government faced up at last to an old and pressing need. The departmental prisons had been the most vulnerable sector of France's penal system; their condition had been a source of chronic embarrassment to French advocates of humane confinement and rehabilitation. Many problems remained, but one of the worst had been partially corrected.

Meanwhile a second reform had been adopted with much less fanfare, in this case by administrative fiat rather than parliamentary action. In 1927 the Penal Administration put an end to the century-old system of contracting with private entrepreneurs for the use of prison labor, and ordered direct state administration of prison workshops (la régie). This change had long been advocated by certain prison reformers, by left-wing politicians, and by budget-cutters. They had argued that if the use of prison labor produced profits, the benefits should go to the taxpayers rather than to private businessmen. They had offered figures to show that in the few prisons where la régie existed, operating costs per inmate were considerably lower than in private-enterprise institutions.[20] Left-wing critics contended that entrepreneurs were indifferent to the rehabilitative values of work and job training—indeed, to everything except private gain. The state in 1895 had abandoned the entrepreneurial system for the supplying of prisons; since then, it had been used only for the organization of work.

The reform of 1927 was a response to collusion on the part of the entrepreneurs. Most contracts were due for renewal in 1926, and the entrepreneurs formed a kind of cartel to enter a single bid in each prison and to double the state's contribution per inmate to the contractors. The Penal Administration compromised by shortening contracts to one year and switching to *la régie* in a few prisons; by 1927 it found its costs reduced by half in the *régie* prisons.[21] Complete conversion followed, but only in the *maisons centrales*, the only prisons where work could be effectively organized. In the short-term prisons, it was generally believed that the only alternative to total idleness was the continued use of private entrepreneurs.[22] And even in the *maisons centrales*, the reform changed things less than one might suppose. Entrepreneurs in recent decades had generally used subcontractors to set up and operate prison workshops; now the prison directors adopted the same practice, simply substituting themselves for the private entrepreneurs and retaining the subcontractors to organize the work.[23]

The impact of the great depression brought some new complications. Work opportunities were reduced in both short-term prisons and *maisons centrales*, and for a time the administration had to reduce prisoners' wages by 20 per cent in order to keep workshops operating.[24] There was also a brief resurgence of the old complaints about unfair competition with free business and labor. But this sort of protest was much milder than it had once been. In part, that was because the product of prison workshops was being used increasingly by the prisons themselves and by other state agencies (including, from 1928 onward, the army and navy).[25] But it also reflected a more widespread acceptance, especially on the part of the labor unions and the Socialists, of the idea that society owed the prisoner the right to work, for his own satisfaction and for its supposed rehabilitative value. Henceforth, the critics of prison labor aimed their complaints in a new direction: they would no longer talk of unfair competition with free workers but rather of unemployment in the prisons and of prisoners' rights to wages and working conditions comparable to those outside.

Still another problem of ancient vintage found its way briefly onto the parliamentary agenda, but was quickly buried. In 1910 a bill designed to "reorganize the fight against vagrancy and begging" had been introduced into the Senate, and parts of the bill were adopted by that body after a judicious delay—in 1921. Article 1 declared that "vagrancy and begging are prohibited on French territory" and proposed severe punishment for professional beggars, but government aid to the infirm and jobless, who would be sent to shelters or to newly created *"établissements d'assistance par le travail."* The Chamber of Deputies also moved deliberately; it finally got round to preliminary action in 1929, when a committee reported out favorably. There matters rested.[26] It was clear that the old obsession with the "plague" of vagrancy no longer possessed French minds.


The emphasis in this chapter has been on the negative—on the stagnancy of the interwar years in both theory and action. Yet some things did change toward the end of that period. Two changes in particular were provoked by press campaigns that grew out of the activity of men whom we would now call investigative journalists: the decision to liquidate the *bagne* in Guiana, and the closure or reform of certain juvenile institutions (Mettray at their head) which had allegedly degenerated from their origins as places of regeneration into something more like *bagnes d'enfants.*

The campaign against Mettray began in 1930 with a sharp attack in the Paris daily *L'Intransigeant.*[27] Visits to the farm colony were forbidden, the journal alleged, in order to conceal its real character as a *"bagne privé"*; it survived because so many important people served on its board. An administrative investigation followed; it reported that the institution had gradually deteriorated since the death of the founder Frédéric Demetz, and that the guards were old, brutal, and often drunk. Mettray had managed to survive a campaign of criticism before 1914, but things had obviously not improved. A crusading journalist named Alexis Danan picked up the issue and embarked during the 1930s on a one-man campaign to expose abuses not only at Mettray but at other juvenile institutions. The death of an inmate at Eysses reformatory in 1937 furthered his cause; other reporters joined the action. Although some of their methods were not always above reproach, they finally achieved results; Léon Blum's minister of public health was persuaded to investigate and to stop sending juvenile offenders to Mettray. The resulting lack of funds forced that institution to close in 1939—a sad end to the dream of one of France's most eminent penal reformers of the nineteenth century. Some reforms were imposed on other juvenile institutions as well.

Much more fundamental was the fate of the *bagne* in Guiana

—the only issue that aroused broad public interest during the inter-war years. Only Portugal and France still had penal colonies in the distant tropics (though the Soviet Union practiced a kind of penal transportation within its own borders). Shipments of convicts to New Caledonia had ended in 1897, since which time the penal pop-ulation there had been steadily shrinking through deaths and occa-sional escapes. On the eve of the Great War there were still about a thousand long-term convicts serving sentences on the island, plus two thousand *libérés* and a thousand *rélégués*. Many of the *libérés*, unable to fend for themselves, returned voluntarily to the detention camp near Noumea as the only safe haven they could find. In 1929–30 the Penal Administration finally withdrew the last of its personnel from New Caledonia and turned over custody of the re-maining prisoners to the local police. Actuarial studies estimated that by 1938 death would carry off the last of the transportees, thus ending an experiment that had lasted three-quarters of a century.[28] In fact, an American journalist who visited New Caledonia in 1942 after American troops landed there was to find a few human scare-crows still tottering about the old penitentiary buildings—the last survivors of the ancient *bagne*.[29]

In Guiana, on the other hand, the *bagne* was still very much alive after the Great War. The penal population there had grown after 1897 to more than eight thousand (4500 hard-labor convicts, 1500 *libérés*, and 2500 *rélégués* confined in a separate camp). The harsh prison rules imposed in 1891 were still in effect. Prisoners re-ceived no wages, but could earn food coupons with which to supple-ment the bread and water diet. Minor rule violations were severely punished; more serious offenses drew cellular confinement or the so-called double chain. Attempts to escape (there were hundreds each year, few of them successful) belonged in the serious category. Most long-term convicts were confined in the camp at Saint-Laurent-du-Maroni, but there were several outlying work camps and three small offshore islands (the Iles du Salut) reserved for special pur-poses. The Ile Saint-Joseph housed mental and disciplinary cases; the Ile Royale was used for new arrivals classed as dangerous; the Ile du Diable was reserved for political deportees. Prisoners were classed in five categories, and in theory they could advance through good conduct; but after 1891 such progression became much more difficult.[30] Counterbalancing the rigorously repressive regime of the

CONVICTS' HOUSING AT THE BAGNE IN GUIANA. Prisoners were locked into these buildings at night and left to their own devices. (Roger-Viollet)

*bagne* was the reality of existence in the camp dormitories. Locked in at night, the convicts were left to their own devices until morning. The strongest and most ruthless dominated; clan rivalries and lovers' quarrels led to frequent fights and silent knifings. Homosexuality, willing or unwilling, was common. A doctor who served at the *bagne* during the 1930s undertook a survey which revealed that only 15 per cent had arrived in Guiana as sexual deviants.[31] The guards, by and large, were a hardened lot, too often inclined to brutality and open to corruption. Who else would choose to assume such service?

Such were the conditions in the Guiana *bagne*—at least as they were described by those ex-prisoners who lived to recount the experience, by a few ex-officials who broke silence, and by an occasional journalist who managed to gain access to the camps. Before 1914 such descriptions had more often taken the line that the *bagne* was a place for rest and recreation, an Eldorado where convicts lazed about and occasionally pretended to work. A quite different note was sounded after the Great War, when the investigative reporter Albert Londres managed to get into the *bagne* and to talk with prisoners as well as officials. Londres made a considerable reputation as a crusader for the underdog and something of a muckraker, and he had a knack for attracting public attention.[32] In 1923 his book, *Au bagne,* and his subsequent articles in the mass-circulation *Petit Parisien,* shocked Frenchmen into an awareness of the seamy side of their penal colony and stirred up hostile criticism abroad. During the budget debate of 1924 in the Chamber, several deputies of both left and right denounced the evils of transportation; the minister of justice named a commission of experts to study the problem, and promised to suspend further shipments of convicts for a year.[33] But the Herriot cabinet fell in 1925, and its successor confined itself to some minor reforms, designed mainly to soften the disciplinary rules of 1891.[34] The government also made a humanitarian gesture; in 1928 it sent an officer of the Salvation Army, Charles Péan, to study conditions on the spot and to propose reforms. Péan's damning report, and his book *Terre de bagne* that followed, sharpened the controversy that had been building. Deputy Maurice Sibille introduced bills to allow judges to substitute imprisonment in France for transportation, and to end the practice of *doublage* that required *libérés* to stay in Guiana, but neither bill won parliamentary approval.[35]

The basic issue, nevertheless, was now out in the open. Was the *bagne* a monstrous aberration, beyond hope of reform? New exposés by ex-*bagnards* and journalists began to pour from the presses in quantity, reinforcing the rising revulsion.[36] Latin American and North American writers joined the campaign, casting aspersions on France's claim to be considered a humane and progressive nation. One semi-fictionalized account of life in the *bagne,* based on interviews with an ex-convict named René Belbenoit, attained bestseller status in the United States, and brought Samuel Goldwyn down from Hollywood to interview Belbenoit and to produce the film *Green Hell* based on his story.[37] Charles Péan embarked in

1933 on a second mission, this time to work with the *libérés* in Guiana; he returned shortly to report in a new book that the *bagne* was a hopeless failure on every count, and could not be reformed. "Never," he wrote, "has the *bagne* rehabilitated a single man. . . . [Its inmates] emerge brutalized, disoriented, desocialized, rootless and devoid of purpose."[38]

There were still defenders of transportation, however, and they fought back more passionately as the threat to their cherished institution increased. The exposés of Londres and the rest were distorted versions of reality, they claimed. Guiana was neither a green hell nor a dry guillotine; Europeans could easily adapt to the climate and could engage in productive work there. If abuses existed, they were the product of the 1925 reforms that had relaxed discipline and permitted a growing anarchy. It was unfair to judge the *bagne* for failure to do much to develop the colony; the fault should be charged to the penal authorities, who had failed to develop a coherent long-term plan and had never understood how to use convict labor effectively. Suppression of the *bagne*, they asserted, would be "a disaster for our colony," for only convict workers could provide the infrastructure of roads and public works.[39] Besides, no one had yet suggested a workable substitute; the cost of building enough prisons in France would be exorbitant, and locking up long-term prisoners in cells would be inhumane. Some pro-*bagne* spokesmen were even more blunt: they swept aside the argument that convicts could help to develop the colony, and the theory that the *bagne* was a place for expiation and rehabilitation. In fact, they said, social defense was the plain and simple issue; certain delinquents were incorrigible and dangerous, and the goal must be "permanent elimination so that honest folk can live in peace."[40] A more moderate set of advocates, aware that the noxious odors arising from Guiana might destroy the principle of transportation itself, began to talk of reopening New Caledonia to convicts or seeking out some thinly populated territory more congenial to Europeans.[41] They also voiced rising resentment at the barrage of foreign criticism, especially Anglo-Saxon, which they claimed was inspired by concealed and despicable motives.[42]

The deadlock lasted until the victory of the Popular Front in 1936. Premier Léon Blum and his ministers were committed to suppression of the *bagne*, and named a special commission which drafted a bill to that effect. It was reported out favorably in 1937, with the deputy from Guiana, Gaston Monnerville, serving as the committee's rapporteur. His brief report endorsed most of the critics' charges, described the *bagne* as a "resounding failure," declared that its existence was damaging to France's international reputation, and rejected any idea of trying to reform the *bagne* ("You can't cure a case of gangrene!" he declared).[43] Once again, however, the process was stalled, this time by the fall of the Blum cabinet. In 1938, therefore, the Daladier cabinet resorted to special decree-law powers to institute the essence of the reform. The decree-law provided that hard-labor convicts would henceforth serve their sentences in a continental French prison, with at least three years of the term to be spent in solitary confinement.[44] It made no provision for the return of convicts and *libérés* currently in Guiana, nor did it suspend the law of 1885 on the transportation of *rélégués*. This latter oversight was corrected four years later by the Vichy regime; in fact, no major criminals or *rélégués* were transported after 1937. The final step—liquidating the *bagnes* by repatriating the last prisoners—was accomplished by the Fourth Republic in 1946.[45]

Thus ended an institution that had endured for almost a full century, and that had seen more than a hundred thousand Frenchmen and several hundred Frenchwomen sent into penal exile and servitude in distant tropical lands. For most Frenchmen, it was not a proud chapter in the history of their search for humane but effective methods of crime control. Yet the idea of penal transportation continued to have its nostalgic defenders. In 1949 Maurice Garçon, one of France's most eminent criminal lawyers, urged its revival, and a generation later, in 1979, a deputy proposed to the Chamber that offenders be shipped to the icebound Kerguelen Islands—that frozen magnet that had attracted hard-liners for a century.[46] Only a few Frenchmen looked back in an attempt at objective judgment of the record: should transportation as operated by the French be viewed as a reasonable experiment or a tragic mistake? One of the exceptions was the eminent criminologist Jean Pinatel; writing in 1950, he arrived at a nuanced but mainly negative conclusion. The *bagne* could be considered successful, he decided, for its contribution to public security and order in France; after all, many potential recidivists were permanently eliminated. Its contribution to the economic development of Guiana he judged dubious at best, though he recognized that some observers differed on this point. As for what he called the "scientific" (i.e., criminological) and human aspects, it was clearly a failure, if one believes that even the worst offenders deserve humane treatment and a chance, however faint, of rehabilitation. And when it came to France's image in the world, Pinatel concluded, there could be no dispute; the balance-sheet was totally negative.[47] No fairer epitaph could be written to the allegedly ideal solution imposed on France by Napoleon III and his advisers.

Ancient institutions sometimes die hard. In 1982 it was reported that the defunct *bagne* in Guiana was about to be resurrected in a new form: an imaginative entrepreneur is said to have refurbished some of the penitentiary buildings to serve as museum and place of entertainment, in the hope of attracting package tours of French tourists.[48] The dictum of Karl Marx seems vindicated: events in history often recur twice, once as tragedy and then as farce.

# IX

## Old Issues, New Ventures
### 1944–1982

> The cause of prison reform is a thankless one, and it remains unpopular. . . . For the general public, prison is a sort of dump-ground, located, like garbage disposal areas, on the outer fringes of cities where society gets rid of its refuse.
>
> EMMANUEL MOUNIER (1945)

> Today's polemics about the penitentiary regime are echoes of talk and projects that are very old indeed. It is no slight surprise to rediscover, still unresolved, problems that so deeply moved Tocqueville, Victor Hugo, Charles Lucas, and that mobilized their reflections and their efforts.
>
> PIERRE DEYON (1975)

LOST WARS, like successful revolutions, are often effective motors for social change. The overwhelming defeat of 1940 and the four years of German occupation that followed left Frenchmen with a smarting sense of humiliation and an urge to transform their political and social institutions. "From resistance to revolution!" was the masthead slogan carried by the Paris newspaper *Combat* after the liberation in 1944. This reformist impulse had its effect on penal policy. The stagnation and drift of the interwar years ended abruptly; French politicians, criminologists, and penal officials all shared in the general desire to build a new and purer republic, responsive to the needs of all its citizens and dedicated to generous and humane goals. For a full generation after the war ended, these reformers were able to pursue their effort to "humanize" French penal policy and to transform its most conspicuous institution, the prison.

Law-and-order critics protested against the trend and at times slowed the process, but the advocates of reform kept the initiative. Then suddenly, in the mid-1970s, the momentum was lost. A wave of destructive riots swept through France's prisons; a surge of social fear altered the public mood; the reformers themselves showed signs of self-doubt as the crime rate rose and the prison population mushroomed. Hard-liners exulted, and seemed once again in control of the crime-control system. Then, even more suddenly, came a still more dramatic reversal: the Socialists' unexpected capture of both the presidency and the parliament in 1981 gave a new impulse to the idea of criminal justice reform, and put a new set of reformers in charge of the process. The story of these advances and retreats constitutes one of the most intriguing chapters in the record of France's long effort to grapple with the crime problem.

The dominant mood in the liberation era was one of enthusiasm and hope. Many of the resistance leaders who now emerged into positions of influence had tasted the bitter reality of prison or detention camp; many more had seen relatives or friends jailed and sometimes tortured. Like the post-1814 reformers, they had a personal interest in prison reform. But their motives were not merely personal; they were also concerned to reassert the principle of due process as against arbitrary action by the state. They felt a deep revulsion against the barbarities of the Nazi conqueror and against the Vichy regime's perversions of justice, such as persecution on "racial" grounds and the use of special courts free of legal restraints.[1] The Vichy government, in a symbolic move to emphasize law and order, had transferred the Penal Administration from the ministry of justice to the ministry of interior, which controlled the police. The restored republic, again symbolically, moved at once to switch it back.[2] Vichy's repressive line was to be replaced by guarantees of civil rights for every citizen, including those persons charged with criminal offenses.

It is true that this high-minded resolve was corroded during the early weeks after the liberation by a wave of spontaneous retaliation against Vichyites and pro-German collaborators; as many as ten thousand may have been liquidated by vigilante-style rough justice.[3] But Charles de Gaulle's new government quickly checked this lawlessness by setting up special courts and imposing such new penalties as "national unworthiness," which suspended the civil rights of those found guilty. For more than a year, the prisons bulged with accused collaborators awaiting judgment—almost 20,000 of them in 1945. The prison system was even more heavily overloaded by a sharp rise in the crime rate during the initial postwar years (following the usual V-curve phenomenon that marks modern wars). The prison population during 1944–47 broke all French records, rising to almost 65,000; the penal authorities coped with the flood only by utilizing many wartime detention camps, and continuing Vichy's experiment in the use of prison labor gangs outside prison walls. This practice was to have some lasting results; the Penal Administration's traditional reluctance to the extramural employment of prisoners was partially broken down, and "open establishments" were to become a permanent though minor aspect of the penitentiary system.[4] Overcrowding also knocked another prop from under the cell system, for there were simply not enough cells to go around, even for prisoners who by law were required to be held in isolation.

In spite of the confusion and crowding of the early postwar era, France's penal authorities moved at once toward fundamental reform. A task force within the ministry of justice was assigned the problem of juvenile delinquency, which had grown to a dismaying level during the occupation years. The report of this group led to an ordinance (February 2, 1945) that drastically altered the structure and spirit of existing law on juvenile offenders. It created special juvenile courts and judges, ordered the reorganization and more rigorous supervision of reform schools and colonies, and substituted (save in rare cases) the concept of treatment for that of punishment for offenders below the age of eighteen.[5]

A much more sweeping action was the appointment of a blue-ribbon commission to study and recommend changes in the prison system. It was chaired by Paul Amor, Director of Penal Administration, and it included the noted criminologist and prison inspector Jean Pinatel along with a leading lawyer, a magistrate, professors of criminal law and medicine, and officials of prisoners' aid societies. The commission brought in its report in May 1945.[6] "The essential purpose of imprisonment," the report declared, "is the rehabilitation and reintegration into society of the prisoner." Such treatment should be carried out in prisons in continental France (thus ruling out a return to the overseas *bagnes*). Prison conditions must be humane and "free of any corrupting promiscuity"; cellular isolation should be the rule for persons awaiting trial and for short-term convicts. Long-term prisons should employ the progressive system and should be specially adapted to different categories of prisoners. Social and medico-psychological services should be provided in all prisons, and all prison personnel should be given special training. Early release on parole should be more extensively used. A new corps of magistrates should be assigned the task of supervising the appropriate treatment for each prisoner. Heretofore, the magistrates' task had ended with the pronouncing of sentence, leaving the penal officials in full charge of punishment. The Amor commission's report thus represented a blend of traditional views, drawn from the leading nineteenth-century reformers of the penitentiary school, and more recent criminological theories that called for individualized treatment of offenders by trained technical experts.

Reports by blue-ribbon commissions have a way of vanishing quietly into some obscure file-drawer. The Amor commission's report was an exception. Although its recommendations were not written into the Code of Criminal Procedure until 1958, they were put into effect at once in gradual and empirical fashion. Many penal officials were dubious about the Amor proposals, but the reformers were in control of the central administration and could press effectively for change. A training school for prison personnel was established; social workers, doctors, and psychologists were appointed; a start was made toward specialized prisons, to which prisoners were assigned after detailed analysis of their individual needs; a small cadre of magistrates was named to supervise the treatment-punishment process and to rule on transfers and early release.[7] Within the prisons, disciplinary rules were relaxed. The rule of silence, imposed in the *maisons centrales* by the Gasparin circular of 1839, was softened; films and radios made their appearance in most large prisons, and choruses, theatrical groups, and sports teams were authorized in some places.[8] The last *bagnards* from Guiana were repatriated in 1946, over the protests of a few diehard advocates of transportation.[9]

The process of empirical reform was helped along after 1946 by an encouraging decline in the crime rate and the prison population. By 1953 general delinquency was down by almost one-third, and by 1956 the number of prison inmates had fallen from 65,000 to 20,000.[10] This trend blunted the warnings of hard-liners and certain neo-classical jurists who had talked ominously of the dangers of "devaluating punishment." "When penalties lose their power to intimidate," one judge declared, "crime rises massively."[11] Since nothing of that sort occurred, law-and-order forces could only grumble. There was no public pressure for a return to severe repression; in fact, to the extent that the public showed any interest at all, it seemed responsive to the reformers' program. The press was more favorable than critical, and film directors found appreciative audiences for pictures that took the side of offenders in their encounters with the courts and the prisons.[12] The neo-classical school of jurists and criminologists seemed to be a dying breed, especially with the emergence in the 1950s of the school of criminal theory that called itself *Défense sociale nouvelle*. Founded in 1949 by Marc Ancel of the Paris law faculty, it was quickly adopted by the postwar reformers as a kind of quasi-official doctrinal base.

*Défense sociale* was a label coined in 1910 by the Belgian penologist Adolphe Prins. It had embodied strictly positivist ideas, and had won few converts in France.[13] The label was taken over in 1945, and the content somewhat modified, by the Italian penologist Filippo Gramatica, but once again its positivist conceptions were too extreme for the French. Gramatica argued for abandoning such terms as "infraction," "delinquent," and "penalty"; he held that study of the offender's personality should take precedence over the effort to prove his guilt or innocence; and he set as his ultimate goal a world without prisons.[14]

Ancel's "new" *Défense sociale*, like the theories of his eclectic predecessors Saleilles and Cuche at the turn of the century, represented a blend of neo-classical and positivist ideas, but it went well beyond the earlier eclectics by relying more heavily on modern criminological theories. The Penal Codes of 1791 and 1810, he argued, had gone wrong by adopting an unrealistic view of man as a free and rational being, master of his own actions and fully responsible for them. (As one of his disciples later put it, "The Penal Code took as its subject a hero from Corneille, but in practice we have only characters out of François Mauriac.")⁵ Ancel denied the charges of some critics that his doctrine was simply a deterministic neopositivism, or that it viewed all delinquents as sick and irresponsible, or that it advocated the suppression of such concepts as "penalty" and "responsibility." His purpose, he insisted, was to see men as they really are, to study the "total man." His goal was to transcend the simple notion of protecting society against malefactors; that goal was valid, but so was the protection of the offender. Above all else, the criminal justice system should aim at the prevention of crime and the "reinsertion" of deviants. Prisons, and the classical idea of punishment as retribution, continued to have a place in his system, but only as part of a panoply of techniques designed to "resocialize" offenders. That process, he contended, could be helped along in some cases by building on the criminal's sense of moral responsibility so cherished by the neoclassical school, and by encouraging his impulse to pay for a fault committed. But for offenders who lacked this potential sense of guilt, punishment would still be useful for intimidation and deterrence. Ancel suggested the concept of *césure*, by which he meant distinguishing sharply between the "legal phase" (trial and sentencing, which would retain overtones of retribution) and the "treatment phase," which would be uncorrupted by any idea of social vengeance. The second phase he regarded as far more important than the first; hence the emphasis on transforming the nature of the prison to become the proper locus of "resocialization."¹⁶

Ancel's *Défense sociale nouvelle* won many adherents beyond the borders of France, but its strongest impact was in France itself. Indeed, the Amor commission's report had already anticipated the doctrine in its general spirit. "The penitentiary," declared a new Director of Prison Administration in 1954, "receives only the man; his offense is dropped off at the door."¹⁷ The new penal policies of course continued to draw fire from neo-classical jurists and penalists, who were able to win occasional counter-victories. In 1950, for example, parliament was persuaded to impose the death penalty for armed robbery involving the use of an automobile; there had been a mild wave of such "*gangsterisme*," imported, it was said, from America.[18] But since the general level of crime and the prison population continued to decline, the reformers could pursue their experiment without arousing a public or political outcry. A few critics on the left complained that the reformers were being too slow and cautious. One journalist who visited thirty prisons before being excluded by the authorities charged in 1953 that the Amor reform program was in fact a dead letter, and that "classic repression" was still the rule. Perhaps, he concluded, the only solution was to abolish all prisons.[19] Another observer agreed in 1955 that the prisons had really changed very little. "In reality," she wrote, "almost all of the prisoners are thrown together in a disastrous mixture of ages, offenses, moral and physical health. . . . Some of them rapidly corrupt the others. . . . An effort has been made to isolate the inmates at night in what are called 'chicken-coops,' used to break up the dormitory rooms; but in most prisons the sleeping quarters continue to be common dormitories, with all that this means in physical and moral promiscuity."[20]

Prison officials could reasonably respond, of course, that their reform program was hampered by the ill-adapted buildings they had inherited, and by the parsimony of parliament. The ministry of justice received less than one per cent of the annual state budget for civil expenditures, and the Penal Administration's share of this appropriation was only one-third.[21] The departmental (short-term) prisons, most of which had at long last been taken over by the central government in 1946, remained for the most part in disgraceful condition; in 1964 the Director of Penal Administration declared that 121 of the 181 prisons in France were "unusable" and ought to be abandoned.[22] It was futile, declared one magistrate, to talk of rehabilitating prisoners in such "medieval" conditions. An official report indicated that 70 per cent of the *maisons d'arrêt* and 40 per cent of the *maisons centrales* were not adequately equipped with basic sanitary facilities; that 55 and 37 per cent respectively were not heated; and that 95 and 57 per cent lacked sufficient space for exercise.[23] Fewer than half of the prisons in 1962 had sports equipment of any kind.[24] Parliament was finally persuaded in 1963 to approve a fifteen-year plan providing for the abandonment or reconstruction of two-thirds of the short-term prisons; but ten years later, only a handful had been closed, and in 1978, 144 of the original 152 *maisons d'arrêt* were

"CHICKEN-COOPS" IN A FRENCH PRISON. In some old prisons, the device called *"cages à poules"* was invented to isolate inmates at night. (From Gaillac, *Les Maisons de correction, 1830–1945*)

still in use.[25] Voting funds for prison maintenance, for experimental programs, or even for prison personnel had little appeal either to politicians or to the voters who elected them. Shortcomings in the reform program could therefore be explained away by penal officials as the consequence of penury and public indifference.

Nevertheless, some changes had really taken place during the years of the Fourth Republic—more changes, indeed, than the system of criminal justice had known for many generations. In 1958 the principles laid down by the Amor commission in 1945 were given *de jure* status in the revised Code of Penal Procedure.[26] The Code now provided for individualized treatment of offenders, based on an elaborate personality profile put together by experts at the time of admission to prison. It legalized the role of the new supervising magistrates in the prisons, giving them the title *juges de l'application des peines* (JAP). (One magistrate hailed this latter innovation as "perhaps the greatest reform in the execution of sentences since the beginning of the century. . . , the keystone of the new edifice.") [27] It placed some restrictions on the length of preventive detention prior to indictment or trial; it further undermined the once-sacred cellular principle by allowing work in common for prisoners awaiting trial; and it introduced for the first time in France a system of supervised probation for offenders given early release or suspended sentences.[28] It also authorized some cautious experiments with "semi-liberty" (mainly allowing work outside the prison for short-term inmates and for some long-termers nearing the end of their sentence) ; and it introduced into the Code such terms as *"reclassement," "réadaptation sociale,"* and *"traitement pénal."* Thus the essential aspects of the great experiment of 1945 seemed to be confirmed, and the future assured for the reformers. "Never," wrote one reforming magistrate, "have such massive breaches been opened in the high walls of the penitentiaries."[29]


Already, however, clouds were gathering. In later retrospect, some disappointed reformers were to blame the war in Algeria for interrupting their experiment and to some extent reversing it.[30] The Algerian revolt against French rule which began in 1954 gradually had its impact on France itself. Factional conflicts among the North Africans living in France brought violent clashes and reprisals; terrorist acts by Algerian activists and police retaliation in Paris and other cities created an atmosphere of insecurity. The homicide rate, which had remained quite stable for a century, rose sharply; so did the prison population, which increased in 1956 for the first time in a decade, and which by 1959 approached 30,000 —one-third of them North Africans. The rise continued, though somewhat more slowly, through the 1960s, reaching a new peak of 33,000 in 1969.[31] It had been only 20,000 when the Algerian war began.

Although the homicide rate returned to what one might call "normal" after the Algerian war ended in 1962, the over-all crime rate continued to rise thereafter, though more slowly. So did the incidence of juvenile and young-adult delinquency; the proportion of prisoners below age 25 reached 48 per cent by 1965.[32] These trends naturally hampered the reformers in their effort to consolidate and broaden the 1945 program; indeed, they blocked all progress throughout the 1960s, and even caused some backsliding. The insecurities of the war period also spurred a resurgence of neo-classical thinking; there was more talk of the need for severe repression and a return to intimidation as the central purpose of punishment.[33] De Gaulle's government responded by restoring the death penalty for certain political crimes, thus reversing a tradition that had endured (with some wartime infringements) since 1848.[34] It also added a new State Security Court to deal with such offenses. De Gaulle's minister of justice, Jean Foyer, gave official weight to the revived hard line in a much-discussed speech to an audience of magistrates; it amounted to a kind of doctrinal manifesto challenging the theories of *Défense sociale nouvelle* as well as the accomplishments of the reformers since 1945.

> The very foundations of penal law contained within the liberal principles of the Revolution are being challenged. A curious doctrine, the product of Italian positivism, preaches a disconcerting system in which the infraction is concealed behind the delinquent, the delinquent' disappears behind the sick person; we see such inventions as *césure* . . . where sentencing conveys no declaration of guilt; we are urged to adopt indeterminate sentences that will allow gradations and modifications in the punishments inflicted. According to this school, every honest man is really an unwitting criminal.
>
> The fundamental vice of such theories is excess; after all, not all delinquents are subnormal or abnormal. The direct result of such systems is a weakening of repression. Besides, the treatment prescribed for curing delinquents and readapting them to life in society is so complicated as to require enormous material resources. . . .
>
> An infraction generally involves an amoral element; the offender knew what he was doing, and acted freely. . . . Too much concern for the individual offender can enervate repression, and can itself be oppressive; it tends to base a debatable therapy upon an uncertain diagnosis. The judge abdicates before the doctor. . . .[35]

Foyer ended his philippic with a blast at almost every aspect of the reformers' program. "The penalists," he charged (quoted an eminent neo-classical jurist) "are no longer interested in the rule of law, but are passionately concerned about the quality of the beans served to the prisoners." In his opinion, the revised Code of 1958 had dangerously relaxed the rules of criminal procedure;

the longtime trend toward "correctionalizing" crimes by converting them into misdemeanors should be halted; the use of the pardoning power and of early release should be restricted; the death penalty must be retained, along with short prison sentences designed to intimidate minor offenders.

Foyer's manifesto was a startling reversal of the stance adopted by successive ministers of justice since 1945. Some observers took it to mean that de Gaulle and his ministers were determined to nullify the postwar reforms and to reinstate neo-classical principles as official doctrine. Apparently President de Gaulle himself leaned in that direction, for in a letter to Foyer he expressed concern about increasing requests for the use of the pardoning power and for early release from prison. Too much attention, he declared, was being given to the personality of the offender, and not enough to the social disturbance caused by the crime. Repression, de Gaulle concluded, must not be weakened at a time when crime was clearly on the rise.[36] No dramatic reversal of policy followed, however— probably because the threat to public order dissipated quickly after the Algerian war ended. Terrorist attacks soon ceased, and the prisons were rapidly cleared of political offenders. It is true that both the over-all crime rate and the prison population continued to rise through the 1960s.[37] But the growth was too modest to alarm the public or the politicians; indeed, the criminologist Jean Pinatel complained in 1965 of the public's indifference to rising crime, reflecting what he called its usual tendency to ignore the entire crime problem.[38] At most, the Algerian war left an aftermath of renewed debate between the theoreticians of *Défense sociale nouvelle* and the partisans of neo-classical ideas. But when a formal debate was organized in 1964 between spokesmen for the two sides, the result was more consensus than conflict. Marc Ancel for *Défense sociale* led off with a somewhat pugnacious statement, but Roger Merle for the neo-classicists stressed his colleagues' acceptance of the principle of individualized treatment of offenders, and urged only that penalties retain their retributive aspect. When the session ended, the chairman summed things up by asking: "Do we have a system of classical penal law influenced by *Défense sociale nouvelle*, or is our system already that of *Défense sociale nouvelle*, with classical penal law acting as a brake?"[39] The reformers were able, therefore, to resume their gradualist effort. The use of suspended sentences and early release became more common, leading from 1968 onward to several years of decline in the prison population. A new round of reform got under way in 1970, when parliament adopted a law that further implemented the 1945 program. It placed additional restrictions on the practice of preventive detention before indictment, authorized freedom on probation for some persons awaiting trial, and increased the authority of the *juges de l'application des peines*.[40]

Meanwhile, however, France had been shaken by the startling upheaval of May-June 1968, which was to have a significant (though delayed) impact on the penal reform movement. The disorders that began in the universities and spread to the factories produced no immediate echo in the prisons. But the aftershock was serious, both directly and in the form of altered public attitudes. The violent confrontation in the streets between students and police, the spontaneous wave of sit-in strikes that paralyzed the country, soon came to an end, but something deeper persisted: a mood of radical challenge aimed at existing institutions and mores. Among those institutions was the system of criminal justice and its most visible manifestation, the prison. Journalists and intellectuals who identified themselves as *"gauchistes"* seized upon the prison as the most representative symbol of "bourgeois oppression," and exalted their inmates as victims of class justice. Jean-Paul Sartre had already provided a rationale for this attitude in his *Saint Genet*—a hagiographic essay on the writer Jean Genet, who had spent much of his life behind bars. A cluster of Paris intellectuals headed by Jean-Marie Domenach, editor of the left-wing Catholic monthly *Esprit*, organized the *Groupe d'Information sur les Prisons* (GIP), dedicated to publicizing prison conditions and agitating for prisoners' rights. Michel Foucault, one of the most influential among left-bank intellectuals, went even further: his goal, he declared, was "to efface the deep frontier [*sic*] between innocence and guilt."[41]

This mood of challenge eventually spread to the prisons. Although the number of inmates continued to decline until the mid-1970s, the proportion of young offenders kept increasing, and some of these were aware of the cultural stresses affecting their age group outside. This atmosphere undoubtedly contributed to the outbreak of prison disorders in the early 1970s that shocked French public opinion, shook the confidence of French penal officials, and helped prepare the way for a return to harsher repression during the years that followed. The wave of riots that began in late 1971 and culminated in the summer of 1974 brought the entire crime-control system into the headlines and profoundly altered public attitudes.

France had known prison disorders before, but never on such a scale. Heretofore they had almost always been localized affairs, provoked by material grievances and quickly repressed by the authorities.[42] The only organized protests had been mounted by political prisoners, usually demanding special status and sometimes achieving it. The new wave of the 1970s was quite unprecedented in both character and scope; its repercussions were therefore that much greater. In September 1971, almost coincident with the Attica prison riot in New York state, a minor outbreak at the antiquated *maison centrale* of Clairvaux ended violently with the murder of two hostages. Three months later came a far more extensive riot at the *maison centrale* of Toul, involving several hundred inmates; other outbreaks followed within a month at three other prisons. An investigating committee was dispatched at once; its chairman, former Director of Prison Administration Robert Schmelck (now a high-ranking magistrate) brought in a remarkably frank report that was promptly published. It recognized some of the rioters' grievances as legitimate, and recommended changes in prison organization and personnel.[43]

Some action did indeed follow: the minister of justice ordered reports on prison conditions throughout France, and set up study groups to consider such questions as prisoners' rights and the development of "open prisons."[44] A series of quite extensive reforms was adopted, embodied in a decree of September 1972 and a law in December of the same year. Prison rules were relaxed considerably: the rule of silence was abolished, disciplinary punishments softened, regulations on correspondence and visits eased, more recreational facilities provided. The December law further broadened such practices as early release, temporary prison leaves, and semi-liberty; it again increased the authority of the JAP; and it restricted the use of the *casier judiciaire* ("rap sheet") that handicapped ex-convicts in their effort to re-enter free society.

THE NEW LOOK IN FRENCH PRISONS. Fleury-Mérogis, opened in 1968 and completed in 1973, is one of only about a dozen new prisons built in France in the 20th century. It was designed to hold more than 3000 inmates from the Paris region: persons awaiting trial, and short-term convicts. The object of criticism by both hard-liners and reformers, it has already been the scene of some disorders, and has the highest suicide rate of any French prison. (Roger-Viollet)

Considerable tension persisted nevertheless; there was a prisoners' strike at Melun in 1973 (for higher wages), a hunger strike at Lyon, involving some material destruction, and a small rebellion at France's newest and most controversial short-term prison at Fleury-Mérogis, near Paris.[46] But the real explosion was still to come. It began in July 1974 at the long-term prison of Clairvaux, where tensions had always been abnormally high. An apparently minor incident rapidly escalated into a full-scale revolt that left two inmates dead and much of the prison a shambles. News of the event spread through the prison system with forest-fire speed; by the time the movement was brought under control two weeks later, outbreaks had occurred in seventy prisons; four *maisons centrales* were completely or partially smashed and burned, and seven inmates were dead.[47] In the midst of this appalling upheaval, the guards in a number of prisons went on strike. Their resentment at low salaries, long hours, and lack of status had been smoldering for some time; they demanded a pay scale equal to that of the police, and some recognition of the importance and dangers of their profession.[48]

This massive wave of rebellion produced a dual response: reformers read its meaning one way, hard-liners in just the opposite fashion. For the reformers, change in the prisons had been too slow and too limited; chronic penury had hampered the realization of the 1945 program, which had raised hopes that had ended in violent frustration.[49] France's newly elected president, Valéry Giscard d'Estaing, publicly espoused this view, and made a much-publicized visit to the prison in Lyon where he talked to inmates as well as officials. Giscard had already announced the creation of a new sub-cabinet position, the state secretariat for prison conditions, and had named a public-health doctor, Madame Hélène Dorlhac, as the first (and only) holder of the post.[50] But the more common reaction among the general public was a mixture of bewilderment and outrage. Minister of Interior Michel Poniatowski, an outspoken advocate of law-and-order, fed this angry spirit by inviting the public to see for itself the damage done to public property. Thousands of citizens lined up for guided tours through the ruined prison at Loos, viewing examples of smashed equipment to which the authorities had thoughtfully attached price tags. The response of these furious taxpayers was not surprising; as one of them put it to a guard acting as guide through the ruins, "why didn't you just cut loose with the machine guns?"[51] Jurists and penal officials of the neo-classical school blamed the riots on the postwar reforms which, in their view, had so softened prison rules that discipline had disintegrated. For them the conclusion was clear: punishment should once more be used to punish, not to seek the will-o'-the-wisp of "resocialization."[52]

The reformers themselves were shaken, and indulged in a good deal of soul-searching.[53] In the end, however, most of them clung to the belief that the 1945 program, reinforced by further social reforms to render the society less "criminogenic," would eventually sap the roots of crime. Thirty years of dedicated effort had of course given them a weighty emotional stake in the success of their program; but they were also convinced that no better alternative existed, either for offenders or for the broader society.

For a time, it seemed that the crisis of 1974 coud be success-fully surmounted. The reform laws of 1970 and 1972 broadened the base for a coherent program, and President Giscard's support seemed to be assured. In 1975 the reformers added another victory; a new law further liberalized the use of temporary prison leaves, ordered the segregation of a few dangerous or incorrigible offend-ers in new maximum-security units (on the theory that officials might then be better able to put their effort into rehabilitating the others) , and—most innovative of all for France—authorized a series of alternative penalties as substitutes for prison (e.g., denial of drivers' licenses, of the right to engage in certain types of work or to reside in certain areas) . One reformer hailed the law as "the most important text of the contemporary epoch for the theory of criminal law."[54] "The scale of punishments is broken," exulted a left-wing lawyer; "prison is no longer the standard penalty."[55]

For a brief period during the mid-1970s the reformed system appeared to be operating smoothly and successfully. Early release became an almost automatic reward for good behavior; in 1973, 34,000 of 38,000 requests were approved. Probation and suspended sentences likewise came into more frequent use, as did the granting of temporary prison leaves and the regime of semi-liberty.[56] Ma-dame Dorlhac, state secretary for prison conditions, reported proudly that more offenders were completing their sentences out-side prison walls than behind bars.[57]

Even the most enthusiastic reformers recognized, however, that there was still a long way to go. The material condition of many prisons remained sub-standard; only a few of the short-term prisons branded ten years earlier as "unusable" had been closed; many JAPs complained that they were overloaded and understaffed for the new burdens they had assumed; some critics charged that few of the reforms were consistently applied in practice.[58]

One time-worn problem that continued to defy solution was the organization of prison labor. As a former prison staff member ironically remarked, perhaps the only time in history when penal labor had not been a problem was in the era of the galleys.[59] Its character had, however, changed over time. The old complaints about private entrepreneurs had ended with the adoption of direct state administration (la régie) in 1927; but in fact, the administra-tion found it necessary to continue contracting with private con-cessionaires for the employment of more than half of the prison workers.[60] The most striking change was the virtual disappearance since the 1930s of complaints about unfair competition with free enterprise and free workers. In part, that change was traceable to the fact that most prison-made products were now consumed by state agencies, notably by the prison system itself. But it also derived from an altered attitude among free workers. The labor unions now complained that too many prisoners were denied the opportunity to work, which they saw as a privilege and a right rather than an onerous burden. They argued also that prison workers should be paid at the same rates as workers outside. Most of the reformers shared the view that prison work should be educational rather than retributive, and that conditions in the prison workshops should resemble as closely as possible those enjoyed by free labor.[61] They did succeed in extending accident and sickness insurance to prison workers, and in raising some of them to the level of the official minimum wage.[62] But they had to admit their failure to provide all convicts with work, as required by the Code. Year after year, successive Directors of Penal Administration reported that about half of the inmates were unemployed, and in 1979 the Director bluntly declared that there was little hope of improving the situation.[63] *Concessionaires*, the authorities asserted, were increasingly hard to recruit; most of them claimed that there was little profit in employing inefficient prison workers, even at below-minimum wages. They repeated too the traditional argument—amply justified by the facts—that the short-term prisons did not lend themselves to work organization; facilities were inadequate, and the turnover of inmates was too rapid to impart skills. Thus a truly satisfactory solution to the wearisome problem of prison labor seemed as distant as ever.

The reformers' successes embodied in the laws of 1970–75 gave them only a short respite. The general public, which had paid little attention to the reform experiment under way since 1945, now began to show signs of growing restiveness and hostility. Already in 1970–71, opinion polls had shown that two-thirds of the respondents were dissatisfied with the effectiveness of their crime-control system, and that 44 per cent favored tougher police repression.[65] The prison riots of 1971–74 reinforced this hard-line stance. Emotions were further stirred by a rash of crime reports in certain segments of the press; the belief spread that France was being inundated by a crime wave without precedent.[66] A few spectacular or grisly crimes got sensational coverage, but much attention was also paid to purse-snatchings, burglaries, and "hold-ups" [sic]. In some small towns in the Paris basin, vigilante groups were formed to patrol the streets at night, and some individual citizens armed themselves or set up booby-traps.[67] An opinion poll in 1975 found that 75 per cent of Frenchmen now found the courts and the police to be too indulgent. Critics seized on the practices of early release and prison leaves, accusing the new JAPs of loosing a horde of unreformed malefactors to prey upon honest folk. The fact that offenses by such released prisoners were extremely rare passed unnoticed. So did statisticians' attempts to estimate the cost of crime to the society; these studies concluded that fiscal fraud was far and away the most costly variety of offense, yet it drew little public attention.[68] For 72 per cent of Frenchmen, an essential weapon in controlling crime was the death penalty—even though there had been no increase in capital crimes as the over-all crime rate rose.[69]

As in earlier periods, it is difficult to untangle the complex interrelationship between the changing level of crime and the public perception of that change. Crime waves can be real, but a distorted belief that crime is rampant can also be artificially whipped up by the press or the politicians, and can become a kind of obsession.[70] Some French criminologists have put forward the hypothesis that there tends to be a three-year lag between a sharp rise in the crime rate and public awareness of that rise.[71] They suggest such a lag during the 1970s; the panicky public reaction was, they say, a response to a real increase in crime, but it was a delayed reaction and it rested on vague notions of the true facts. The over-all crime rate had in truth been rising well before public attention became riveted on the issue. The rise had begun in the early 1960s—slowly at first, then somewhat more rapidly, then (after 1970) more rapidly still. From 1963 to 1975 the overall rate (crimes and misdemeanors per capita) quadrupled—though almost all of this increase was confined to offenses against property rather than against persons, aid was not accompanied by violence.[72] Even though public perceptions of this trend were delayed and distorted, there was enough evidence to provoke serious concern. The upsurge of crime since the 1960s reflected a worldwide phenomenon. "Almost everywhere," declared the criminologist Jean Pinatel, "crime has exceeded the level at which it ceases to be a residual phenomenon and becomes a political issue." It was the product, he suggested, of unusually rapid social change.[73]

It is hardly surprising that the authorities responded promptly to the public's growing sense of insecurity. Some magistrates did so by imposing longer prison sentences (especially on young offenders) and granting fewer suspended sentences; some prison officials did so by cutting back on prison leaves and early release.[74] President Giscard did so by appointing an experts' commission (1976) to study the interlocking problems of crime and violence and to recommend solutions. The commission, chaired by the prominent politician Alain Peyrefitte, included some of France's leading criminologists, penologists, and penal officials, along with magistrates, social scientists, a psychiatrist, an urbanist, and a high police official.[75] Further buttressed by several task forces, the commission met for almost a year, and in 1977 produced a blockbuster of a report—the most elaborate official study of the crime problem since that of Haussonville's commission in 1875. It put forward 105 recommendations, intended not only to reduce the level of crime but also that of violence generally.[76] Most of these recommendations proposed various social reforms (such as limiting the size of cities and the height of apartment buildings, and controlling television violence) ; a few, however, sought to grapple directly with the crime-control problem.

The Peyrefitte report reflected, on the whole, the views of the gradualist reformers who had shaped penal policy since 1945. True, it did suggest greater caution in according such privileges as temporary prison leaves, and it favored the use of very brief prison sentences for first offenders, intended to administer "a necessary shock."[77] But it also recommended further experiments in reform: the development of additional penalties as alternatives to prison, broader reliance on the expertise of doctors and psychologists throughout the judicial process, an increase in the number of JAPs, the creation of some small low-security prisons adapted to the regime of semi-liberty, tighter controls on the possession of weapons, and (by a split vote) abolition of the death penalty. It further suggested a "modernization" of the Penal Code to take account of "the evolution of mores," and the establishment of permanent national and regional commissions to monitor the criminal justice system.

Although the commission recognized that Frenchmen had some reason to feel insecure (crimes and misdemeanors, according to its calculations, had doubled in ten years, burglaries had increased two and a half times, armed robbery fivefold, "holdups" twentyfold) ,[78] it reminded the government and the public that waves of panic were cyclical phenomena that did not accurately reflect reality. Rather, according to the commission, such waves reflected sensational coverage of crime in the mass media.[79] Nor did the commission find much correlation between the public's beliefs about crime and the personal experience of most citizens. Polls conducted in 1976 for the commission revealed that more than 80 per cent of the respondents were gravely concerned by what they saw as a threatening growth of violence and crime, yet only a small proportion said that they had recently been victims of criminal aggression or knew any such victim.[80] Nevertheless, a large majority of respondents ranked crime, along with high prices and unemployment, as one of the three most important domestic issues of the time. The commission's polls also gave added proof of rising impatience with the "excessive indulgence" allegedly shown by the courts and the penal authorities; the respondents were blithely unaware of the fact that judges had increased the number of prison sentences by 40 per cent during the previous three years.[81] Three out of four respondents shared this hard-line view; many of them would surely have applauded the splenetic outburst of a contributor to the *Journal du Dimanche* who wrote in 1976, under the headline *"Assez de Pitié pour les Monstres!"*: "Society, society, society! How many times have we not read and heard that word of late. Well, yes! Society is guilty. It is guilty of pity."[82]

When the commission's experts analyzed the poll more closely, however, they found that Frenchmen's reactions to the crime problem were too complex to be contained within the simplistic dichotomy, hard-liners versus reformers. They distinguished five general categories of public response:[83]

I. "Alarmist-repressives":
   (a) "Sensitive persons," mainly older respondents; crime

and violence seen as the product of lack of affection; favor censorship of television violence and more effective policing. (18%)

(b) Hard-liners, including a large proportion of young respondents; most crime and violence seen as the work of certain social categories; tougher policing essential. (20%)

(c) "Moralizers," showing the highest average age; crime and violence seen as the product of a decline of religious belief and of parental authority, plus an excessive taste for luxury; emphasize the need to restore moral order; ask for more effective police protection. (18%)

II. "Militants and moderates":

(a) Militants, predominantly young and *gauchiste*; crime and violence seen as products of inequality and social injustice; some violence a normal and acceptable thing; police already have too much authority. (17%)

(b) Moderates: dislike all forms of violence, discount the current wave of panic about crime as excessive. (27%)

If this analysis is valid, it may suggest that differences among Frenchmen about the crime problem may have been similarly complex in the past. And it may suggest also that a French consensus on ways to deal with the crime problem will not be easy to achieve in the future.

Shortly after the Peyrefitte commission finished its work in 1977, its chairman was named to the post of minister of justice. The appointment seemed to indicate that the government intended to push ahead with the reform program outlined in the report; and indeed, Peyrefitte himself appeared at first to be committed to such action. Instead, a brusque reversal soon occurred. The government pushed through parliament in November 1978 a bill retracting some of the postwar reforms.[84] The law cut back the authority of the JAPs, transferring decisions on early release and prison leaves to a committee controlled by penal officials. It imposed harsher penalties on those guilty of violent crimes, and restricted early release for such offenders. A second law dropped from the Code all reference to the progressive system which had enabled prisoners to earn better conditions through good behavior. Peyrefitte, questioned about the commission's proposal to abolish the death penalty, replied somewhat equivocally; he expressed personal sympathy for abolition, but declared that French opinion was not yet ready for such a step. If capital punishment were abolished, he declared, people would take the law into their own hands.[86] More startling was the new line adopted by the minister after a brief visit to the United States in 1979. The Americans, Peyrefitte told the press, had led the way in rehabilitation experiments, but had now concluded that all such programs were failures. They were returning, therefore, to the idea that prison's essential purpose should be to punish.[87]

In 1980 Peyrefitte brought to parliament an elaborate bill revising many sections of the Code of Criminal Procedure; he described this measure as a guarantee of "security and liberty." Somewhat amended but not basically altered, the bill was adopted and went into effect in 1981. It aroused a small storm of denunciation among both moderate and radical reformers, for its main thrust was again in the direction of more severe repression.[88] It cut back on the practices of suspended sentences and prison leaves; it restricted the use of attenuating circumstances to justify reduced penalties, and it restored to prosecutors and prison officials some of their lost power to keep accused persons under preventive detention. The new law, one critic concluded, "upsets most accepted ideas on penal questions . . . ; the policy based on rehabilitation is replaced by a philosophy that sees the penalty as the alpha and omega of penal doctrine."[89] Peyrefitte responded by arguing that his only purpose was to restore a proper balance between the rights of the offender and those of society. Besides, he asserted, "Vengeance is a fundamental impulse among men. If it's neglected, the effect is simply to breed doubts about justice."[90]

The new governmental hard line was reinforced by an increased severity on the part of the judges, juries, and penal officials. Fewer early releases were granted; sentences were longer, and the death penalty imposed more often by juries. Ironically, a reform of the jury-selection system in 1978 had replaced the former blue-ribbon juries by "popular" juries chosen by lot; Peyrefitte reported with pleasure that their verdicts were much more severe.[91] One result of all this was a dramatic rise in the prison population; from a low point of 27,000 in 1975, it climbed steadily to 35,000 in 1979 and then to a new peak of 42,000 in 1981—the highest figure since the immediate postwar years.[92] In part the increase was the product of a continuing rise in the crime rate (burglaries in 1980, for example, rose 25 per cent over the preceding year), but mainly it was the consequence of the new penal policy that kept offenders in jail longer.[93] The pressure on prison facilities approached the danger point; even the 1975 figure of 27,000 had meant overcrowding, yet now the same facilities were required to handle over 40,000 inmates. But, as Peyrefitte jauntily remarked, "A cell built for two can always hold three, and one built for three can hold four."[94]

Throughout the 1970s, the penal reformers had been under fire not only from the advocates of more rigorous repression but also from radical critics on the left. There had been such critics in the past, but most of them had been isolated figures whose ideas had had little resonance. Now, for the first time, a vigorous movement emerged to challenge the criminal justice system as a whole and, more particularly, its central institution, the prison. Its main source of strength was a growing sentiment that the prison had failed, either as a mechanism to rehabilitate or as an agency to intimidate and deter. The weaknesses of the movement were a lack of coherence and an inability to win much sympathy among the general public.

The idea of radical reform was in part a by-product of the upheaval of May 1968, which crystallized some burgeoning discontents with the values and institutions of "bourgeois" society. The movement first took organized form with the founding in 1971 of the *Groupe d'Information sur les Prisons*, which denounced the prison as a "lawless" institution and set out to educate both the public and the prisoners about the issue of prisoners' rights. Torn by factional differences from the start, the GIP survived for only two years. Its extremist wing rejected the idea of "humanizing" prisons as hypocritical and futile; since prisons were merely agencies for social control by the ruling elites, the goal should be the abolition of prisons as one aspect of a total transformation of society. This faction looked for inspiration to Jean-Paul Sartre, whose political writings seemed to imply "a general revolt against the concentration-camp universe in which we all live," and to Michel Foucault, advocate of erasing the line that divided innocence from guilt.[95] For Jean-Marie Domenach, editor of the monthly *Esprit* and founder of the GIP, such an attitude was self-defeating. "To reverse the existing manicheism by transforming all prisoners into innocent men is to remain within the vicious circle of guilt. The ideological alibi 'It's society that is guilty' leads in fact to glorifying the condemned person—which blocks all reform and puts off the revolution to the apocalypse."[96] The GIP was dissolved in 1973, and the Domenach wing reorganized as the *Association pour la Défense des Droits des Prisonniers*, which brought together a small band of Catholic and Socialist intellectuals. Some ex-prisoners meanwhile formed their own *Comité d'Action des Prisonniers*; it campaigned for prisoners' rights and for drastic changes in the criminal justice system, and sought to provide aid and advice to prisoners and their families.[97] In Lyon a small coterie of leftist lawyers and prison officials assumed a similar task.

None of these organizations, however, won much support. Far more significant, potentially at least, was the formation in 1968 by a group of young magistrates of a judges' union called the *Syndicat de la Magistrature*, which by 1980 claimed a membership of 900 (from the total of 5500 French magistrates). At the outset the *Syndicat* had a broad and varied ideological base; among the founders were many young Catholics of moderately reformist temper, products of the postwar Catholic youth movement that had strongly affected local politics and farmers' unions in rural France. That group, however, was outmaneuvered during the 1970s by men of Socialist or *gauchiste* outlook, so that the *Syndicat* moved farther to the left.[98] The "red judges," as the press soon dubbed them, became the spearhead of opposition to the new repressive trend after the mid-1970s. Its leaders accused the government of consciously exaggerating the threat of crime, thus artificially creating a public psychosis that would enable it to "perpetuate the extraordinary privileges of the class that took power in the 19th century and has kept it ever since."[99] The *Syndicat* vigorously attacked Peyrefitte's "law of security and liberty" and campaigned against the death penalty. The conversion of so many young magistrates to the idea of radical reform of the criminal justice system had some precedent: in the years before 1789, most young judges had so absorbed the Enlightenment outlook of Beccaria that they followed the new doctrines rather than the letter of *ancien régime* law.[100] That transformation had speeded the reform process after 1789; members of the *Syndicat* hoped that history might repeat.

For the gradualist penal reformers who had been at work since 1945, the stance of their leftist critics was much too extreme. Wedged between those critics and the hard-liners, they had less and less room to maneuver. Difficult problems still faced them as they sought to transform the penal system. A few ultra-modern prisons had been built, but most facilities remained ill-adapted to "resocialization." As crowding increased, prison personnel was stretched thin, and even the new prisons threatened to explode. Guards were skimpily trained for their changing functions, and resented their low pay and status.[101] Auxiliary personnel—teachers, social and psychiatric workers, probation officers—remained in short supply. Three hundred probation officers aided by two hundred part-timers were expected to handle a case load of 48,000 probationers.[102] The ministry of justice continued to receive less than one per cent of the state budget for civil affairs.[103] When the government in 1980 decided to expand the nation's police force over a five-year period by an additional 10,000 officers, no provision was included for an increase in prison personnel.[104]

These persistent problems were frustrating enough in themselves, but they were made worse by the self-doubts that began to assail the reformers during the 1970s. Do the ideas of 1945 still fit our needs? mused the criminologist Jean Pinatel; perhaps the initial mistake was made two centuries ago, when our ancestors burdened the prison with a set of responsibilities far beyond its capacity to fulfill.[105] Perhaps, wrote the penal official Pierre Arpaillange, the penal sanction has become equivocal; the courts, pulled between the concepts of punishment and treatment, often make decisions that achieve neither purpose; we no longer dare to punish, but we lack the means to treat.[106] Perhaps, suggested Judge Perdriau, the postwar reforms had been thwarted by the "rigid and unitary straightjacket" of a system still run autocratically by a "quasi-military hierarchy."[107] Perhaps, added the former Director of Penal Administration Robert Schmelck, it was simply irrational to assume that rehabilitation can be carried out in prison —"as senseless as trying to prepare someone for a footrace by keeping him in bed."[108] Even the members of the revived *Société des Prisons*, celebrating in 1976 the centennial of that bastion of the penitentiary movement, listened politely to a paper by a left-wing lawyer denouncing the prison as a demonstrated failure.[109] In spite of all the experiments, a disillusioned former JAP declared, the daily reality of prison had not really changed very much. We must admit, concluded Robert Schmelck in 1980, that the reforms adopted since 1945 have ended in "relative failure."[110] Some reformers began to speculate about abandoning prisons except for a few incorrigibles, and trying to resocialize the rest in some fashion outside prison walls.

This pervasive mood of gloom and doubt was brusquely interrupted in May-June 1981 by the unexpected and sweeping victory of the Socialists at the polls. Although the party's program and the campaign speeches of the new president François Mitterrand had placed little emphasis on penal reform, save for formal opposition to the death penalty, many Socialist militants were known to favor either moderate or radical reforms. Mitterrand had publicly espoused changes in the system of criminal justice, and one leader of the party's left wing, Jean-Pierre Chevènement, had at one time advocated the abolition of prisons as the ultimate goal of a socialist society.[111] Few Frenchmen or foreign observers, however, foresaw the dramatic actions that swiftly followed the Socialist victory.

Mitterrand chose as minister of justice (over the mild objections of his prime minister Pierre Mauroy) the brilliant but controversial criminal lawyer Robert Badinter, a member of the *Syndicat de la Magistrature* and an outspoken crusader for criminal justice reform, human rights, and abolition of the death penalty. Badinter had won notoriety as defense attorney in a number of sensational murder cases in which he had saved his clients from the gallows. He had not been a party activist, but identified himself as a social democrat. Along with his dazzling forensic skills went a passionate temperament and a reputation for inflexibility. Hard-liners were stunned by the appointment, and by Badinter's choice of several colleagues from the *Syndicat* for high posts in the ministry.[112] They anticipated the worst, and from their point of view, they soon got it.

Badinter's first move, with Mitterrand's solid support, was to present parliament with a bill to abolish capital punishment. It was promptly approved, despite the Senate's bitter opposition and despite renewed evidence through an opinion poll that almost two-thirds of the public continued to favor the death penalty.[113] Thus the long crusade against capital punishment that had begun even before the Great Revolution culminated at last in victory; France fell into line with most other European nations. Badinter also took prompt emergency action to relieve prison crowding, ordering the liberation of many minor offenders and prisoners nearing the end of their sentences. Within three months, the prison population dropped from 42,000 to just over 30,000.[114]

These immediate actions were followed by the announcement of a long series of reforms designed to reverse the recent trend toward more rigorous repression. Badinter's goals, as embodied in his first press conference, included abrogation of Peyrefitte's "law of security and liberty"; suppression of de Gaulle's State Security Court (which had dealt with cases of political subversion and terrorism); abolition of the maximum security quarters in prisons; and sweeping revisions of the Penal Code and the Code of Criminal Procedure.[115] Badinter himself assumed the chairmanship of the Penal Code commission, while Jacques Léauté, the eminent criminologist at the University of Paris, chaired the prodecural reform body. A third commission was assigned the task of studying ways to aid the victims of crime.

So sudden and drastic a reversal in the realm of criminal justice was almost without precedent in France. Advocates of law-and-order naturally responded with expressions of shock, outrage, and panic. The *Syndicat*, they charged, was scheming to infiltrate and regiment the entire corps of magistrates through its grip on key positions in the Ministry of Justice—an accusation that *Syndicat* leaders angrily denied, pointing out that only about fifteen of their members had been named to posts in the ministry.[116] Conservative politicians in the Paris city council complained of "rising violence and insecurity," and cited an insurance group that had called Paris "the burglary capital" (of Europe, presumably).[117]

Communist spokesmen chimed in to support the conservative critics; the Communists had, during the past couple of years, assumed a strong law-and-order stance, especially in towns of the "red belt" surrounding Paris. "The fight against delinquency and crime," party leader Georges Marchais had declared in 1980, "is a concern of Frenchwomen and Frenchmen. They insist on living in security; their liberty depends on it."[118]

A rash of terrorist bombings and assassinations during the spring and summer of 1982 fed public fears and gave the hard-liners new ammunition. So did the official crime statistics for 1981, which showed a global increase of 9.99 per cent over 1980. Armed robberies were up almost 12 per cent, housebreakings over 16 per cent.[119] Opposition politicians stepped up their warnings, charging that the government's laxity was responsible for the terrorist atrocities. From within the government as well came a new challenge to Badinter's reform program; Minister of Interior Gaston Defferre, whose responsibilities included the police and public order, demanded that some provisions of the Peyrefitte law be retained— notably those that authorized the police to make spot identity checks. Badinter reluctantly conceded the point, but continued to press for early abrogation of other repressive provisions in the "law of security and liberty." He achieved that goal in July 1982; the National Assembly approved his bill over vigorous opposition led by Peyrefitte himself.[120]

Meanwhile the Badinter program for reform of the criminal codes was also making steady progress. Chairman Jacques Léauté told the press that his commission on criminal procedure would propose "a radically new philosophy" that would introduce something like the Anglo-Saxon practice of *habeas corpus,* would create special tribunals of magistrates to rule on early release, and would establish a new set of courts to which offenders might appeal from the verdict of a *cour d'assises*.[121] Léauté's commission was scheduled to report in the autumn of 1982, Badinter's commission on Penal Code reform in the spring of 1983. If this pace could be maintained, it would mean that France's criminal justice system had been dramatically transformed in less than two years since the Socialists took power.

The achievement has been impressive. But of course, France's newest venture in the realm of crime control remains to be tested by time and experience. As usual, Frenchmen are sharply divided as to its probable effects. Will the retreat from rigorous repression cause the crime rate to rise precipitously, as the hard-liners predict? Will it level off instead, or even decline, as fewer first offenders are sent to prison to be irremediably corrupted in these "crime factories?" Or will the statistics continue to provide ammunition for both sides through creative manipulation? Forecasts lie beyond the historian's sphere—though it is probably safe to suggest that when all the facts are in, Frenchmen and foreign observers alike will continue to disagree about what those facts mean. Chronic social problems such as crime have never allowed for easy answers. That, at least, is not likely to change.

# Postface

JUST OVER A CENTURY AGO, at the first session of the National Assembly's commission on penal reform in 1872, the jurist Jean-Charles Babinet warned his fellow commissioners: "We can be sure that every possible system has already been tried somewhere, and that there's nothing left to invent."[1] Babinet was overly skeptical about the inventiveness of later generations; the past century has not been empty of new theories and techniques of crime control. Yet the dominant mood of our own day seems to represent a reversion to Babinet's grim conclusion: everything has been tried, nothing works. "We have moved into an era of penological pessimism," remarks the eminent Oxford legal scholar Rupert Cross.[2] "The incidence of crime seems to be going up in all parts of the world . . . and among all segments of society," writes the Cambridge expert Sir Leon Radzinowicz.[3] If we extrapolate from recent trends in France's crime rate, says the leading criminologist Jacques Léauté, every Frenchman may be a criminal eight years hence.[4]

It is tempting at the end of this survey of France's historical experience to adopt this defeatist position. Not that France's record is peculiarly disillusioning; with a few variations, the French experience parallels that of other Western nations. The most striking variable is France's long and stubborn reliance on transportation of convicts to overseas penal colonies. In France as elsewhere, prisons (and penal colonies) have been more criminogenic than curative, and such alternative penalties as have been cautiously tried have produced debatable results. Everywhere, public disillusionment stimulates a visceral urge to abandon the reformist efforts of the past two centuries in favor of simple and extreme solutions. On one wing, the cry is for harsh repression and more certain punishment; retribution and intimidation are demanded in place of the "illusory" goal of rehabilitation. On the other wing, the abolition of prisons together with a sweeping transformation of society is offered as the only possible action that will clear away the wreckage of past failures and will permit daring new departures in the "resocializing" of offenders.

Buffeted between these two extremes, French politicians and crime specialists are likely to cling to a traditional zigzag middle course of moderate reformism. Past failures have had a sobering effect, but have not destroyed the conviction of leading experts and of many citizens that the effort is worth pursuing. Something, they believe, can be done to limit the growth of crime and to make the techniques of punishment at least marginally more humane. Although experience seems to prove that most lawbreakers have not been successfully rehabilitated by any methods so far tried, it also proves that a significant minority of first offenders, for whatever reason, manage to stay out of further trouble. For most reformers, this partial success justifies the continued effort to maintain and increase the size of the non-recidivist minority.

The test of France's newest experiment—the changes introduced in 1981–82 by the Socialist government—is of course still to come. It stands in sharp contrast to the prevailing law-and-order trend in most Western nations, and that contrast may permit a more valid judgment of the relative effectiveness of these two approaches to the crime problem. Whatever the outcome, the French example should—as usual—be worthy of the world's attention.

# Notes

## Preface

1. Rupert Cross, *Punishment, Prison and the Public* (London: Stevens, 1971), pp. 40–41.
2. Antoine Jay in the Chamber of Deputies, November 22, 1831. *Archives parlementaires*, 2d series, LXXI, 762.
3. Louis Moreau-Christophe, *De l'état actuel des prisons en France* (Paris: Desrez, 1837), pp. xxxi–xxxiii.
4. Labour Party leader (and future prime minister) James Callaghan, unpaged preface to Anthony Babington, *The English Bastille: A History of Newgate Gaol* (New York: St. Martin's, 1972).
5. Henri Joly, *Le Combat contre le crime* (Paris: Cerf, 1892), p. 217.

## Chapter I:  The Challenge to Tradition

1. Arlette Farge, *Délinquance et criminalité: le vol d'aliments à Paris au XVIIIe siècle* (Paris: Plon, 1974), p. 26.
2. A gruesome contemporary description of Damiens's execution forms the introduction to Michel Foucault's *Surveiller et punir: naissance de la prison* (Paris: Gallimard, 1975), pp. 9–11. Cf. also Robert Anchel, *Crimes et châtiments au XVIIIe siècle* (Paris: Perrin, 1933), pp. 223–25.
3. The classic description of the departure of *la chaîne* from Bicêtre is that of Victor Hugo in *Le Dernier Jour d'un condamné* (Paris: Hetzel, 1889), pp. 75–77. For writers of the time, it was a favorite subject.
4. John Howard, *The Works of John Howard* (London: Johnson, 1791), II, 54.
5. Creditors were required to pay a small daily sum for the debtor's food while in prison. Debtors were released after five years, or earlier if they or their friends paid off the debt.

6. Farge, *Délinquance*, p. 66.

7. Ibid., p. 89.

8. Louis Sébastien Mercier, *Tableau de Paris* (Amsterdam, 1782–88), VI, 69–70.

9. Quoted in John Mackrell, "Criticism of Seigniorial Justice in Eighteenth-Century France," in *French Government and Society 1500–1850* (ed. J. F. Bosher, London: Athlone, 1973), p. 123.

10. A. Esmein, *A History of Continental Criminal Procedure* (tr. John Simpson, Boston: Little, Brown, 1913), pp. 352–57.

11. Baron Charles de Montesquieu, *Oeuvres complètes* (ed. Roger Cailloix, Paris: Gallimard, 1951), II, 318–30, 433.

12. Cesare Beccaria, *Traité des délits et des peines, traduit de l'italien d'après la sixième édition* (Paris: Bastien, 1773), pp. 139–45 and passim.

13. Voltaire, "Commentaire sur le livre *Des délits et des peines*," *Oeuvres complètes* (Paris: Gernier, 1879), pp. 41–42.

14. J. J. Rousseau, *Du contrat social* (ed. J. Ehrard, Paris: Garnier, 1975), p. 257.

15. Quoted in Yves Castan, *Honnêteté et relations sociales en Languedoc, 1715–1780* (Paris: Plon, 1974), p. 63.

16. F. M. Vermeil, *Essai sur les réformes à faire dans notre législation criminelle* (Paris: Demonville, 1781), pp. 31–32.

17. Charles Dupaty, *Mémoire justificatif pour trois hommes condamné à la roue* (Paris: Pierres, 1786), pp. 243–45.

18. Charles Dupaty, *Lettres sur la procédure criminelle de la France* ("En France": no publisher listed, 1788), pp. 6, 165–68.

19. Jacques-Pierre Brissot de Warville, *Théorie des lois criminelles*, I (Berlin, 1781), 37–38, 98; II (Paris: Aillaud, 1836), 276.

20. Mercier, *Tableau de Paris*, I, 42; III, 223.

21. P.-F. Muyart de Vouglans, *Réfutation des principes hasardés dans le "Traité des délits et peines"* (Paris: Desaint, 1767), pp. 5, 17, 20, 76, 90, 102, 118.

22. Quoted in Jean-Marc Varaud, *La Prison, pour quoi faire?* (Paris: La Table Ronde, 1972), pp. 19–20.

23. Quoted in Mackrell, "Criticism of Seigniorial Justice," p. 142.

24. Brissot de Warville, *Théorie*, II, 107.

25. John H. Langbein, *Torture and the Law of Proof* (Chicago: Univ. of Chicago Press, 1977). The gradual withering of the use of judicial torture is also demonstrated by current research under way in Brittany under the direction of Louis-Bernard Mer, "Réhabilitation de la justice de l'Ancien Régime," *Le Monde Dimanche*, July 19, 1981.

26. Pierre Deyon, *Le Temps des prisons* (Villeneuve: Univ. de Lille III, 1975), p. 34.

27. F.-A. Isambert (ed.), *Recueil général des anciennes lois françaises*

*depuis l'an 420 jusqu'à la révolution de 1789* (Paris: Belin-Leprieur, 1827), XXVIII, 526–32.

28. Marcello T. Maestro, *Voltaire and Beccaria as Reformers of Criminal Law* (New York: Columbia Univ. Press, 1942), p. 143.

29. Emmanuel Le Roy Ladurie, "La décroissance du crime au XVIIIe siècle: bilan d'historiens," *Contrepoint*, no. 9 (1973), p. 232.

30. Among these studies are Farge, *Délinquance*; A. Abbiateci et al., *Crimes et criminalité en France sous l'Ancien Régime* (Paris: Colin, 1971); Nicole Castan, *Justice et répression en Languedoc à l'Epoque des Lumières* (Paris: Flammarion, 1980); Pierre Deyon, *Le Temps des prisons*; Iain Cameron, *Crime and Repression in the Auvergne and Guienne, 1720–1790* (Cambridge: Cambridge Univ. Press, 1981); N. W. Mogenson, "Crimes and Punishments in Eighteenth-Century France: The Example of the Pays d'Auge," *Histoire Sociale/Social History*, X (1977), 337–53; R. Muchembled, *Culture populaire et culture des élites* (Paris: Flammarion, 1978); and several studies done by students of Pierre Chaunu at Caen and summarized in the *Annales de Normandie* for 1962, 1966, and 1971.

31. Le Roy Ladurie, "La décroissance du crime," pp. 231–32. Recent research in provincial archives by Iain Cameron and Robert Muchembled casts considerable doubt on what Cameron calls "the Authorized Version" of 18th century crime—that theft was replacing physical violence.

32. Mercier, *Tableau de Paris*, I, 196–97; Abbiateci, *Crimes et criminalité*, pp. 220–21.

33. Louis Chevalier, *Classes laborieuses et classes dangereuses* (Paris: Plon, 1958), p. 47.

34. Le Roy Ladurie, "La décroissance du crime," pp. 227–30.

35. Mercier, *Tableau de Paris*, I, 205.

36. G. Le Trosne, *Mémoire sur les vagabonds et sur les mendiants* (Soissons: Simon, 1764), pp. 4, 8–10, 39, 46–47.

37. G. Le Trosne, *Vues sur le justice criminelle* (Paris: Debure, 1777).

38. J.-P. Gutton, *La société et les pauvres: Lyon 1534–1789* (Paris: Les Belles Lettres, 1971), p. 441.

39. Iain G. Cameron, "The Police of Eighteenth-Century France," *European Studies Review*, VII (1977), 69–70.

40. G. Rusche and O. Kirchheimer, *Punishment and Social Structure* (New York: Russell, 1968), p. 5.

41. Ibid., p. 73.

42. Ibid., pp. 76, 78.

43. Foucault, *Surveiller et punir*, esp. pp. 61–72 and Parts II and IV.

44. Marquis de Condorcet, *Esquisse d'un tableau historique des progrès de l'esprit humain* (Paris: Editions Sociales, 1966), p. 220.

## Chapter II: Laboring on a Volcano (1789–1814)

1. Georges Lefebvre and Anne Terroine (eds.), *Recueil de documents relatifs aux séances des Etats-Généraux, mai–juin 1789*, I (Paris: Editions du C.N.R.S., 1953), 287, 340–41.

2. J-B. Duvergier (ed.), *Collection complète des lois, décrets, ordonnances, règlemens, avis du Conseil d'Etat depuis 1788* (2d edition, Paris: Guyot, 1836), III. 240.

3. J. Ancel, "La politique criminelle de l'Assemblée constituante," (typewritten thesis, Paris: Faculté de Droit, 1966), pp. 102ff., 110–15, 136ff., 189; Jacques Godechot, *Les Institutions de la France sous la Révolution et l'Empire* (Paris: Presses universitaires, 1968), p. 144; Esmein, *History of Continental Criminal Procedure*, pp. 402–3, 407.

4. The texts of these laws may be found in Duvergier, *Collection complète*, I, 310–33; III, 289–304 and 352–66.

5. Ibid., 313ff., 327ff.

6. *Archives parlementaires de 1787 à 1860: recueil complet des débats législatifs et politiques des chambres françaises* (Paris: Dupont, 1879–    ), 1st series, XV, 343. Duport's report is in ibid., XXI, 42–61; the subsequent debate dragged on through late 1790 and 1791.

7. Ibid., XXIII, pp. 38–39. A report by the Marquis de Mirabeau on the organization of prisons (1790) was not discussed by the Assembly. It proposed far-reaching reforms, most of which were far ahead of their time; the goal would be rehabilitation rather than punishment. Vicomte H. Begouin, "Un rapport inédit de Mirabeau sur le régime des prisons," *Revue d'Economie Politique*, I (1887), 491–512.

8. Le Pelletier's report appeared in the *Procès-verbal de l'Assemblée Nationale* (Paris: Baudouin, 1789–1901), LVI, 1–121. While the influence of Beccaria is plain, that of the English reformer Jeremy Bentham is more uncertain. Bentham bombarded the National Assembly with memoranda, including one that proposed his model prison called the Panopticon; he offered his own services as its first unpaid director. The Assembly ordered the memorandum published in translation (Paris: Imprimerie nationale, 1791), but took no further action. The Convention later voted Bentham honorary French citizenship as one of several foreigners "distinguished by their actions or writings in favor of liberty, humanity, and morality" (*Archives parlementaires*, le série, LIX, 10), but Bentham's disappointment was not assuaged.

9. Rusche and Kirchheimer, *Punishment and Social Structure*, p. 68.

10. Foucault, *Surveiller et punir*, pp. 229, 269–88.

11. *Procès-verbal de l'Assemblée*, LVI, 2–11.

12. Ibid., pp. 13, 16, 32–34, 44.

13. Ibid., pp. 13, 33–35, 39–41.

14. Camille Bloch, *L'assistance et l'état en France à la veille de la Révolution* (Geneva: Slatkine, 1974), p. 51; Deyon, *Le Temps des prisons*, p. 43.

15. *Procès-verbal de l'Assemblée*, LVI, 43–44.

16. Capital offenses retained in the new code were treason, conspiracy, destruction of public property by arson or bombing, parricide, premeditated murder, certain mutilations, and acceptance of a bribe by a legislator (ibid., LVII, no. 667; Duvergier, *Collection complète*, III, 324f.). One anonymous pamphleteer had urged the lawmakers to adopt a standard punishment for all offenders—painless death by the administration of a fatal dose of opium. Criminals were immune to reform, he argued, and certain death for all crimes would be an effective deterrent (Anon., *La Mort de tous les criminels* [Paris: Barrois, 1790]).

17. Duvergier, *Collection complète*, III, 352ff.

18. *Procès-verbal de l'Assemblée*, LVI, 48–50.

19. The Code of 1791 is carefully analyzed in the Paris law thesis of Mlle J. Ancel: "La politique criminelle de l'Assemblée Nationale." Two older studies are also useful: Henri Rémy, *Des principes généraux du Code Pénal de 1791* (Paris: Sirey, 1910), and Edmond Seligman, *La Justice en France pendant la Révolution* (2 vols., Paris: Plon, 1901–13).

20. The new machine was adopted in 1792 on the advice of Dr. Louis of the Academy of Medicine. Designed by him, it was initially called the Louisette in his honor; later it reverted to the name of its first sponsor, Dr. Guillotin. Within six months after its adoption by the Legislative Assembly, eighty-three of the new machines had been built and installed throughout France.

21. Godechot, *Institutions*, pp. 379–84; Marcel Marion, *Le Brigandage pendant la Révolution* (Paris: Plon, 1934), pp. 40, 70, 76–77, 82–86, 100–101.

22. Marion, *Le Brigandage*, pp. 77, 86, 100; Maurice Agulhon, *La Vie sociale en Provence intérieur au lendemain de la Révolution* (Paris: Société des Etudes Robespierristes, 1970), p. 378; Denis Woronoff, *La République bourgeoise* (Paris: Seuil, 1972), pp. 22–23, 129–32.

23. *Moniteur Universel*, Dec. 20, 1796.

24. Ibid.

25. Duvergier, *Collection complète*, IX, 366; X, 177–78, 181–82; Godechot, *Institutions*, pp. 477–79.

26. Marion, *Le Brigandage*, pp. 100–101.

27. Ibid., pp. 114–15, 123; Agulhon, *La Vie sociale*, pp. 372–78.

28. Agulhon, *La Vie sociale*, pp. 384, 390; Marion, *Le Brigandage*, pp. 372–78.

29. Esmein, *History of Continental Criminal Procedure*, pp. 453ff.; Godechot, *Institutions*, p. 628.

30. O. Pozzo di Borgo (ed.), *Benjamin Constant: écrits et discours politiques* (Paris: Pauvert, 1964), pp. 156–89; Paul Bastid, *Benjamin Constant et sa doctrine* (Paris: Colin, n.d.), I, 159; Esmein, *History of Continental Criminal Procedure*, p. 456.

31. Esmein, *History of Continental Criminal Procedure*, pp. 453–58.

32. Duvergier, *Collection complète*, XVII, 4345; G. Vauthier, "Les prisons d'état en 1812," *Revue Historique de la Révolution et l'Empire*, 1916, pp. 84–94. According to Jacques Godechot (*Institutions*, p. 637), the number had risen to 2500 by 1814.

33. *Moniteur Universel*, February 19 to March 1, 1810.

34. Ibid., February 7, 1810.

35. Ibid., February 7, 16, 18, 1810; Louis Tripier (ed.), *Les Codes français* (Paris: Cotillon, 1859), pp. 824–31. For any second offense, the penalty was raised one level in the scale of punishments. Vagrancy was punishable by a prison term of three to six months, followed by police surveillance; penalties for begging varied from three months to two years of prison, depending on the circumstances.

36. *Moniteur Universel*, February 18, 1810.

37. Ibid., 8 pluviose An IX.

38. Esmein, *History of Continental Criminal Procedure*, pp. 465–87; Maurice Sabatier, "Napoléon et les Codes criminelles," *Revue Pénitentiaire*, XXXIV (1910), 911ff.

39. Duvergier, *Collection complète*, III, 303.

40. Quoted in Richard Cobb, *Reactions to the French Revolution* (London: Oxford Univ. Press, 1972), p. 166.

41. Archives Nationales, $F^{16}1018$.

42. Ibid.; Duvergier, *Collection complète*, XII, 357.

43. Archives Nationales, $F^{16}1018$.

44. Quoted in Cobb, *Reactions to the Revolution*, p. 166.

45. Duvergier, *Collection complète*, XVI, 283–84.

46. Archives Nationales, $F^{16}308$.

47. G. Stefani et al., *Criminologie et science pénitentiaire* (Paris: Dalloz, 1972), p. 350.

48. Camille Bloch and Alexandre Tuetey (eds.), *Procès-verbaux et rapports du Comité de Mendicité de la Constituante 1790–1791* (Paris: Imprimerie nationale, 1911), pp. 531–32.

49. Michel Devèze, *Cayenne: déportés et bagnards* (Paris: Julliard, 1965), pp. 40–41.

50. Etienne Dupont, *Les Prisons de Mont-Saint-Michel* (Paris: Perrin, 1913), pp. 181–96. During the Empire, royalist dissidents were also confined at Mont-Saint-Michel while awaiting transportation.

51. Devèze, *Cayenne*, pp. 38–39; Jean Ollier, *Convient-il d'abolir la transportation à la Guyane?* (Paris: Mechelinck, 1932), pp. 9–11.

52. Devèze, *Cayenne*, pp. 51–71.

53. Jean-Marie Destrem, *Les Déportations du Consulat et de l'Empire* (Paris: Jeanmaire, 1885), pp. 35, 56, 66, 94, 126, 151.

## Chapter III: Age of the *Philanthropes* (1789–1814)

1. Théodore Homberg, *Etudes sur le vagabondage* (Paris: Forestier, 1880), p. 109.

2. Louis Chevalier, *Classes laborieuses*, esp. pp. iii–xiv. J.-H. Donnard, in *Les Réalités économiques et sociales dans la Comédie Humaine* (Paris: Colin, 1961), also cites evidence of social fear in the Paris press of the 1840s (p. 208), and H.-A. Frégier, in a classic study of the time, estimated that as many as one-third of the working class could be described as potentially vicious or dangerous. *Des classes dangereuses dans la population dans les grandes villes* (Paris: Baillière, 1840). Cf. also the alarmist reaction of the journalist Léon Faucher, who called for immediate measures "to clear out of our streets and public squares the bandits who have taken possession of them" ("De la réforme des prisons," *Revue des Deux Mondes*, February 1, 1844, p. 377).

3. On Hugo, Savey-Casard, *Le Crime et le peine dans l'oeuvre de Victor Hugo*; on Vidocq and Lacenaire, Gordon Wright, *Insiders and Outliers* (San Francisco: Freeman, 1982), ch. 2.

4. On the highly controversial question of the relationship between urbanization and crime, see especially Denis Szabo, *Crimes et villes: étude statistique de la criminalité urbaine et rurale en France et en Belgique* (Paris: Cujas, 1960). There is also a detailed discussion in Léauté, *Criminologie et science pénitentiaire*, pp. 308–44.

5. Comte Adrien de Gasparin, *Rapport au roi sur les prisons départementales* (Paris: Imprimerie royale, 1837), pp. 8–12.

6. Ibid.

7. Léauté, *Criminologie et science pénitentiaire*, p. 209; Henri Joly, *La France criminelle* (Paris: Cerf, 1889), ch. I. Alexis de Tocqueville, in the Chamber of Deputies on June 20, 1840 (*Moniteur Universel*, June 24, 1840), reported that the number of arrests and/or indictments from 1827 to 1838 had increased from 65,000 to 89,000—five times as fast as the growth in population. But most of the increase, he added, was in misdemeanors.

8. *Moniteur Universel*, June 24, 1840; April 25, 1844.

9. Louis Marquet de Vasselot, *Ethnographie des prisons* (Paris: Boutarel, 1854), p. 9. The novelists Balzac and Sue reinforced this view with their lurid descriptions of the physical traits that made criminals, in their opinion, a kind of race apart. Balzac also found a close relationship be-

tween criminals and madmen: "When you look at the prisoners in the courtyard of the Conciergerie and the madmen in the garden of an asylum, it's the same thing" (*Splendeurs et misères des courtisanes* [Paris: Gallimard, 1948], pp. 1041, 1049). Eugène Sue, in *Les Mystères de Paris* (Brussels: Méline, 1844), III, 412–15, described a series of convicts as resembling a fox, a tiger, a bird of prey, a serpent: ". . . almost all of them bore a frightful resemblance to wild beasts."

10. Moreau-Christophe, *De la réforme des prisons*, p. 360.

11. C. Granier, "Un réformatoire en 1814," *Revue Pénitentiaire*, XXII (1898), 219.

12. Duc F.-A.-F. de La Rochefoucauld-Liancourt, *Des prisons de Philadelphie, par un européen* (Paris: Du Pont, 1796); later editions 1799, 1800, 1819.

13. Savey-Casard, *Le Crime et la peine dans l'oeuvre de Victor Hugo*, p. 12.

14. Comte Joseph de Maistre, *Les Soirées de Saint-Petersbourg, ou entretiens sur le gouvernement temporel de la providence* (Paris: La Colombe, 1960), pp. 39–41.

15. Foucault, *Surveiller et punir*, pp. 61–67, 104–5. Michelle Perrot has also suggested that the idea of a criminal class was a bourgeois device to divide the working class (Michelle Perrot [ed.], *L'Impossible Prison* [Paris: Seuil, 1980], pp. 291, 299).

16. Archives nationales, F⁷6960. There are two full-scale biographies of Liancourt: Ferdinand Dreyfus, *Un Philanthrope d'autrefois: La Rochefoucauld-Liancourt, 1747–1827* (Paris: Plon, 1902), and J.-D. de La Rochefoucauld, *Le Duc de La Rochefoucauld-Liancourt, 1747–1827* (Paris: Perrin, 1980).

17. The committee's reports, most of them written by Liancourt, have been edited by Bloch and Tuetey, *Procès-verbaux et rapports du Comité de Mendicité*.

18. Rochefoucauld-Liancourt, *Des prisons de Philadelphie* (1819 edition), *passim*.

19. Dreyfus, *Un Philanthrope*, pp. 463–64. On this abortive experiment, see also C. Granier, "Un réformatoire," pp. 219–38.

20. Rochefoucauld-Liancourt, *Des prisons de Philadelphie*, p. ix.

21. Dreyfus, *Un Philanthrope*, pp. 465–66.

22. Alphonse Bérenger, *De la justice criminelle en France* (Paris: L'Huillier, 1818), pp. iii, 2, 384–88.

23. Charles Daru and Victor Bournat, "La Société Royale des Prisons, 1819–1830," *Bulletin de la Société Générale des Prisons*, II (1878), 55–60; Benjamin Appert, *Bagnes, prisons, et criminels* (Paris: Guilbert, 1836), IV, 189ff. Hard-liners scoffed at the members of the society as "cousins of

Tartuffe, playing the charity comedy" (G.-G Claveau, *De la police de Paris* (Paris: Pillot, 1831), p. 239).

24. Daru and Bournat, "La Société Royale," pp. 70–71.

25. Ibid., pp. 288–91.

26. Ibid., pp. 288–91. Barbé-Marbois's reports are preserved in the Archives Nationales, dossier C2749. These accounts of prison conditions were confirmed in the prefects' replies to a ministerial questionnaire; most prisons, they declared, were "breeding-places of physical and moral infection" (Daru, pp. 61–66). As late as 1837 Minister of Interior de Gasparin admitted that many insane persons were still incarcerated in prisons and in the worst quarters there. Gasparin, *Rapport au roi*, p. 17. Prison Inspector Moreau-Christophe retorted, however, that this practice could not be abandoned because it was financially impossible to build a mental hospital in each department. Jean Bancal, "L'oeuvre pénitentiaire de la Restoration et de la Monarchie de Juillet," *Revue de Science Criminelle,* VI (1941), 222.

27. Gasparin, *Rapport au roi*, pp. 10–12.

28. *Moniteur Universel*, August 2, 1829.

29. Ibid., January 31, 1830. Montbel's suggestions were limited to special treatment for juveniles and increased severity for recidivists. There is some irony in the fact that only a few months later Montbel himself was a fugitive from justice, condemned in absentia to a life sentence in prison and permanent loss of civil rights *(mort civile)* .

30. Martignac reported in 1829 that of the 17,378 inmates of the *maisons centrales,* 14,800 were now working regularly for private entrepreneurs, at a wage 20 per cent below that of free workers. Inmates of all prisons, he declared, now received a daily ration of 1½ pounds of bread and vegetable soup; clothing was provided for the most indigent; in the *maisons centrales* bedsheets were changed monthly and nightshirts weekly; and the Sisters of Charity were beginning to provide nursing services in some prisons.

31. The best account of the *Société's* activities may be found in Dreyfus, *Un Philanthrope,* pp. 492ff.

32. Archives Nationales, F⁷6960. A list of professors who belonged to this organization "judged dangerous by the government" was sent by the minister of interior to the Grand Master of the University, who promised to take appropriate action (February 26, 1824) .

33. Dreyfus, *Un Philanthrope,* pp. 498–500. The *Société's* membership included fifteen Protestant pastors but only two priests.

34. Ibid., pp. 356–70. In 1823 when the *Conseil général des prisons* was purged, Liancourt had angrily resigned rather than continue to serve in what he called "this phantom council." The government promptly dis-

missed him from five other advisory or administrative posts, whereupon Liancourt pointed out ironically that the authorities had overlooked one (ibid., pp. 331–32).

35. Lucas (1803–89) was the son of a civil servant stationed in Brittany. The best account of his career is Jean Pinatel, "La vie et l'oeuvre de Charles Lucas," *Revue Internationale de Droit Pénal*, XVIII (1947), 121–54; see also the eulogy in the *Bulletin de la Société Générale des Prisons* (1886), 417ff. The most influential of his many writings were his essay *Du système pénal et du système répressif en général* (Paris: Béchat, 1827) and his massive work *De la réforme des prisons ou de la théorie de l'emprisonnement* (3 vols., Paris: Legrand, 1836–38). His last book appeared shortly before his death: *De l'état anormal de la répression en matière de crimes capitaux* (Paris: Pédone, 1885).

36. Savey-Casard, *Le Crime et la peine dans l'oeuvre de Victor Hugo*, pp. 28f; Herbert J. Hunt, *Le Socialisme et la romantisme en France: étude de la presse socialiste de 1830 à 1848* (Oxford: Clarendon Press, 1935); E. Fournière, *Les Théories socialistes au XIXe siècle* (Paris: Alcan, 1904).

37. Ibid., pp. 269–70; Jean Savant, *La Vie fabuleuse et authentique de Vidocq* (Paris: Seuil, 1950); François-Eugène Vidocq, *Mémoires* (Paris: Tesson, 1828).

38. Gasparin, *Rapport au roi*, p. 14.

39. George W. Pierson, *Tocqueville and Beaumont in America* (New York: Oxford Univ. Press, 1938), pp. 27–33. The two men seized upon the current interest in prison reform to justify their real purpose, which was to visit the United States and, incidentally, to escape service with the new monarchy, of which they disapproved.

40. Alphonse Bérenger, *De la répression pénale, de ses formes et de ses effets* (Paris: Cosse, 1855), I, 212.

41. *Archives parlementaires*, 2d série, LXXI, 475ff. For the debate in the two chambers, ibid., LXXI, 759ff.; LXXII, 16ff.; LXXVI, 149ff., 441ff., 516ff., 622ff.; LXXVII, 344.

42. Moreau-Christophe, *De la réforme des prisons*, pp. 111, 212; *Moniteur Universel*, April 25–26, 1844 (Peyramont). During the 1844 debate in parliament, the lawyer-deputy Crémieux vigorously challenged the critics of the 1832 reform; his statistics suggested that repression since that time had been more effective and certain than before. Likewise the reformer Alphonse Bérenger, reminiscing twenty years after the reform, concluded that it had definitely increased the proportion of convictions by juries (Bérenger, *De la répression pénale*, I, 216).

43. Pierson, *Tocqueville*, pp. 681ff.

44. Beaumont and Tocqueville, *On the Penitentiary System*, passim.

45. André Normandeau, "Politique et réforme pénitentiaire: le cas

de la France (1789–1875)," *Revue de Science Criminelle*, n.s. XXV (1970), 613–14.

46. Léon Faucher, *De la réforme des prisons* (Paris: Angé, 1838), pp. 7–10.

47. Marquis de la Rochefoucauld-Liancourt, *Examen de la théorie et de la pratique du système pénitentiaire* (Paris: Delaunay, 1840).

48. Marquet de Vasselot, *Ethnographie des prisons*, p. 155; Vingtrinier, *Des prisons*, p. 19; Marquis Ernest de Blosseville, *Histoire de la colonisation pénale* (Evreux: Hérissey, 1859), p. xxiii.

49. Moreau-Christophe, *De la réforme des prisons*, pp. 359–60.

50. Alexandre de la Ville de Mirmont, *Observations sur les maisons centrales de détention, à l'occasion de l'ouvrage de MM. de Beaumont et de Tocqueville* (Paris: Crapelet, 1833).

51. Moreau-Christophe, *De l'état actuel des prisons en France* (Paris: Desriz, 1837), pp. 345–46; *De la réforme des prisons*, pp. 120, 168, 212, 236, 246–47, 360, 364.

52. *Moniteur Universel*, November 6, 1839.

53. Archives parlementaires, 2d série, LXXXXVIII, 465–66. Guizot's stance was in sharp contrast with his view expressed in 1822: "Laws find their strength more in men's consciences than in their fears. The reprobation and shame that are publicly attached to certain actions are more effective than fear of the punishments that might follow" (François Guizot, *De la peine de mort en matière politique* [Paris: Béchet, 1822], pp. 34–35).

54. Balzac, *Splendeurs et misères des courtisanes*, pp. 933–36.

55. Sue, *Les Mystères de Paris*, III, 424.

56. André Dupin, *Observations sur plusieurs points importans de notre législation criminelle* (Paris: Baudouin, 1821), pp. 228–29. Dupin borrowed the passage from an eighteenth-century Rouen lawyer named Servin.

57. The new prison was so named to distinguish it from La (Grande) Roquette next door, where executions by guillotine were carried out until 1903. La Petite Roquette was demolished in 1974, despite a campaign by architectural specialists to preserve it as a unique monument of its time.

58. The reformer Alphonse Bérenger told a special commission in 1846 that the experience at La Roquette had converted him from a critic to an advocate of the cell system; the health of young offenders there had improved, he said, and they had been taught a trade as well as the three R's. Archives Nationales, C928 (March 27, 1846).

59. Marquis de La Rochefoucauld-Liancourt, *Conséquences du système pénitentiaire* (Clermont: Corbon, 1841), p. 122.

60. *Moniteur Universel*, July 13, 1838.

61. Ibid., May 15, 1839.

62. Moreau-Christophe, *De la réforme des prisons*, pp. 433–37.

63. Beaumont and Tocqueville, *On the Penitentiary System*, pp. 33, 84.

64. The government boasted that after only four months, the new disciplinary rules had already restored order in the prisons (*Moniteur Universel*, October 4, 1839). Criticism continued nevertheless: see, for example, the debate in the Chamber of Deputies in 1844 (ibid., April 23, 1844 [Corne]). The prison official Jean Bancel, writing in 1941, observed that most of the rules established by the Gasparin circular were still in effect a century later and that they had proved effective (Bancel, "L'oeuvre pénitentiaire," pp. 244–45). On the issue of crimes committed in prison in an effort to get transfer to the *bagnes*, see Bérenger, *De la répression pénale*, I, 330, and the debate in the Chamber of Deputies in 1844 (*Moniteur Universel*, April 25, 1844 [Peyramont and Duchâtel]).

65. Rochefoucauld-Liancourt, *Conséquences*.

66. Ibid., pp. 81–82.

67. Bérenger, *De la répression pénale*, I, 297. Bérenger recalled having seen a prisoner at Mont-Saint-Michel who had been confined for eleven months in a dark and humid *cachot* cut into the rock. Visitors to the abbey in our day are sometimes shown these *cachots*, in which few men can stand upright.

68. *Moniteur Universel*, March 5 and July 7, 16, 20, 1837. The officials admitted that the first consignment of convicts had to be carried from the *voiture cellulaire* on arrival; their heavy chains and cramped quarters had left their legs so swollen and scarred that they could not walk. These technical flaws were corrected before the next shipment (ibid., July 20, 1837).

69. Naval authorities repeatedly urged the government or the parliament to suppress the *bagnes* and usually proposed transportation of their inmates: e.g., Caffareli in 1809, the Simeon commission in 1818–19, du Hamel in 1826, Tupinier in 1838. Tupinier described the *bagnes* as costly, corrupting, and "a veritable plague" for the navy (Vénuste Gleizes, *Mémoire sur l'état actuel des bagnes en France* (Paris: Imprimerie royale, 1840), part II, pp. 8–27).

70. Ibid., part I, pp. 4–31; part III, pp. 18ff., 37ff.

71. Archives Nationales, C928 (minutes of the special commission on prison reform, February 14, 1846).

72. Frédéric Demetz and Abel Blouet, *Rapports à M. le comte de Montalivet sur les pénitenciers des Etats-Unis* (Paris: Imprimerie royale, 1837).

73. Bancal, "L'oeuvre pénitentiaire," p. 241.

74. *Moniteur Universel*, May 10, 1840; Charles de Rémusat, *Mémoires de ma vie* (ed. C. H. Pouthas, Paris: Plon, 1960), III, 179–80, 326.

75. *Moniteur Universel,* June 24, 1840.

76. Ibid., April 17–18, 1843.

77. Ibid., July 6, 1843.

78. Ibid., April 27, 1844.

79. Ibid., April 25, 1844.

80. Ibid., May 9, 1844.

81. Ibid., April 24, 1844.

82. Ibid., May 8, 1844..

83. Ibid., April 25 and 25, 1844.

84. Ibid., May 7, 1844.

85. Blosseville, *Histoire de la colonisation pénale,* pp. 499–508; *Moniteur Universel,* April 15, 1819; June 7, 1826; November 24–25, 1831.

86. *Moniteur Universel,* May 7, 1844.

87. Ibid., April 23, 1844.

88. Ibid., April 24, 1844.

89. Ibid., April 25, 1844.

90. Ibid., May 3, 1844.

91. Ibid., May 7, 1844.

92. In the confusion of the final voting, the exhausted Chamber accepted a sub-amendment presented by Odilon Barrot authorizing the courts to limit solitary confinement prior to transportation to five rather than ten years. The longer period in solitary, Barrot argued, would make a prisoner a kind of vegetable, unfit to make a new start overseas. This change appears to have slipped through almost unnoticed (*Moniteur Universel,* May 16, 1844) .

93. Ibid., May 15, 1844.

94. The minutes of the special commission are in the Archives Nationales, dossier C928.

95. *Moniteur Universel,* May 1, 1847.

96. The best account of the Mettray experiment is in Henri Gaillac, *Les Maisons de correction, 1830–1945* (Paris: Cujas, 1971) . There is a hostile description in Foucault's *Surveiller et punir,* 300ff.

97. La Petite Roquette, intended originally as a prison for women, was diverted instead to juvenile offenders. At first it was organized on the Auburn plan, with isolation at night and common workshops; in 1838 it was converted to the Philadelphia plan of day-and-night isolation with work and lessons in the cell. Recidivism declined sharply during the next decade, strengthening the case of the advocates of solitary confinement. But new problems emerged in the 1850s, throwing doubt on the great experiment (Géo. Bonneron, *Notre Régime pénitentiaire: les prisons de Paris* [Paris: Firmin-Didot, 1898], pp. 211–14) .

## Chapter IV: Two Steps Forward, Two Steps Back (1848–1870)

1. Comité National du Centenaire de 1848. *Procès-verbaux du Gouvernement Provisoire et de la Commission du Pouvoir Exécutif (24 février–22 juin 1848)* (Paris: Imprimerie nationale, 1950), p. 12. Cited hereafter as *Procès-verbaux 1848*. The rhetoric was surely that of Alphonse de Lamartine, the leading figure in the new government.

2. *Procès-verbaux 1848*, p. 92; Michelle Perrot (ed.), *L'Impossible Prison: recherches sur le système pénitentiaire au XIXe siècle* (Paris: Seuil, 1980), p. 300.

3. Perrot, *L'Impossible Prison*, p. 301.

4. Ibid., pp. 287–92.

5. Ibid., pp. 287–90; Archives Nationales, BB$^{18}$1466. This dossier in the Archives contains a bulky file on the *maison centrale* at Clairvaux, where the entrepreneur was charged with involuntary homicide and was eventually convicted (see below, p. 87). In August 1848 a serious riot occurred at Clairvaux, provoked by an outbreak of illness from tainted food. Charles Lucas, who had been sent in as temporary director a few days earlier, was credited with bringing the rioters under control by seizing the two ringleaders, one with each hand, and herding the inmates back into their sleeping quarters (Archives Nationales, BB$^{18}$1466; *Moniteur Universel*, August 23, 1848).

6. *Procès-verbaux 1848*, p. 12. In fact, no political offenders had been executed since 1822.

7. Jean Pinatel, "La Révolution de 1848 et le système pénal," *Revue de Science Criminelle*, IX (1948), 552.

8. *Moniteur Universel*, August 20, 1848.

9. Ibid., June 16–17, 1848; Archives Nationales, C918 and C2780; *Procès-verbaux 1848*, pp. 52, 60, 276; Jules Lalou, *De l'emprisonnement pour dettes* (Paris: Cotillon, 1857), pp. vi–vii.

10. *Moniteur Universel*, August 20, 1848.

11. See below, pp. 102–3.

12. Duvergier, *Collection complète*, XXI, 139.

13. Barbé-Marbois, reporting in 1821 to the Royal Prison Society, strongly endorsed the treadmill for use in all French prisons (Archives Nationales, C2749); but some years later he rejected it just as strongly as "repugnant to French mores" (*Moniteur Universel*, August 4, 1829). Alphonse Bérenger, reporting to the peers in 1847 on the prison reform bill, suggested the use of some modified form of the treadmill in individual cells (ibid., May 1, 1847).

14. Archives Nationales, BB$^{18}$1466.

15. Hennequin, "Du travail dans les prisons," pp. 632–33. Hennequin scoffed at the government's argument and insisted that consumers did in

fact depress prices by threatening to buy prison-made products. He proposed borrowing the Belgian system, which confined prison production to items not manufactured by free Belgian workers. He was also critical of the entrepreneurial system, yet at the same time skeptical of state operation of prison workshops.

16. *Procès-verbaux 1848*, pp. 93–94.

17. Hennequin, "Du travail dans les prisons," p. 631; *Moniteur Universel*, August 19, 1848.

18. Perrot, *L'Impossible Prison*, pp. 287–90; cf. also fn. 5 above.

19. Pinatel, "La Révolution de 1848," pp. 554–55.

20. *Moniteur Universel*, August 19, 1848; November 15, 1851.

21. Ibid., November 15, 1851.

22. Ibid., March 11, 1851.

23. Ibid., February 26, 1852.

24. J.-J. Baude, "Du système pénal en France," *Revue des Deux Mondes*, September 1, 1855, p. 1037; Berlier de Vauplane, "Le cinquantenaire de Mettray," *Le Correspondant*, n.s. CXXV (October–December 1890), 855.

25. The best work on French policy toward juvenile offenders is Henri Gaillac, *Les Maisons de correction 1830–1945*. Jean Lebrun has studied another of these agricultural colonies, La Trappe, in Perrot, *L'Impossible Prison*, pp. 236–76. Lebrun lists fifty-eight such colonies for male juveniles—most of them privately established but a few state-operated.

26. Archives Nationales, C2875 (December 19, 1873).

27. Berlier de Vauplane, "Le cinquantenaire de Mettray," p. 868. Alphonse Bérenger in 1855 put the number of recidivists from Mettray at less than 10 per cent. *De la répression pénale*, I, 436–37.

28. Ibid., pp. 867–69; Gaillac, *Les Maisons de correction*, pp. 284ff.

29. The text of the law, with commentary, may be found in Gaillac, *Les Maisons de correction*, pp. 100–107.

30. Pinatel, "La Révolution de 1848," p. 558.

31. Gaillac, *Les Maisons de correction*, pp. 85–86.

32. Perrot, *L'Impossible Prison*, p. 305.

33. Devèze, *Cayenne*, p. 118.

34. *Procès-verbaux de l'Assemblée Législative*, April 4 et seq., April 18 et seq., June 7–8, 1850. Archives Nationales C*I 367.

35. *Moniteur Universel*, November 13, 1850.

36. Archives Nationales, C1002 (Léon Faucher's report on behalf of the commission).

37. Vincent Wright, "The Coup d'Etat of 1851," in Roger Price (ed.), *Revolution and Reaction* (London: Croom Helm, 1975), pp. 308–9.

38. *Moniteur Universel*, May 5, 1854. A sizable minority of the Mac-

kau commission had doubts about Guiana and proposed the annexation of New Caledonia for this purpose.

39. Ibid., February 21, 1852.

40. Ibid., February 21 and March 29, 1852.

41. Ibid., May 4–5, 1854.

42. Blosseville, *Histoire de la colonisation*, p. 562.

43. Devèze, *Cayenne*, p. 135.

44. Ibid., pp. 136–37; Ollier, *Convient-il d'abolir la transportation?*, pp. 104–5.

45. Devèze, *Cayenne*, p. 141.

46. Ibid., p. 142.

47. France, Ministère de la Justice, *Compte générale de l'administration de la justice criminelle, 1865* (Paris: Imprimerie Impériale, 1867), pp. xiv–xx. Cited hereafter as *Compte générale*, with relevant date. Retrospective surveys covering most of the nineteenth century include an official analysis by the ministry's statistician Yvernès in *Compte générale 1880*; Henri Joly, *La France criminelle* (Paris: Cerf, 1889); and Comte Othenin d'Haussonville, "Le combat contre le vice: la criminalité," *Revue des Deux Mondes*, April 1, 1887, pp. 564–98. "The oasis of criminality" was Alfred Fouillée's phrase, in his *La France au point de vue moral* (Paris: Alcan, 1906).

48. On the problems of interpreting criminal statistics, see Léauté, *Criminologie et science pénitentiaire*, pp. 195ff.; Thorsten Sellin and Marvin Wolfgang, *The Measurement of Delinquency* (New York: Wiley, 1964); and V. A. C. Gatrell and T. B. Haddon, "Criminal Statistics and Their Interpretation," in E. A. Wrigley (ed.), *Nineteenth Century Society* (Cambridge: Cambridge Univ. Press, 1972). I am aware of no two historical studies of French crime rates that agree, except when one copies the other's findings.

49. Alphonse Bérenger, *De la répression pénale*, I, v.

50. *Compte générale 1865*, pp. vii, xx. A recent study by a French sociologist finds that the total number of accused and indicted persons per 100,000 population dropped from 729.4 in 1854 to 455.1 in 1865. A. Davidovitch, "Criminalité et répression en France depuis un siècle (1851–1952)," *Revue Française de Sociologie*, II (1961), p. 39.

51. The ministry of justice's retrospective study in *Compte générale 1880* concluded that the number of major crimes (i.e., cases brought to jury trial) had remained fairly stable from 1826 to 1855, then had declined for a decade, and had fluctuated thereafter. Crimes against property, on the other hand, were down by 57 per cent over the half-century 1830–80; but the report concluded that both this decline and the relative stability of jury cases reflected the downgrading of many offenses to *délit* or police-court status. The analysis found that crimes against persons followed a more variegated pattern: during the half-century, homicide de-

clined slightly and serious assaults more rapidly (in the latter case through "correctionalization," at least in part), but infanticide and abortion increased, and morals offenses (especially rape and child molestation) tripled. The report was challenged as too optimistic by a number of writers of the time. Henri Joly (*La France criminelle*, p. 10) calculated that *criminalité générale* had risen by 133 per cent in fifty years; Louis Barthou, in his introduction to Louis André, *La Récidive* (Paris: Plon, 1892), pp. v ff., asserted that total crime had tripled; and Vicomte d'Haussonville in the *Revue des Deux Mondes*, April 1, 1887, pp. 566–72, claimed that major crimes had doubled and that misdemeanors had quadrupled. A recent study by Howard Zehr concludes that while the homicide rate declined during the nineteenth century, the assault rate rose and that this latter increase was greatest in 1855–70 ("The Modernization of Crime in Germany and France, 1830–1913." *Journal of Social History*, VIII [1975], 128, 140). The statistics obviously lend themselves to what one might call creative manipulation.

52. The eminent magistrate Arnould Bonneville de Marsangy asserted in 1864 that both crimes and misdemeanors had declined markedly during the Second Empire, but with two exceptions: infanticide and morals offenses against adults. His great concern, however, was "the frightening increase" in recidivism (*De l'amélioration de la loi criminelle*, II [Paris: Cotillon, 1864], 4–10, 20–21, 29). Another magistrate, Raymond Aylies, claimed that not only infanticide and rape but also fraud and insults to public officials were up sharply ("La question pénitentiaire en 1865," *Revue des deux mondes*, June 1, 1865, p. 710).

53. Léon Vidal, *Coup d'oeil sur la science pénitentiaire* (Paris: Chaix, 1869), pp. 40–44, 64–65; Jules Lalou, *Aperçu sur les motifs de la progression des cas de récidive en matière de criminalité* (Paris: Chaix, 1870).

54. *Compte générale 1880*, p. 98.

55. Ibid., pp. 55–56.

56. Ibid., pp. ix, xviii–xx. The lengthy debate over revision of the Code may be found in *Moniteur Universel*, April 11 to 19, 1863.

57. Ibid., April 11, 1863 (Baron de Beauverger).

58. Joseph Ortolan, *Eléments de droit pénal* (Paris: Plon, 1855), p. 75; cf. also Dr. Guillaume Ferrus, *Des prisonniers, de l'emprisonnement et des prisons* (Paris: Baillière, 1850), p. vi.

59. Bérenger, *De la répression pénale*, II, 25–55 (text of the Persigny circular). The critic quoted was a deputy, Léonce Hallez-Claparède, speaking in parliament: *Moniteur Universel*, April 11, 1863.

60. Dr. Prosper de Pietra Santa, *Mazas: études sur l'emprisonnement cellulaire* (Paris: Masson, 1853), pp. 1–31.

61. Fernand Desportes, *La Réforme des prisons* (Paris: Le Clerc, 1862), pp. 1, 58, 72ff.

62. Blosseville, *Histoire de la colonisation pénale*, p. xxi.

63. Leading advocates of cellular confinement during the Second Empire included the lawyer and reformer Fernand Desportes, the magistrates Alphonse Bérenger, Raymond Aylies, and Isidore Alauzet, the doctor and deputy Louis-François Lelut, and the deputy Léonce Hallez-Claparède. Opponents of the cell, headed by Charles Lucas, were equally persistent. A few reformers advocated more drastic changes: e.g., that all closed prisons be replaced by agricultural colonies. This was suggested by the republican deputy Jules Simon (*Moniteur Universel*, June 14, 1865) and by the jurist Edouard Desprez (*De l'abolition de l'emprisonnement* [Paris: Dentu, 1868], p. 151). The empire tried one experiment with an "agricultural penitentiary" in Corsica, but malaria decimated the inmates. The noted editor Emile de Girardin put forward the most sweeping proposal—namely, to replace most existing penalties by what he called *la publicité pénale*. This involved the recording and publicizing of any criminal act, which would follow the offender throughout his life in the form of a yellow identity card. *Du droit de punir* (Paris: Plon, 1871), pp. 307–8, 355.

64. Bérenger, *De la répression pénale*, I, 287; II, 252–55.

65. Desportes, *La Réforme des prisons*, p. 16.

66. Lalou, *Aperçu*, pp. 1–3.

67. Vidal, *Coup d'oeil*, pp. 6, 34–36.

68. Aylies, "La question pénitentiaire en 1865," *Revue des Deux Mondes*, Jan. 1, 1865, p. 708.

69. Ibid., pp. 716–20; *Revue Pénitentiaire*, XVI (1892), pp. 504–19; *Annales du Sénat et du Corps Législatif*, Session ordinaire de 1870, I, 329; III, 46–48, 71–76.

70. *Moniteur Universel*, April 11, 1863. Léon Vidal, on the other hand, admitted that recidivism was up even though the crime rate (he said) was down; but he rejected the charge that recidivism was traceable to the Empire's return to the common prison (Vidal, *Coup d'oeil*, pp. 45–46).

71. See above, p. XX.

72. Archives Nationales, C2780. The Baroche papers in the Bibliothèque Thiers contain a collection of press clippings supporting or attacking the government's proposal.

73. *Revue Pénitentiaire*, XXIII (1909), p. 324.

74. *Compte générale 1880*, p. 121.

75. Etienne Dupont, *La Bastille des mers* (5th ed., Paris: Perrin, 1933), pp. 42–50.

76. Ibid., p. 67.

77. Ibid., pp. 181–96.

78. Archives Nationales, F$^{16}$355A (director's reports 1818–22).

79. Jean B. Lechat, "Les prisons du Mont-Saint-Michel pendant la

Révolution," *Revue de l'Avranchin et du Pays de Granville* (September 1966), pp. 175–84.

80. Archives Nationales, F¹⁶355B (Duruisseau to Minister of Interior, undated); Prisoner Bonnet to Minister of Interior (June 15, 1823). Barbé-Marbois, who visited the prison in 1821, called it "healthy" and "the most secure prison in the world" (Archives Nationales, C2749).

81. Archives Nationales, F¹⁶355A (Prefect to Minister of Interior, August 28, 1818).

82. Duruisseau's reports to Paris, in dossier F¹⁶355A at the Archives Nationales, provide us with his side of the running battle with Vidal.

83. Archives Nationales, F¹⁶355B (Prefect to Minister of Interior, August 14, 1826).

84. La Rochefoucauld-Liancourt, *Conséquences du système péniten-tiaire*.

85. *Moniteur Universel*, April 27, 1844; Rochefoucauld-Liancourt's rebuttal in ibid., May 1, 1844.

86. Bérenger, *De la répression pénale*, I, 297.

87. *Moniteur Universel*, May 19, 1844.

88. Ibid.

89. Roger Jouet, "La maison centrale du Mont-Saint-Michel entre 1846 et 1853: tentatives de réformes et conflits administratifs," *Revue de l'Avranchin et du Pays de Granville* (September 1966), pp. 185–237. Among Régley's innovations was the preparation of the first visitor's guide to Mont-Saint-Michel.

90. Dupont, *La Bastille des mers*, pp. 339–41.

91. Roger Jouet, "Les Montois devant la suppression de la maison centrale (1863–1864)," *Annales du Mont-Saint-Michel* (1965), pp. 108–12. One of the most vigorous complainers was a merchant named Victor Poulard—a name familiar to modern tourists, who still savor the omelettes of Mère Poulard.

## Chapter V: Theory and Practice: From the Classical to the Positivist Era (1814–1914)

1. Quoted in Léauté, *Criminologie et science pénitentiaire*, p. 736.

2. Ortolan, *Eléments de droit penal*, p. 83; Rusche and Kirchheimer, *Punishment and Social Structure*, p. 101.

3. Michael Ignatieff, *A Just Measure of Pain: The Penitentiary in the Industrial Revolution* (New York: Pantheon, 1978), pp. 47–63.

4. Foucault, *Surveiller et punir*, esp. Part III.

5. Moreau-Christophe, *De la réforme des prisons*, pp. 62–72.

6. Baude, "Du système pénal en France," pp. 1050–51.

7. La Ville de Mirmont, *Observations*, p. 5.

8. Faucher, *De la réforme des prisons*, p. 6.

9. Gleizes, *Mémoire*, p. 33.

10. Vingtrinier, *Des prisons*, p. 173.

11. Archives Nationales, BB$^{18}$1466 (June 18, 1847).

12. The term "neo-classical" is a bit slippery, since French writers on crime have used it (and continue to use it) in different ways. Some of them employ it to describe the eclectic school of criminology that emerged at the end of the nineteenth century with Saleilles and Cuche. Others prefer to apply it (as I have done) to those theorists who, from the early nineteenth century, began to modify the "pure" classical doctrine.

13. Ortolan, *Eléments de droit pénal*, pp. 80–92.

14. Adolphe Franck, *Philosophie du droit pénal* (Paris: Baillière, 1864).

15. Quoted in Robert Castel, *L'Ordre psychiatrique: l'âge d'or de l'aliénisme* (Paris: Editions de Minuit, 1976), p. 40.

16. Outside of Paris, insane persons continued to be locked up in prisons (and often chained) for another generation. On Pinel's career see Castel, *L'Ordre psychiatrique*, pp. 85ff. Pinel's pioneering work has been denigrated recently by Michel Foucault and his school: Foucault, *Histoire de la folie à l'âge classique* (Paris: Gallimard, 1972), pp. 490–501. They accuse Pinel of substituting a new form of cruel repression for the old.

17. On Esquirol see Castel, *L'Ordre psychiatrique*, pp. 158ff.

18. Dr. Prosper Despine, *Psychologie naturelle: étude sur les facultés intellectuelles et morales* (Paris: Savy, 1868), II, 165ff., 245–47. The evolution of psychiatric ideas about crime during the nineteenth century is surveyed in Paul Broussole, *Délinquance et déviance: brève histoire de leurs approches psychiatriques* (Toulouse: Privat, 1978).

19. On Gall, see Georges Lantéri-Laura, *Histoire de la phrénologie* (Paris: Presses universitaires, 1970), and Erwin H. Ackerknecht, *Franz Joseph Gall, Inventor of Phrenology* (tr. Claire St. Leon, Madison: Univ. of Wisconsin Medical School, 1956).

20. See below, pp. 119–20.

21. Dr. Prosper Lucas, *Traité philosophique et psychologique de l'hérédité naturelle* (Paris: Baillière, 1847–50), I, 494.

22. Ibid., pp. 486, 494–500, 526–27.

23. Dr. Benedict Morel, *Traité des dégénérescences physiques, intellectuels et morales de l'espèce humain* (Paris: Baillière, 1857), pp. viii–ix.

24. Ibid., pp. 4, 688–91.

25. Dr. Charles Féré, *Dégénérescence et criminalité: essai physiologique* (Paris: Alcan, 1888), pp. 80, 120–29. For a fine analysis of the impact and broader implications of degeneracy theory, see Robert A. Nye's unpublished essay "Degeneration and the Medical Model of Cultural Crisis in the French *Belle Epoque*," in Seymour Drescher et al. (eds.), *Politi-*

*cal Symbolism in Modern Europe* (New Brunswick, N.J.: Transaction Press, 1982), pp. 19–41.

26. Dr. Eugène Dally, *Remarques sur les aliénés et les criminels au point de vue de la responsabilité morale et légale* (Paris: Masson, 1864), pp. 3, 37.

27. Drs. Valentin Magnan and Paul-Marie Legrain, *Les Dégénérés (état mental et syndromes épisodiques)* (Paris: Rueff, 1895), pp. 214–15.

28. Fernand Desportes, February 6, 1874 (Archives Nationales, C3008). Cf. E.-M. Caro, "La responsabilité morale et le droit de punir," *Revue des Deux Mondes*, August 1, 1873, p. 504.

29. Yvonne Marx, "Le mouvement de la 'Défense Sociale,'" *Esprit*, October 1954, pp. 450–51.

30. Cesare Lombroso, *L'uomo delinquente* (Turin: Bocca, 1876).

31. Lombroso's most eminent followers were the jurists Enrico Ferri (who coined the term "born criminal") and Raffaele Garofalo (who is supposed to have invented the word "criminology"). Lombroso subsequently expanded his book until it approached two thousand pages, and softened the sharp edges of his theory. On the centenary of *L'uomo delinquente* in 1976, French criminologists gathered in Paris to commemorate his work in warmly sympathetic spirit (*Revue de science criminelle*, XXXXII [1976], pp. 285–89; XXXVIII [1977], pp. 541–49).

32. Quoted in Louis Proal, *Le Crime et la peine* (3d ed., Paris, Alcan, 1899), p. 300. Unless otherwise noted, this edition will be cited henceforth.

33. Ibid., p. 2.

34. For an excellent analysis of this contest, see Robert A. Nye, "Heredity or Milieu: The Foundations of Modern European Criminological Theory," *Isis*, LXVII (1976), 335–55.

35. Ibid., p. 339. On Lacassagne's subsequent work and influence, see Henri Souchon, "Alexandre Lacassagne et l'Ecole de Lyon," *Revue de Science Criminelle*, XXXV (1974), pp. 533–59.

36. Nye, "Heredity or Milieu," p. 340.

37. Quoted in Arthur Desjardins, "Crimes et prisons," *Revue des Deux Mondes*, January 1, 1891, p. 173.

38. Gabriel Tarde, *La Philosophie pénale* (5th ed., Paris: Masson, 1900), pp. 49–50.

39. Nye, "Heredity or Milieu," pp. 344–53. The French school of criminal sociology was anticipated by the statistical studies of Adolphe Quételet (a Belgian) and A.-M. Guerry during the 1830s. Using the Ministry of Justice statistics, they sought correlations between crime levels and various social, economic, and geographical factors.

40. Letourneau's introduction to Cesare Lombroso, *L'homme criminel* (1st French edition, Paris: Alcan, 1887), pp. i–vii.

41. Ibid. (2d French edition, Paris: Alcan, 1896), pp. i–iii.

42. Georges Vacher de Lapouge, *Les Sélections sociales: cours libre de science politique professé à l'Université de Montpellier 1888–1889* (Paris: Thorin, 1896), pp. 320–24.

43. Joseph Maxwell, *Le Crime et la société* (Paris: Flammarion, 1912), pp. 262–74.

44. Louis Proal, *Le Crime et la peine* (Paris: Alcan, 1892); Georges Vidal, *Principes fondamentaux de la pénalité dans les systèmes les plus modernes* (Paris: Rousseau, 1890).

45. Proal, *Le Crime et la peine*, pp. xx–xxxii, 231–33.

46. Camoin de Vence, "Des erreurs et des dangers de l'anthropologie criminelle," *Revue Pénitentiaire*, XVI (1892), 311.

47. Quoted in *Revue Pénitentiaire*, XVI (1892), 311.

48. Ibid.

49. Gabriel Tarde in *Revue Pénitentiaire*, XXVII (1903), 159.

50. Haussonville, "Le combat contre le vice," p. 588. The theme of moral decay recurred constantly in discussions of the crime problem from the 1880s to 1914: e.g., *Revue Pénitentiaire*, XXXVI (1912), 659–60, 829ff., 841–44.

51. Dr. Emile Laurent, *L'Anthropologie criminelle et les nouvelles théories du crime* (2d ed., Paris: Société d'éditions scientifiques, 1893), pp. 76–79. Alfred Fouillée, *La France au point de vue morale* (Paris: Alcan, 1900), pp. 163–70; Vacher de la Pouge, *Les Sélections sociales*, pp. 122–25 (arguing that education had increased the level of crime and the sophistication of criminals); Camoin de Vence in *Revue Pénitentiaire*, XVI (1892), p. 311.

52. Proal, *Le Crime et la peine*, p. 240; Fouillée, *La France au point de vue morale,* p. 156; Henri Joly, "Le problème criminelle au moment présent," *Revue des Deux Mondes*, December 1, 1907, p. 703.

53. Haussonville, "Le combat contre le vice," p. 592; Fouillée, *La France au point de vue morale*, pp. 171–72. In 1910 the popular magazine *La revue* solicited answers from a number of leading experts and politicians on "criminality and the press"; most respondents shared the editor's view that the responsibility of the press for rising crime was too obvious to doubt. *La revue*, December 15, 1910, to February 15, 1911.

54. Adolphe Guillot, *Paris qui souffre* (Paris: Dentu, 1889), pp. 22–24.

55. Proal, *Le Crime et le peine*, p. 272.

56. Fouillée, *La France au point de vue morale*, pp. 185–86; Paul Cuche, *Traité de science et de législation pénitentiaire* (Paris: Librairie générale de droit, 1905), pp. 22–23; Tarde, *La Philosophie pénale*, p. 457; *Revue Pénitentiaire*, XXXVI (1912), 678–9, 841.

57. E.g., *Journal Officiel, Débats de la Chambre*, December 5, 1889, pp. 306–10; November 4, 1903, pp. 202–3.

58. Emile Durkheim, *Les Règles de la méthode sociologique* (Paris: Alcan, 1895), and *De la division du travail social* (Paris: Alcan, 1893). On Durkheim's crime theories see Jean Pinatel, "La pensée criminologique d'Emile Durkheim et sa controverse avec Gabriel Tarde," *Revue de Science Criminelle*, XX (1959), 435–42; and W. A. Lunden's essay in Hermann Mannheim (ed.), *Pioneers in Criminology* (Chicago: Quadrangle, 1960), pp. 288–40.

59. Fernand Brunetière, "Savans et moralistes," *Revue des Deux Mondes*, November 1, 1891, pp. 205–16; Fouillée, *La France au point de vue morale*, pp. 399ff.; Gabriel Tarde, *La Philosophie pénale*, pp. 1–6.

60. Robert A. Nye, "Degeneration and the Medical Model"; Théodule Ribot, *Les Maladies de la volonté* (Paris: Alcan, 1884), p. 150.

61. Raymond Saleilles, *The Individualization of Punishment* (tr. Rachel Gastrow, Boston: Little, Brown, 1911), pp. 9–10, 126–27, 165–68.

62. Cuche, *Traité de science*, pp. 14, 38–39.

63. Paul Cuche, "L'avenir de l'intimidation," *Revue Pénitentiaire*, XVIII (1894), 800–3.

64. Paul Cuche, "Le conflit des doctrines et la législation pénale," *Revue Pénitentiaire*, XXXVI (1912), 1178–83.


## Chapter VI: Incarcerators versus Transporters (1871–1914)

1. Jacques Rougerie, *Procès des communards* (Paris: Gallimard, 1978), pp. 17–21. Rougerie's detailed analysis shows that 3417 were sentenced to simple deportation, 1169 to deportation in a fortified enclosure, and 251 to hard labor. But the number who actually reached New Caledonia was somewhat smaller: cf. George Pisier, *Les Déportés de la Commune à l'Ile des Pins, 1872–1880* (Paris: Société des océanistes, 1971), pp. 7, 17–18, 37.

2. Archives Nationales, C2875.

3. Ibid., C3008. Most of Lucas's rare interventions during the commission's sessions were devoted to criticism of foreign observers, who had allegedly failed to credit France with the progress made since the 1820s.

4. The commission's hand-written minutes are bound in seven volumes, preserved in carton C3008 at the Archives Nationales. Minutes, reports, and supporting data were published at the time in a 1000-page volume, (XLV) of the *Annales de l'Assemblée Nationale* (Paris: Imprimerie du Journal Officiel, 1876).

5. Archives Nationales, C3008 (May 14, 17, 21, 24, 28, 1872).

6. Ibid., June 18, 1872.

7. Ibid., June 28 and July 2, 1872.

8. Ibid., May 7, 1872, and January 21, 1873.

9. Ibid., June 28, July 2 and 5, 1872.

10. Ibid., May 24 and 28, June 28, 1872.

11. Ibid., January 10, 14, 28, and 31, 1873.

12. Ibid., February 7, 1873 et seq.

13. Ibid., July 23 and 30, November 22 and 29, December 7, 1872.

14. Ibid., July 17, 1872.

15. Ibid., March 7 and 11, 1873.

16. Ibid., March 14, 18, 21, and 28, 1873.

17. Ibid., March 21 and April 1, 1873.

18. Ibid., March 21, 1873.

19. Comte Othenin d'Haussonville, "Le combat contre le vice," *Revue des Deux Mondes*, January 1, 1888, p. 159.

20. *Bulletin de la Société Générale des Prisons*, I (1877), 1–4, 42. Cited hereafter as BSGP.

21. Henri Joly, *Le Combat contre le crime* (Paris: Cerf, 1892), p. 160; Cuche, *Traité de science*, p. 264.

22. Ministère de la Marine, *Notice sur la transportation à la Guyane et à la Nouvelle Calédonia pendant les années 1868, 1869 et 1870* (Paris: Imprimerie nationale, 1874), pp. 30–31. Subsequent volumes in this irregularly published series will be cited henceforth as *Notice sur la transportation*, with appropriate date.

23. Rougerie, *Procès des communards*, pp. 17–21.

24. Pisier, *Les Déportés de la Commune*, pp. 7–43.

25. *Notice sur la transportation 1884*, p. 12.

26. Archives Nationales, C3008, July 19, 1872.

27. Ibid., June 7, 12, and 14, 1872.

28. Hubert-Ernest Michaux, *Etude sur la question des peines* (Paris: Challamel, 1872), preface.

29. *Compte général 1880*, p. 51.

30. Ollier, *Convient-il d'abolir la transportation?*, pp. 37–38.

31. Archives Nationales, C3276.

32. Ollier, *Convient-il d'abolir la transportation?*, p. 37; BGSP III (1880), 674ff.

33. The fullest account of Pallu de la Barrière's governorship may be found in the archives of the former Ministry of Colonies, Nouvelle Calédonie cartons 32 and 38.

34. Ibid., carton 32.

35. Ibid. (extract from *La Gironde*'s correspondent in Noumea, February 1, 1883).

36. L. Gauharou, *Rapport de la commission nommée par M. le Capitaine Pallu de la Barrière* (Noumea: Imprimerie du Gouvernement, 1884), pp. 3–5.

37. *Notice sur la transportation 1884*, p. 11.

38. Léon Moncelon, *La Bagne et la colonisation pénale en Nouvelle-*

*Calédonie* (Paris: Bayle, 1886), p. 56. Moncelon had been in New Caledonia for eleven years as a free colonist, and represented his fellow colonists on the advisory Conseil Supérieur des Colonies.

39. Ibid., p. 123. Moncelon's idea of appropriate punishment for insubordinate convicts was incarceration in a solitary cell for up to five years, with no work or distractions; the prisoner would be "completely abandoned to himself, face to face with his conscience." These "tombs of stone" would be, he admitted, "a frightful punishment." But "when a society wants to survive, its first duty to its citizens is security; it must not hesitate to rid itself of the monsters who ruin and devour it" (ibid., p. 35).

40. Archives Coloniales, Nouvelle Calédonie carton 38.

41. E.g., Jean Carol, *La Bagne* (Paris: Ollendorff, 1903), pp. 131–32; Emile Garçon in *Revue Pénitentiaire*, XXXIII (1909), 817; ibid., XXXIV (1910), 180.

42. This was the so-called Dislère commission. Ministère du Commerce, de l'Industrie et des Colonies, *Compte-rendu des travaux de la commission permanente du régime pénitentiaire pendant les années 1889 et 1890, par M. Dislère* (Melun: Imprimerie administrative, 1891). Chairman Dislère reported that the commission, "discarding the excessively humanitarian ideas that were dominant when the decree of 1880 was issued," had based its work on the idea that the real purpose of punishment was expiation, with rehabilitation a doubtful second goal. His commission not only imposed severe disciplinary rules, but also abolished wages for work in the *bagnes* and restricted the convicts' chances of access to agricultural concessions. Intimidation was needed, said Dislère, to restore order in the *bagnes*.

43. The official *Compte général* for 1880 contained a retrospective study of crime trends since 1825; it stimulated a great deal of interest and discussion. Most analysts concluded that both crime and recidivism had grown at an alarming rate, though Charles Lucas argued that crime had actually declined since 1825 and that petty offenders rarely became major criminals (BGSP, VI, 725–30).

44. BGSP, VI (1882), 295; Joseph Reinach, *Les Récidivistes* (Paris: Charpentier, 1882), pp. 7–8.

45. According to the Barodet for 1881, the electoral platforms of some thirty republican candidates included the proposal to transport recidivists.

46. Reinach, *Les Récidivistes*, pp. 1–10.

47. The *Société des Prisons* repeatedly discussed the bill at great length, with most members strongly against it (BGSP, VI [1882], 850–926; VII [1883], 12–21, 137; IX [1885], 676–713). The Chamber of Deputies debated the bill during a series of sessions in 1883 (April to July), and again in 1885 (May 9–12).

48. BGSP, IX (1885), 900.

49. Ibid., p. 688; *Journal Officiel, Débats de la Chambre*, May 9, 1885, p. 41.

50. BGSP, VI (1882), 876–77; IX (1885), 688, 696, 702.

51. BGSP, VII (1883), 20–21.

52. *Journal Officiel, Débats du Sénat*, February 6, 1885, p. 55.

53. *Journal Officiel, Débats de la Chambre*, April 26 and May 1, 1883, pp. 124 and 192. The term "relegation" was proposed by Deputy Marcou.

54. Ibid., May 12, 1885, pp. 80–83. The amendment was proposed by Monsignor Freppel, Bishop of Angers and a deputy. It was adopted by a wide margin, 334–70.

55. BGSP, IX (1885), 678, 706; *Revue Pénitentiaire*, XXXIII (1909), 673. Jules Leveillé, professor of criminal law in the Paris Faculty, was credited with lobbying this amendment through parliament. Cuche, *Traité de science*, p. 469.

56. The Chamber's list consisted of New Caledonia, the Marquesas Islands, the island of Phu-Quoc in Indochina, and Guiana (*Journal Officiel, Débats de la Chambre*, May 7, 1883, p. 217; BGSP, IX [1885], 680–81).

57. Among the most vigorous opponents of the bill in the Chamber were the monarchists Mgr. Freppel and Albert de Mun and the Socialists Martin Nadaud and Charles Amouroux. Amouroux, a member of the Commune, had been condemned to hard labor for life in New Caledonia. Elected a deputy in 1885, he insisted on speaking against the relegation bill although he was seriously ill. He was carried home from the Chamber after his speech, and he died two weeks later.

58. Albert de Mun, quoted in BGSP, IX (1885), 711.

59. Ibid., p. 702. Socialist Deputy Nadaud scolded his colleagues for succumbing to this "wave of public panic." The law ordered automatic relegation after two condemnations during a ten-year period for serious crimes (excluding those punishable by death or hard labor), or after three to seven convictions for lesser offenses, depending on their gravity.

60. "Paul Mimande" [Vicomte Paul-Marie La Loyère], *Criminopolis* (Paris: Lévy, 1897), p. 272; "Paul Mimande," *Forçats et proscrits* (Paris: Lévy, 1897), pp. 140ff.; Emile Chautemps, "La suppression de la rélégation," *Revue Bleue*, June 20, 1908, pp. 775–78; *Revue Pénitentiaire*, XXXII (1908), 1122–33.

61. *Revue Pénitentiaire*, XXXII (1908), 1122.

62. Ibid., XXXVII (1913), 108–12.

63. Louis André, *La Récidive* (Paris: Plon, 1892), pp. 48–52; Paul Cuche in *Revue Pénitentiaire*, XXXV (1911), 103–10; ibid., XXXVI (1912), 670, 83–84.

64. Ibid., XXVII (1903), 505.

65. *Journal Officiel, Débats de la Chambre*, February 25, 1888, p. 584.

66. *Revue Pénitentiaire,* XXIV (1900), 1451–66; ibid., XXVII (1903), 171–72; Cuche, *Traité de science,* pp. 428–30.

67. BGSP, XIII (1889), 875ff.; XV (1891), 119–20; Cuche, *Traité de science,* pp. 428ff.

68. *Revue Pénitentiaire,* XIX (1895), 1184ff.

69. Carol, *Le Bagne,* pp. 170–71. On the other hand Carol was appalled at the severity of the disciplinary punishments meted out to rule-breakers (pp. 203ff.).

70. *Revue Pénitentiaire,* XVI (1892), 97–101.

71. Ibid., XXII (1898), 721.

72. Ludovic Beauchet, *Transportation et colonisation pénale à la Nouvelle Calédonie* (Paris: Revue politique et parlementaire, 1898), p. 92; *Revue Pénitentiaire,* XXXI (1907), 164; XXXIII (1909), 510.

73. *Revue Pénitentiaire,* XXXVII (1913), 458.

74. Ollier, *Convient-il d'abolir la transportation?,* pp. 25, 247; *Notice sur la transportation 1884,* pp. 14, 95–96.

75. Ollier, *Convient-il d'abolir la transportation?,* pp. 239–73.

76. Jules Leveillé, *La Guyane et le question pénitentiaire coloniale* (Paris: Colin, 1886), pp. 35–40. Leveillé calculated a 6 per cent average, but official reports showed considerable fluctuation. In 1902 and 1903, for example, a yellow fever epidemic drove the rate up to 15 per cent, forcing suspension of *bagnard* convoys for a year (*Notice sur la transportation 1902–04,* pp. 1–10).

77. Leveillé, *La Guyane,* pp. 12–42.

78. *Revue Pénitentiaire,* XIX (1895), 49–50, 450.

79. "Mimande," *Forçats et proscrits,* pp. 315–128.

80. *Notice sur la transportation 1905–07,* p. 67; Devèze, *Cayenne,* p. 217; Ollier, *Convient-il d'abolir la transportation?,* pp. 104–5.

81. Henri Joly, "Le problème pénitentiaire au moment présent," *Revue des Deux Mondes,* February 1, 1910, p. 638.

82. Beauchet, *Transportation et colonisation pénale,* p. 8.

83. "Mimande," *Forçats et proscrits,* p. 21.

84. Gabriel Tarde, in *Revue Pénitentiaire,* XXVII (1903), 171–74, expressed serious doubts. An official of the Ministry of Interior argued that recidivism actually increased during the decade that followed adoption of the law on relegation, because of New Caledonia's reputation as a paradise (ibid., XXVII [1903], 307).

85. Emile Chautemps, "La faillite de la transportation des condamnés aux travaux forcés," *Revue Bleue,* June 6, 1908, pp. 709–11; June 13, 1908, pp. 741–43; June 20, 1908, pp. 775–78.

86. The debate occupied three long sessions, which were fully recorded

in the *Revue Pénitentiaire*, XXXIII (1909), 481–520, 641–81, and 793–850.

87. Ibid., pp. 509, 804–26.

## Chapter VII: Vagrants, Workers, Executioners (1880–1914)

1. Quoted in Henri Joly, *Le Crime: étude sociale* (Paris: Cerf, 1888), pp. 36ff.

2. Some crime specialists did show a lively and presumably genuine sympathy for citizens down on their luck; among them were Moreau-Christophe, Alphonse Bérenger, and the Comte d'Haussonville.

3. Camille Bloch, *L'Assistance et l'état en France à la veille de la Révolution* (Paris: Picard, 1908), pp. 47–48; Louis Moreau-Christophe, *Du problème de la misère et de sa solution chez les peuples anciens et modernes* (Paris: Guillaumin, 1851), III, 359, 376.

4. "Versailles de la misère" was Moreau-Christophe's phrase (*Misère*, p. 340). The *hôpitaux*, mostly founded by the church, had existed since the Middle Ages as refuges for the sick, aged, and indigent; Louis XIV sought to upgrade them by imposing central control, but his reform was ineffective.

5. Moreau-Christophe, *Misère*, p. 379; Bloch, *L'Assistance*, p. 51.

6. Bloch, *L'Assistance*, pp. 34–35; Le Trosne, *Mémoire*, pp. 4–9.

7. Le Trosne, *Mémoire*, p. 10.

8. Moreau-Christophe, *Misère*, p. 381; Bloch, *L'Assistance*, pp. 161–67.

9. Bloch and Tuetey, *Procès-verbaux du Comité de Mendicité*, pp. 523ff.

10. Fernand Dubief, *La Question du vagabondage* (Paris: Pasquelle, 1911), p. 309.

11. J. Ancel, "La politique criminelle," p. 224.

12. Bloch and Tuetey, *Procès-verbaux*, pp. 529–30; Moreau-Christophe, *Misère*, p. 389.

13. Moreau-Christophe, *Misère*, pp. 414ff.; Théodore Homberg, *Etudes sur le vagabondage* (Paris: Forestier, 1880), pp. 88–92.

14. Archives Nationales, C7487; Moreau-Christophe, *Misère*, pp. 433–36.

15. Archives Nationales, C7487.

16. Archives Nationales, C2749; Moreau-Christophe, *Misère*, pp. 450–52, 502–4.

17. Archives Nationales, F² I 1290–93.

18. Moreau-Christophe, *Misère*, p. 514. Among the classic private surveys of crime in that era were: H.-A. Frégier, *Des classes dangereuses dans la population dans les grandes villes* (Paris: Baillière, 1840); Dr.

Louis-René Villermé, *Tableau de l'état physique et morale des ouvriers* (Paris: Renouard, 1840); Baron Joseph de Gérando, *De la bienfaisance publique* (Paris: Renouard, 1839); Baron Bigot de Morogues, *Du pauperisme, de la mendicité et des moyens d'en prévenir les funestes effets* (Paris: Dondey-Depré, 1834); and Eugène Buret, *De la misère des classes laborieuses en Angleterre et en France* (Paris: Paulin, 1840).

19. Moreau-Christophe, *Misère*, p. 514 (citing Leroux); Karl Marx, "The Eighteenth Brumaire of Louis Bonaparte," in Robert C. Tucker (ed.), *The Marx-Engels Reader* (New York: Norton, 1972), p. 519.

20. Moreau-Christophe, *Misère*, pp. 514–19; Bérenger, *De la répression pénale*, II, 157. Moreau-Christophe calculated that if the average beggar took in two francs a day the cost to Frenchmen was 46 million francs a year—far higher than the cost of adequate state and private aid. Misery, he contended, could be eradicated in France if people would stop confusing it with poverty, which could not be ended.

21. Moreau-Christophe, *Misère*, p. 519.

22. Archives Nationales, C7487.

23. Adolphe Thiers, for example, urged in 1850 that the "vile multitude" of vagabonds be expelled from Paris; they were the most dangerous sector of society, he said, and they had brought down every republic to date (Chevalier, *Classes laborieuses*, p. 459).

24. Homberg, *Etudes sur le vagabondage*, preface. The Haussonville commission of 1872–75 had given only passing attention to the problem of vagrancy. One commissioner urged that they be placed in special workhouses rather than in prisons. Public security required their confinement, he said, but since they could not be moralized, they would only waste valuable prison space (Archives Nationales, C3008).

25. *Journal Officiel, Débats de la Chambre*, June 17, 1889; *Revue Pénitentiaire*, XIX (1895), 651ff.; XXII (1898), 98ff.; Alexandre Bérard, "Le vagabondage en France," *Archives de l'Anthropologie Criminelle*, XIII (1898), 601–4.

26. *Revue Pénitentiaire*, XXII (1898), 98ff.

27. Homberg, *Etudes sur le vagabondage*, p. 243. On the Freemasons' petition, Reinach, *Les Récidivistes*, p. 7.

28. *Journal Officiel, Débats de la Chambre*, May 12, 1885, pp. 80–83.

29. *Compte générale* (1880), p. 59; Henri Joly, *La France criminelle*, p. 20. Joly calculated that 72 per cent of the vagrants and beggars held for trial in a typical year (1883) were recidivists. Joly, *Le Combat contre le crime*, p. 340.

30. BSGP, VI (1882), 725–30.

31. Bérard, "Le vagabondage en France," pp. 601–14. Henri Joly took a more nuanced view of vagrancy as a fatal springboard to crime. Joly, *Le Crime*, pp. 36ff.

32. Bérard, "Le vagabondage en France," p. 607.

33. *Revue Pénitentiaire*, XIX (1895), 651ff.; XXII (1898), 1–40, 98ff.; XXIII (1899), 572–84. During the centennial year of the Great Revolution, whose leaders had set out confidently to extirpate begging, the Chamber spent some time discussing "the grave problem of vagrancy and begging, resurgent in central France" (BSGP, XIII [1889], 872ff.).

34. M. Lecour, "De la répression du vagabondage," BGSP, XV (1891), 570–88.

35. Georges Berry, *Les Mendiants* (Paris: Arnould, 1891), pp. 4–8. In the Chamber of Deputies, Berry was a vigorous advocate of severe controls on begging. The tiny Place Georges-Berry near the Opéra commemorates this long-forgotten politician.

36. Dr. Armand Pagnier, *Du vagabondage et des vagabonds: étude psychologique, sociologique et médico-légale* (Lyon: Storck, 1906), pp. 195ff.; Dr. Armand Marie and Raymond Meunier, *Les Vagabonds* (Paris: Girard, 1908), pp. 24–36 and Ch. II. The man who assumed the beggar's role was Louis Paulian, who published his experience in *Paris qui mendie: mal et remède* (Paris: Ollendorff, 1893).

37. Bérard, "Le vagabondage en France," pp. 602–4.

38. Dr. Armand Pagnier, *Le Vagabond* (Paris: Vigot, 1910).

39. Henri Joly, "Le problème criminel au moment présent," *Revue des Deux Mondes*, December 1, 1907, p. 685.

40. Archives Nationales, C7487; *Revue Pénitentiaire*, XXIV (1900), p. 1350; Joly, "Le problème criminel," p. 685. The official *Compte générale* for 1900 also blamed the magistrates for laxity.

41. *Revue Pénitentiaire*, XXIV (1900), 1350; XXVI (1902), 734–36; XXXVI (1912), 670.

42. Archives Nationales, C7487. On the various bills pending in the Chamber, see also *Journal Officiel, Documents de la Chambre*, LXXIX (1909), 524, and LXXX (1910), 8off., 118ff., 207ff.

43. Archives Nationales, C7487.

44. The minutes of this abortive commission, chaired by the single-minded Georges Berry, are in the Archives Nationales, C7775.

45. BSGP, II (1878), 392.

46. *Revue Pénitentiaire*, XXV (1901), 1120.

47. Karl Marx, "Critique of the Gotha Program," in Tucker (ed.), *The Marx-Engels Reader*, p. 398.

48. *Journal Officiel, Débats de la Chambre*, February 16, 1878, pp. 286–88; November 29, 1878, pp. 253–55.

49. Archives Nationales, C924.

50. For example, *Journal Officiel, Débats de la Chambre*, January 18, 1887, pp. 51–56; December 6, 1888, pp. 835–41.

51. BSGP, II (1878), 992; *Journal Officiel, Débats de la Chambre*, January 31, 1889; *Revue Pénitentiaire*, XXV (1901), 961.

52. *Revue Pénitentiaire*, XXV (1901), 963.

53. Roger Roux, *Le Travail dans les prisons* (2d edition, Paris: Rousseau, 1902), pp. 38, 134, 154ff.; Armand Mossé, *Les Prisons et les institutions d'éducation correctives* (3d edition, Melun: Imprimerie administrative, 1939), p. 246.

54. BSGP, XV (1891), 123–37; *Revue Pénitentiaire*, XVI (1892), 715–16.

55. BSGP, XV (1891), 1237.

56. *Revue Pénitentiaire*, XVI (1892), 716.

57. Ibid., XXV (1901), 1111.

58. *Journal Officiel, Débats de la Chambre*, January 31, 1899, pp. 314–18; Roux, *Le travail*, p. 152.

59. *Revue Pénitentiaire*, XXV (1901), 946; XXVII (1903), 1130–31; Roux, *Le travail*, p. 152.

60. *Revue Pénitentiaire*, XXV (1901), 964.

61. Brief and unsuccessful experiments in the use of outdoor work gangs were tried during the July Monarchy and the Second Empire. The Socialist deputy François Jourde (an ex-Communard) proposed it again in 1899, but other deputies protested that such gangs would compete with farm workers and manual laborers. Jourde responded rather lamely that since many workers of this sort were not Frenchmen, less damage would result (*Journal Officiel, Débats de la Chambre*, December 5, 1899, pp. 197–98).

62. For a fuller treatment of prison labor in the nineteenth century, see Patricia O'Brien, *The Promise of Punishment* (Princeton: Princeton Univ. Press, 1982), ch. 5.

63. Beccaria, *Traité*, pp. 139–45.

64. Brissot de Warville, *Théorie*, I, 147.

65. *Réimpression de l'Ancien Moniteur*, XV, 720–22, 733–36, 740, 751 (sessions of March 18 and 19, 1793). It was during this session that a member named Duhem delivered himself of a memorable mixed metaphor: "The ship of state is leaking at every seam. I ask for a solemn discussion of ways to heal the republic's wounds—for a philosophic report that will enlighten us and enable us to save the country."

66. Jean Imbert, *Peine de mort* (Paris: Presses universitaires, 1972), p. 145.

67. Georges O. Junosza-Zdrojewski, *Le Crime et la presse* (Paris: Jouve, 1943), p. 176; Jean-Claude Chesnais, *Les Morts violentes en France depuis 1826* (Paris: Presses universitaires, 1976), pp. 35–36.

68. Imbert, *Peine de mort*, p. 188.

69. Karr, in his memoirs, reminisced proudly about the impact of his phrase, and used it as his title: *Messieurs les assassins* (Paris: Lévy, 1885), p. 2.

70. *Revue Pénitentiaire*, XVIII (1894), 924ff.; XXXI (1907), 298ff.

71. Corps législatif 1870, *Compte rendu analytique*, pp. 123–31. Archives Nationales, C* I 414.

72. BSGP, II (1879), 398–402.

73. *Revue Pénitentiaire*, XVIII (1894), 924ff.; XXXVII (1913), 630; Junosza-Zdrojewski, *Le Crime et la presse*, pp. 180–81.

74. Chesnais, *Les Morts violentes*, pp. 35–38.

75. As usual, crime statistics at the time were interpreted in a variety of ways, though the Ministry of Justice and most criminologists agreed that there was a downward trend for a few years after 1896. Even in retrospect, there are uncertainties: see, for example, Jacques Léauté's analysis in his *Criminologie et science pénitentiaire*, pp. 211–12.

76. *Journal Officiel, Débats de la Chambre*, December 13, 1906, pp. 1036–43; *Gazette des Tribunaux*, December 9, 1908.

77. Archives Nationales, C7356 (Reinach's *exposé des motifs*).

78. Ibid. (bill introduced by Deputy Auguste Failliot).

79. *Revue Pénitentiaire*, XXXI (1907), 800–801. The government's revised version added a provision for six years of solitary confinement, followed by transportation for life to a penal colony.

80. The activities of two bandit gangs, the bande Pollot and the bande de la Drôme, were given extensive coverage. Both gangs were arrested, tried, and convicted, but their executions were suspended pending the outcome of the death penalty debate.

81. *Revue Pénitentiaire*, XXXI (1907), 400, 847, 1324.

82. Ibid., p. 1104.

83. Ibid., p. 1224.

84. Ibid., pp. 847–48; XXXII (1908), 1331; *Gazette des Tribunaux*, December 9, 1908.

85. Henri Joly, "Le problème criminel au moment présent," *Revue des Deux Mondes*, December 1, 1907, pp. 679, 686; *Gazette des Tribunaux*, December 7–8, 1908.

86. *Revue Pénitentiaire*, XXXII (1908), 1167.

87. Ibid., XXXI (1907), 848.

88. Ibid., XXXII (1908), 1162; *Gazette des Tribunaux*, December 9, 1908.

89. Ibid.

90. My account of this Chamber debate is drawn from the *Journal Officiel, Débats de la Chambre*, July 3, 1908, pp. 655–82; November 4, 11, and 18, pp. 379–415, 615–30, 850–63; December 7 and 8, pp. 1329–64; and

from the contemporary commentaries in the *Revue Pénitentiaire*, XXXII (1908), 1164-66, 1325-38, and the *Gazette des Tribunaux*, December 7-8 and 9, 1908.

91. Ibid.

92. Junosza-Zdrojewski, *Le Crime et la presse*, p. 182. The depredations of the Pollot gang are recounted in Philippe Kah, *Aux enfers du crime* (Lille: Bresle, 1930), pp. 63ff.

93. Chesnais, *Les Morts violentes*, pp. 35-38. In 1910 the Socialists attracted 8000 Parisians to a mass meeting to protest the imminent execution of a young "apache" who had killed a policeman. Speakers claimed that he was a victim of injustice through false arrest. This was apparently the only major public protest against the death penalty in the immediate prewar years (*Revue Pénitentiaire*, XXXIV [1910], 457, 828).

## Chapter VIII: Ebb Tide (1918-1940)

1. *Revue Pénitentiaire*, XLVI (1922), 916-17. Cf. also J.-A. Roux in *Revue Internationale de Droit Pénal*, III (1926), 189-98.

2. *Revue Pénitentiaire*, XLVI (1922), 916-17.

3. *Revue de Science Criminelle et de Droit Pénal Comparé*, I (1936), 1-3.

4. The *Revue Pénitentiaire* was resurrected in 1947 and has continued to appear alongside the *Revue de Science Criminelle*; it focuses more strongly on penal questions.

5. *Revue Pénitentiaire*, XLVI (1922), 46.

6. Henri Donnedieu de Vabres, *La Justice pénale d'aujourd'hui* (Paris: Colin, 1929), pp. 38-39, 147; Léauté, *Criminologie et science pénitentiaire*, pp. 210-13.

7. J.-A. Roux, *La Défense contre le crime: répression et prévention* (Paris: Alcan, 1922), pp. 14-16.

8. Donnedieu de Vabres, *La Justice pénale*, pp. 38-39. Retrospective studies of the statistics, as usual, make things more complicated. They agree that crime declined after 1922 and then fluctuated until World War II. They also suggest that while *crimes* (cases taken to the assize courts) were down as compared with the nineteenth century, *délits* (cases taken to the correctional courts) were up. The total number of cases tried per 10,000 population varied within a rather narrow range. The total number of offenses reported was considerably higher than it had been in the past, but so was the proportion of cases that were never brought to trial (Léauté, *Criminologie et science pénitentiaire*, pp. 205-14); A. Davidovitch, "Criminalité et répression en France," pp. 36-47; Otto Kirch-

heimer, "Remarques sur la statistique criminelle de la France d'après-guerre," *Revue de Science Criminelle*, I (1936), 363–96; *Annuaire statistique*, LIII (1937), 46*–47*, LVII (1946), 68*ff.

9. *Journal Officiel, Documents du Sénat*, 1928, p. 927.

10. Jean Pinatel, "La crise pénitentiaire," *L'Année Sociologique*, 3d series, no. 24 (1974), 29; Léauté, *Criminologie et science pénitentiaire*, pp. 792–93.

11. For example, Archives Nationales, C3008 (Haussonville commission minutes, December 17, 1872); Henri Joly, "Le problème pénitentiaire," pp. 659–65.

12. *Revue Pénitentiaire*, XLVI (1922), 69.

13. Ibid., 43–76, 352–75; Paul Cuche, "Examen de conscience pénitentiaire," *Revue de Science Criminelle*, I (1936), 4–8.

14. *Revue Pénitentiaire*, XLVI (1922), 46.

15. Armand Mossé, *Les Prisons et les institutions d'éducation corrective* (3d ed., Melun: Imprimerie administrative, 1939), p. 121.

16. Armand Mossé, *Les Prisons, exposé pratique du régime pénitentiaire en France* (Paris: Boccard, 1926), pp. 62–64; *Revue Pénitentiaire*, LIII (1929), 100–102.

17. *Revue Pénitentiaire*, LIII (1929), 100.

18. Ibid., pp. 102–3; Mossé, *Les Prisons* (3d ed.), pp. 84–85.

19. *Revue Pénitentiaire*, LIII (1929), 106–7; Mossé, *Les Prisons* (3d ed.), pp. 84–85, 133.

20. *Journal Officiel, Documents du Sénat*, 1928, pp. 928–29.

21. Ibid., pp. 928–29: *Documents de la Chambre*, 1929, p. 54.

22. Mossé, *Les Prisons* (3d ed.), pp. 170–72.

23. *Revue Pénitentiaire*, LXXXVIII (1964), 873–74; *Revue de Science Criminelle*, XXXI (1976), 732–35 (annual reports of directors of prison administration).

24. *Revue de Science Criminelle*, I (1936), 93–94, 572; II (1937), 712; *Revue Pénitentiaire*, LVII (1933), 203.

25. *Journal Officiel, Documents de la Chambre*, 1929, p. 54.

26. *Etudes criminologiques*, V (1930), 204.

27. My account in this paragraph is drawn from H. Gaillac, *Les Maisons de correction*, pp. 261–99.

28. Archives des Colonies, New Caledonia carton 233.

29. *The Nation*, CLIV (1942), 653.

30. The fullest account of policy zigzags at the *bagne* from 1854 to 1932 is Ollier's *Convient-il d'abolir la transportation?*

31. *Revue de Science Criminelle*, XI (1950), 225–26.

32. There is a recent journalistic study of Londres's career: Paul Mousset, *Albert Londres: ou, l'aventure du grand reportage* (Paris: Grasset, 1972).

33. *Journal Officiel, Débats de la Chambre*, November 12, 1924, pp. 129–39; Mossé, *Les Prisons* (1st ed., p. 211).

34. *Revue Pénitentiaire*, LV (1931), 108ff.

35. *Journal Officiel, Documents de la Chambre*, 1929, p. 55; *Etudes criminologiques*, V (1930), 27; *Revue de Science Criminelle*, II (1937), 89–91.

36. Some examples of this literature: Antoine Mesclon, *Comment j'ai subi quinze ans de bagne* (Paris: l'auteur, 1924); Jacques Dhur, *Visions de bagne* (Paris: Ferenczi, 1925); Louis Merlet, *Au bout du monde* (Paris: Delpeuch, 1928); L. Le Boucher, *Ce qu'il faut connaître du bagne* (Paris: Boivin, 1930); Géo. London, *Aux portes du bagne* (Paris: Portiques, 1930); Dr. Louis Rousseau, *Un Médecin au bagne* (Paris: Fleury, 1930); Georges Ferré, *Bagnards, colons et casaques* (Paris: Jouve, 1932); Henri Huchon, *Quand j'étais au bagne* (Bordeaux: Delmas, 1933); Marius Larique, *Dans la brousse* (Paris: Gallimard, 1933); Paul Roussenq, *Vingt-cinq Ans au bagne* (Paris: La Défense, 1934); Mireille Maroger, *Bagne* (Paris: Denoel, 1937).

37. The best-seller was Blair Niles, *Condemned to Devil's Island* (New York: Harcourt, 1928); it was enthusiastically praised by almost all American reviewers. Belbenoit himself eventually managed to leave Guiana and published his own memoirs: *Dry Guillotine: Fifteen Years Among the Living Dead* (New York: Dutton, 1938). It drew even more extravagant praise; critics used such terms as "shocking, awesome, exciting, monumental"; one reviewer outdid the rest by declaring that "nothing, in fact or fiction, has ever approached it" (*Book Review Digest*, 1938, p. 76). The *bagne* continued to exert its morbid fascination even after it had been liquidated—witness the literary success of Henri Charrière's *Papillon* (Paris: Laffont, 1969; New York: Morrow, 1970). Charrière's melodramatic tale of his own heroics earned him a half-million dollars for the movie rights as well as selection by the Book-of-the-Month Club.

38. Charles Péan, *Le Salut des parias* (Paris: Gallimard, 1935), pp. 47–50, 217.

39. *Revue Pénitentiaire*, XLIX (1925), 10–16, 25; Louis Hugueney, "Un projet de dispenses de la transportation," *Revue Internationale de Droit Pénal*, III (1926), 98–103; Ollier, *Convient-il d'abolir la transportation?*, pp. 2–8, 44ff., 273, 290.

40. Maurice Garçon, "Les bagnes," *Mercure de France*, CLXXCII (1925), 315–17.

41. *Revue Pénitentiaire*, XLIX (1925), 13; LX (1931), 110, 128; Armand Rouilleault, *La Suppression de la transportation* (Lyon: Grosjean, 1938), p. 66.

42. Rouilleault, *La Suppression*, pp. 105–6.

43. *Journal Officiel, Documents de la Chambre*, 1937, Annexe no. 2669.

44. *Revue de Science Criminelle*, III (1938), 512; Mossé, *Les prisons* (3d ed.), pp. 20, 373ff.

45. *Revue de Science Criminelle*, XI (1950), 225–28.

46. Maurice Garçon, in *Le Monde*, September 18–19, 1949; *Esprit*, November 1979, pp. 134–35.

47. *Revue de Science Criminelle*, XI (1950), 225–28.

48. *Le Monde*, April 24, 1982.

## Chapter IX: Old Issues, New Ventures (1944–1982)

1. See, for example, Michael R. Marrus and Robert O. Paxton, *Vichy France and the Jews* (New York: Basic Books, 1981), and Hervé Villeré, *L'Affaire de la section spéciale* (Paris: Fayard, 1973).

2. *Revue de Science Criminelle*, I nouvelle série (1946), 132–34. The Third Republic in 1911 had transferred the Penal Administration from its traditional locus in the Ministry of Interior to the Ministry of Justice, on the assumption that the new atmosphere would breed a spirit of penal reform. Instead, the Penal Administration remained intact in personnel and methods. Vichy, in a symbolic action, restored the agency to the Ministry of Interior.

3. Peter Novick, *The Resistance versus Vichy* (New York: Columbia Univ. Press, 1966), pp. 202–8.

4. Charles Germain, "Les nouvelles tendances du système pénitentiaire française," *Revue de Science Criminelle*, IX (1954), 43, 50. In 1962, a typical year, only 1,147 of 28,404 prisoners were working outside the prisons (*Revue Pénitentiaire*, LXXXVII [1963], 643).

5. *Revue de Science Criminelle*, I (1946), 276; XXX (1975), 891ff.

6. Ibid., I (1946), 141–43.

7. Ibid.; Léauté, *Criminologie et science pénitentiaire*, p. 100.

8. *Revue de Science Criminelle*, I (1946), 327–28; (1954), 57ff.

9. Georges Arnaud, *Prisone 53* (Paris: Julliard, 1953), p. 84. The relegation law of 1885 was not repealed until 1946. *Relégués* were imprisoned in France from 1946 until 1970, when the term "relegation" was removed from the criminal code.

10. Jean Pinatel, "L'évolution de la criminalité en France depuis la libération," *Revue de Science Criminelle*, IX (1954), 159; *Revue Pénitentiaire*, LXXXVII (1963), 629–30.

11. André Sauvageot, "Dévaluation de la peine," *Revue Politique et Parlementaire*, October 10, 1946, p. 19.

12. Several films directed by the ex-lawyer André Cayatte were harshly

critical of various aspects of the criminal justice system; two of them—
"*Justice est faite*" (1950) and "*Nous sommes tous des assassins*" (1952) —
won major film prizes.

13. Adolphe Prins, *La Défense sociale et les transformations du droit
pénal* (Brussels: Misch and Thron, 1910).

14. Gramatica founded his Center for the Study of Social Defense at
Genoa in 1945, and followed up with an International Society of Social
Defense in 1947.

15. Quoted in *Revue de Science Criminelle*, XXIV (1969), 914.

16. Ancel's manifesto, in *Défense sociale nouvelle* (Paris: Cujas,
1954), was extensively revised and expanded in a second edition dated
1966. He further elaborated his ideas in a series of papers read at subsequent penal congresses and round tables. A Festschrift by his admirers
was published in 1975: *Recueil d'études en hommage à Marc Ancel: aspects nouveaux de la pensée juridique* (2 vols., Paris: Pédone, 1975).

17. *Revue de Science Criminelle*, IX (1954), 41.

18. Roger Merle (ed.), *Les Mondes du crime* (Toulouse: Privat,
1968), pp. 29–30. The remedy appears to have been effective; armed
hold-ups declined thereafter.

19. Arnaud, *Prisons 53*, pp. 10–12, 91.

20. Jacqueline Peyron, "Institutions et réformes: quelques chiffres,"
*Esprit*, April 1955, p. 569.

21. Jean-Marc Théolleyre, "Ces inconnus dans la cité: nos prisons,"
*Le Monde*, April 11, 1967.

22. Annual report of Director of Penal Administration Robert
Schmelck, *Revue de Science Criminelle*, XIX (1964), 870. Of the 152
*maisons d'arrêt*, Schmelk scheduled 102 to be closed or rebuilt.

23. Jacques Vérin, "Faut-il encore des maisons d'arrêt et de correction?," ibid., XXI (1966), 635–36.

24. Annual report of Robert Schmelck, ibid., XVIII (1963), 618.

25. Jean-Marie Domenach, "Le détenu hors la loi," *Esprit*, February
1962, p. 164n; *Annuaire statistique de la France*, 1978, p. 154.

26. *Revue de Science Criminelle*, XIV (1959), 421–3; XV (1960),
101, 312–17.

27. Ibid., XIV (1959), 433 (Pierre Cannat).

28. In the past, parliament had repeatedly rejected proposals to adopt
probation—notably in cases of suspended sentences—on the ground that it
smacked of the old system of *surveillance de la haute police*, abolished
during the 1880s (Ahmed Lourdjani, "La probation en France," *Revue
Pénitentiaire*, CI [1977], 43–58).

29. Pierre Cannat in *Revue de Science Criminelle*, XV (1960), 317.

30. Jean-Marc Varant, *La Prison, pour quoi faire?* (Paris: Table
Ronde, 1972), p. 57. *Revue de Science Criminelle*, XXIX (1974), 426–27.

31. Annual reports of the Director of Penal Administration, *Revue de Science Criminelle*, XIII (1958), 880; XIV (1959), 369; XXIV (1969), 895; *Revue Pénitentiaire*, LXXXVII (1963), 620, 629–30.

32. J.-M. Théolleyre in *Le Monde*, April 11, 1967.

33. Jacques Léauté (ed.), *La Responsabilité pénale* (Paris: Dalloz, 1961), pp. 351ff.; Marc Ancel, "Défendre la Défense sociale?," *Revue de Science Criminelle*, XIX (1964), 194–203.

34. Ibid., XV (1960), 399.

35. Jean Foyer, "La doctrine de la cinquième république en matière de répression," *Revue Pénitentiaire*, LXXXVII (1963), 281–87.

36. Quoted in Alain Peyrefitte, *Les Chevaux du lac Ladoga* (Paris: Plon, 1981), pp. 355–56.

37. Raymond Salingardes, "Les caractéristiques de la criminalité en France," *Revue Pratique de Psychologie de la Vie Sociale*, 1970, pp. 145–58.

38. *Revue de Science Criminelle*, XVIII (1965), 923.

39. Ibid., XIX (1964), 799. The debate and the subsequent discussion were printed *in extenso* on pp. 188–204 and 733–99. Merle, an articulate and balanced spokesman for neo-classical ideas, insisted that its contemporary exponents in France might properly be labelled "new neo-classicists," so far had they evolved. He also claimed the 1945 reform program as an expression of neo-classical ideas. Roger Merle and André Vitu, *Traité de droit criminel* (Paris: Cujas, 1967), pp. 39, 48.

40. Bernard Dutheillet-Lamonthézie, "Les modifications récentes du régime d'exécution des peines," *Revue de Science Criminelle*, XXVIII (1973), 567.

41. Michel-Antoine Burnier (ed.), *C'est demain la veille* (Paris: Seuil, 1973), p. 343 (interview with Foucault, 1971).

42. Robert Schmelck, "Une nouvelle politique pénitentiaire," *Revue de Science Criminelle*, XXVII (1972), 417. Mention of prison disorders is scattered through the archives and the press during the nineteenth and twentieth centuries, but such incidents were not consistently reported and apparently drew little public notice. Students of Michelle Perrot have recently done unpublished master's theses on revolts in Paris prisons during the first half of the nineteenth century and on a wave of outbreaks in 1886 (*L'Impossible Prison*, p. 63). The *Revue Pénitentiaire* reported another rash of disorders during the years 1909–12, including what appears to have been France's first hunger strike.

43. The Schmelck report was published in *Revue de Science Criminelle*, XXVII (1972), 136–49.

44. Ibid., pp. 417–21.

45. Ibid., XXVIII (1973), 568–74.

46. Fleury-Mérogis, opened in 1968–73, was designed to be a model

prison. Some critics denounced it as an extravagant luxury, the Ritz or the Hilton (as earlier complainers had done when the Santé and Fresnes prisons were built). Others were repelled by its massive size (more than 3000 inmates) and its coldness.

47. *Le Monde,* July 21 to August 13, 1974; M. Perdriau, "La crise des prisons en 1974," *Revue de Science Criminelle,* XXXI (1976), 226–35.

48. *Le Monde,* July 30, 1974 et seq.

49. For example, Dutheillet-Lamonthézie in *Revue de Science Criminelle,* XXVIII (1973), 578, 588–89; M. Vérin in ibid., 734–39.

50. Madame Dorlhac served from June 1974 until August 1976; her position was eliminated, without explanation, when the Chirac cabinet resigned.

51. *Le Monde,* August 7, 1981; *Revue de Science Criminelle,* XXVII (1972), 847–55.

52. *Revue Pénitentiaire,* C (1976), 161.

53. *Revue de Science Criminelle,* XXVII (1972), 419–20; XXVIII (1973), 578; XXXIII (1976), 230–31.

54. André Decocq, ibid., XXXIII (1976), 5.

55. Jean-Marc Varant, in *Revue Pénitentiaire,* C (1976), 675.

56. Annual report of Director of Penal Administration Jacques Mégret, *Revue Pénitentiaire,* C (1976), 45, 111, 117, 129; Bernard Dutheillet-Lamonthézie, "L'évolution actuelle des fonctions du JAP en prison," ibid., 162–63.

57. Ibid., 660.

58. Domenach, in *Esprit,* February 1972, p. 164n.; Jean Schewin (a former JAP), "L'équilibre et la complémentarité," *Revue de Science Criminelle,* XXVIII (1972), 463–64.

59. Simone Buffard, *Le Froid Pénitentiaire, ou l'impossible réforme des prisons* (Paris: Seuil, 1973), p. 126.

60. Annual report of Director of Prison Administration Robert Schmelck, *Revue de Science Criminelle,* XIX (1964), 873–74. Schmelck calculated that prisoners working for *concessionaires* outnumbered those employed by *la régie* by seven to one.

61. Charles Germain, ibid., XIX (1954), 59; Buffard, *Le Froid Pénitentiaire,* p. 126.

62. Germain, in *Revue de Science Criminelle,* IX (1954), 59.

63. Annual report of Director of Prison Administration Christian Daublanc, *Revue Pénitentiaire,* CIV (1980), 171. For a brief survey of the problem of prison labor, see Jean Favart, *Le Labyrinthe Pénitentiaire* (Paris: Centurion, 1979), pp. 122–37.

64. Annual report of Director of Prison Administration, *Revue Pénitentiaire,* C (1976), 97; M. Talbert, ibid., 732–35.

65. *Sondages,* 1971, pp. 89–92, 96–97.

66. Ministère de la justice, *Comité d'études sur la violence, la criminalité et la délinquance; réponses à la violence* (Paris: Presses pocket, 1977), I, 46. Cited hereafter as Peyrefitte Report.

67. Claude Lecomte, "Les milices privées," *La Nef*, no. 57 (1975), 103–7.

68. Thierry Godefroy and Philippe Robert, *Le Coût du crime en France en 1974 et 1975* (Paris: S.E.P.C., 1977). The authors calculated that the total cost of crime in France in 1975, borne by the state and by individual citizens, was fr. 112,210 million. Of this total, fr. 44,483 million was attributed to fiscal fraud (evasion of consumption tax and income tax). The cost to individuals of offenses against persons and property was estimated at fr. 11,786 million.

69. Jacques Léauté, *Notre Violence* (Paris: Denoel, 1977), p. 30; Jean-Claude Chesnais, *Les Morts violents en France depuis 1826* (Paris: Presses universitaires, 1976).

70. One journalist spoke of *"la France figée dans son obsession de la criminalité"* (*Le Monde*, June 17, 1981); another referred to an emerging "psychosis" (Philippe Boucher, *Le Ghetto judiciaire* [Paris: Grasset, 1978], p. 122). Perhaps such terms were excessive; still, the experts who made up the Peyrefitte commission clearly accepted the idea if not the word (Peyrefitte Report, I, 48–63).

71. Ibid., 67.

72. Léauté, *Notre Violence*, pp. 26–30, 48.

73. Jean Pinatel, *La Société criminogène* (Paris: Calmann-Lévy, 1971), p. 1. Crime, Pinatel argues, is a "social malady," yet the value judgments embodied in the law until 1945 remained rooted in Christian morality, with its conception of good and evil (ibid., p. 13). On the worldwide rise in crime, cf. Sir Leon Radzinowicz and Joan King, *The Growth of Crime* (London: Hamish Hamilton, 1977), pp. 3–9.

74. Léauté, *Notre Violence*, p. 63; J.-M. Caroit, "Le grand refus des jeunes," *Le Nef*, no. 57 (1975), 131; M. Beauvais, "Bilan de la réforme de 1975," *Revue Pénitentiaire*, CII (1978), 163.

75. The commission included the criminologist Jacques Léauté, the former Director of Penal Administration Robert Schmelck, the economist Jean Fourastié, and the sociologist Jacques Ellul.

76. The Peyrefitte Report was published for public consumption in two paperback volumes; these were supplemented by eight volumes of reports and statistics (Paris: La Documentation Française, 1977).

77. Peyrefitte Report, I, 216–17.

78. Ibid., 31; vol. II, 449. The figures in the two volumes differ somewhat, since the base periods used were not the same.

79. Ibid., I, 50–52.

80. Ibid., 47–50. Respondents were asked whether they had experi-

enced or observed crimes during the preceding month. But when the period was extended to the past three years, the result was quite different: 41 per cent claimed to have been victims at least once. In half of these instances, however, no violence was involved (ibid., II, 457).

81. Ibid., II, 488; Boucher, *Le Ghetto judiciaire*, p. 122.

82. Quoted in Jean-Marc Théolleyre, *Tout condamné à mort aura la tête tranchée* (Paris: Téma, 1977), p. 1.

83. Peyrefitte Report, Annex I, p. 75. A French sociologist, analyzing attitudes toward crime as revealed in several recent polls, classifies the results somewhat differently:

(1) (27%) More severe repression needed; individuals, not society, responsible for crime.

(2) (37%) The social order must be protected, but shortcomings in the system of criminal justice and the structure of society are more important; fearful about the future.

(3) (11%) Liberty more important than order; crime the product of social maladjustments; re-education of offenders needed.

(4) (14%) Radical changes in the system needed; society and criminal justice flawed and unfair.

(5) (11%) Refused to answer.

This analyst detected the recent growth of what he called "skeptical repressiveness"—a desire for more severe punishment combined with profound doubts about its probable effects (Philippe Robert, "La justice pénale et l'opinion publique," *Revue Pénitentiaire*, CIV [1980], 211–38).

84. P. Slavski, "La nouvelle loi pénitentiaire," ibid., CIII (1979), 31–36; Gilbert Marc, in *Revue de Science Criminelle*, XXXIV (1979), 139–41; Robert Schmelck, ibid., XXXV (1980), 585.

85. Annual report of the Director of Penal Administration, *Revue Pénitentiaire*, CIV (1980), 139.

86. Quoted in Théolleyre, *Tout condamné à mort*, p. 49.

87. Paul Thibaud in *Esprit*, November 1979, p. 5; Peyrefitte, *Les Chevaux du lac Ladoga*, pp. 339–45. Peyrefitte's statement was applauded by conservative magistrates: one wrote, "So we're returning, after some sorry experiments, to the robust idea that punishments must be quite simply punitive" (*Le Figaro*, September 27, 1979).

88. The *Syndicat de la magistrature* led the attack in a collectively written book, *Justice sous influence* (Paris: Maspero, 1981). A summary of the law's content, hostile in tone, appeared in *Le Monde* for February 4, 1981. Peyrefitte toured the country during the spring, debating the merits of the law with hostile lawyers and judges. He also came out for short prison terms for adolescents, to shock them into good behavior (*Le Monde*, June 7, 1981).

89. Bertrand Le Gendre in *Le Monde*, February 4, 1981.

90. *L'Express*, October 4, 1980.

91. Peyrefitte, *Les Chevaux du lac Ladoga*, p. 263.

92. *Le Monde*, June 20, 1981.

93. Annual report of the Director of Penal Administration, *Revue de science criminelle*, XXXV (1980), 168, 183; Boucher, *Le Ghetto judiciaire*, p. 122; François Colcombet, "Vivre avec les prisons," *Esprit*, November 1979, p. 127.

94. *Le Monde*, May 17–18, 1981.

95. Domenach in *Esprit*, February 1972, p. 167; Foucault in Burnier (ed.), *C'est demain la veille*, p. 34.

96. Domenach in *Esprit*, February 1972, p. 168. The GIP's brief history is recounted in ibid., November 1979, pp. 3–4, 102ff.

97. *Esprit*, November 1979, pp. 10–11.

98. François Colcombet, "La croix dans la balance," *Esprit*, April–May 1977, pp. 185–92. On the *Syndicat*, see also Marc Robert, *On les appelle les juges rouges* (Paris: Téma, 1976), and Philippe Meyer, "A quoi sert le Syndicat de la Magistrature?" *Esprit*, November 1977, pp. 112–13.

99. Roland Kessous (a former vice-president of the *Syndicat*) "Le rictus d'une société," *Le Nef*, no. 57 (1975), p. 160.

100. See above, chapter I.

101. The prison guards' strike of August 1974 failed to achieve its goals; although the minister of justice recommended an upgrading of their salaries and status, the minister of finance rejected it as too costly (*Le Monde*, August 2, 1974). The rise in the prison population was not matched by an increase in personnel; from 1954 to 1966 the number of prisoners rose by 49 per cent, the number of guards by 2½ per cent (Annual report of the Director of Penal Administration, *Revue de Science Criminelle*, XXVII [1972], 909).

102. In 1976 there were 9,763 prison guards, 532 educators, 326 "technical personnel," 260 social workers, 296 full-time and 187 part-time probation officers (Ministère de la justice, *Compte général 1976* [Paris: Documentation française, 1981], pp. 36, 67).

103. Roger Errera, *Les Libertés à l'abandon* (Paris: Seuil, 1975), p. 159.

104. *Revue de Science Criminelle*, XXVII (1972), 420.

105. Jean Pinatel, "La crise pénitentiaire," *L'Année Sociologique*, 1973, pp. 36, 47ff.

106. Quoted in Errera, *Les Libertés*, p. 157.

107. *Revue de Science Criminelle*, XXXI (1976), 231–31.

108. Ibid., XXVII (1972), 420.

109. Jean-Marc Varaut, "La prison pour qui?," *Revue Pénitentiaire*, C (1976), 671–81.

110. *Revue de Science Criminelle*, XXXI (1976), 230; XXXV (1980), 585.

111. *Politique d'Aujourd'hui*, April–May 1972, pp. 85–87.

112. Notable among these appointees was Michel Jéol as director of criminal affairs and pardons. Jéol, a Socialist magistrate in his mid-forties, had published in 1978 a vigorous critique of the criminal justice system: *Changer la justice* (Paris: Firmin-Didot).

113. *Le Monde*, September 19 and 20–21, 1981. Sixty-three of the respondents favored retaining the death penalty (ibid., November 26, 1981).

114. Ibid., October 31, 1981.

115. Ibid., July 11 and November 8–9, 1981.

116. Ibid., December 1, 1981.

117. Ibid., February 24, 1982.

118. Ibid., June 24, 1980. During 1981 several Communist mayors, strongly endorsed by the party leadership, suddenly embarked on a campaign against immigrant workers in their municipalities, accusing them of drug trafficking and thievery. See, for example, *France-Observateur*, February 23, 1981, pp. 31–32.

119. *Le Monde*, August 14, 1982. The *rate* of increase declined, however, from 12.74 percent in 1980 to 9.99 percent in 1981.

120. Ibid., June 3, 1982.

121. Ibid., November 8–9, 1981; February 26, 1982.

## Postface

1. Archives Nationales, C3008 (minutes of the Haussonville commission, May 3, 1872).

2. Rupert Cross, *Punishment, Prison and the Public* (London: Stevens, 1971), p. 100.

3. Sir Leon Radzinowicz and Joan King, *The Growth of Crime: The International Experience* (London: Hamish Hamilton, 1977), p. 3.

4. Jacques Léauté, *Notre Violence* (Paris: Denoel, 1977), p. 7. Léauté's remark was of course a bit of French irony.

# Bibliography

## Archives and Private Papers

*Archives Nationales*
BB$^{18}$ 1466.
BB$^{20}$ 12, 50, 145.
C 661, 708–9, 845, 918, 924–26, 928, 1002–3, 1088, 2749, 2766, 2780, 2875–76, 3008–17, 3276, 5565, 7356, 7644, 7775.
C*I 34, 367, 395.
F$^{2}$I 1293.
F$^{7}$ 6960. .
F$^{16}$ 1018, 102, 106–8, 308, 355A, 355B.
*Archives Nationales: Section d'outre-mer* (formerly Ministère des Colonies)
Nouvelle Calédonie cartons 32, 38, 55, 166, 233.
*Bibliothèque de l'Institut de France*
Papers of Charles Benoist, dossiers 42, 49.
*Bibliothèque Thiers*
Papers of Jules Baroche, dossier 1081.

## Official Publications

*Parliamentary Debates and Documents*
*Archives parlementaires de 1787 à 1860: recueil complet des débats législatifs et politiques des chambres françaises.* Paris: Dupont, 1879– . Published to date: 1st series, 1787–94; 2d series, 1814–39.
Assemblée nationale 1789–91. *Procès-verbal de l'Assemblée nationale.*
Assemblée législative 1849–51. *Procès-verbaux de l'Assemblée législative.*
Corps législatif 1852–70. *Annales du Sénat et du Corps législatif* (1870).
Assemblée nationale 1871–75. *Annales de l'Assemblée nationale.*

Chambre des députés 1875–1940. *Journal officiel, débats de la Chambre des députés.*

———. *Journal officiel, documents de la Chambre des députés.*

Sénat 1875–1940. *Journal officiel, débats du Sénat.*

———. *Journal officiel, documents du Sénat.*

Assemblée nationale 1946–82. *Journal officiel, débats de l'Assemblée nationale.*

Official Newspapers

*Le Moniteur Universel.* 1789–1868.

*Réimpression de l'Ancien Moniteur* (1789–99). Paris: Plon, 1858–63.

Official Reports

Ministère du commerce, de l'intérieur et des colonies. *Compte-rendu des travaux de la commission permanente du régime pénitentiaire pendant les années 1889 et 1890, par M. Paul Dislère.* Melun: Imprimerie administrative, 1891.

Ministère de l'économie nationale, Direction de la statistique générale et de la documentation.

*Annuaire statistique*, vols. 53, 56, 57, 84. Paris: Imprimerie nationale, 1937–46, 1978.

Ministère de l'intérieur

Demetz, Frédéric, and Abel Blouet. *Rapports à M. le comte de Montalivet sur les pénitenciers des Etats-Unis.* Paris: Imprimerie royale, 1837.

Gasparin, Comte Adrien. *Rapport au roi sur les prisons départementales.* Paris: Imprimerie royale, 1837.

Perrot, Louis. *Rapport à M. le Ministre de l'Intérieur sur un projet de transportation . . . en Algérie et en Corse.* Paris: Imprimerie nationale, 1852.

Ministère de la justice

*Compte général de l'administration de la justice criminelle.* Annual since 1826.

*Statistique pénitentiaire.* Annual since 1853.

Comité d'études sur la violence, la criminalité et la délinquance. *Réponses à la violence.* 2 vols. Paris: Presses pocket, 1977.

———. *Réponses à la violence: annexes au rapport du Comité d'études présidé par Alain Peyrefitte.* 8 vols. Paris: La Documentation française, 1977–78.

Ministère de la marine

*Notice sur la transportation à la Guyane française et à la Nouvelle Calédonie.* Published at irregular intervals from 1867 until 1910.

[Gauharon, L.] *Rapport de la Commission nommée par M. le Capitaine de Vaisseau Pallu de la Barrière, gouverneur de la Nouvelle Calédonie.* Noumea: Imprimerie du gouvernement, 1884.

*Documentary collections*

Bloch, Camille, and Alexandre Tuetey (eds.). *Procès-verbaux et rapports du Comité de mendicité de la Constituante 1790–91.* Paris: Imprimerie nationale, 1911.

Comité national du centenaire de 1848. *Procès-verbaux du Gouvernement Provisoire et de la Commission du Pouvoir Exécutif (24 février–22 juin 1848).* Paris: Imprimerie nationale, 1950.

Duvergier, J.-B. (ed.). *Collection complète des lois, décrets, ordonnances, règlemens, avis du Conseil d'Etat depuis 1788.* 2d ed. Paris: Guyot, 1836.

Isambert, François A. et al. (eds.). *Recueil général des anciennes lois françaises depuis l'an 420 jusqu'à la Révolution de 1789.* Paris: Belin-Leprieur, 1822–33.

Lefebvre, Georges, and Anne Terroine (eds.). *Recueil de documents relatifs aux séances des Etats-généraux mai–juin 1789.* Paris: C.N.R.S., 1953–62.

Tripier, Louis (ed.). *Les Codes français collationnés sur les textes officielles.* Paris: Cotillon, 1859.


## Books

Abbiateci, André et al. *Crimes et criminalité en France sous l'Ancien Régime, 17e–18e siècles.* Paris: Colin, 1971.

Ackerknecht, Erwin H. *Franz Joseph Gall, Inventor of Phrenology.* Tr. Claire St. Leon. Madison: Univ. Wisconsin Press, 1956.

Acollas, Emile. *Philosophie de la science politique.* Paris: Maresq, 1877.

Agulhon, Maurice. *La Vie sociale en Provence intérieure au lendemain de la Révolution.* Paris: Société des études robespierristes, 1970.

Alauzet, Isidore. *Essai sur les peines et le système pénitentiaire.* 2d ed. Paris: Cosse, 1863.

Alcindor, Emile. *Questions diverses d'administration pénitentiaires.* Montpellier: Midi, 1909.

Alhoy, Maurice, and Louis Curine. *Les Prisons de Paris, histoire, types, moeurs, mystères.* Paris: Havard, 1846.

Ancel, Jacqueline. "La politique criminelle de l'Assemblée constituante." Typescript, Univ. of Paris, 1966.

Ancel, Marc. *La Défense sociale nouvelle.* 2d ed. Paris: Cujas, 1971.

Anchel, Robert. *Crimes et châtiments au XVIIIe siècle.* Paris: Perrin, 1933.

André, Louis. *La Récidive, théorie d'ensemble et commentaire détaillée.* Paris: Plon, 1892.

Appert, Benjamin. *Bagnes, prisons et criminels.* 4 vols. Paris: Guilbert, 1836.

Arnaud, Georges. *Prisons 53.* Paris: Julliard, 1953.

Ballanche, Pierre-Simon. *La Ville des expiations.* Paris: Ed. des Presses Françaises, 1926.

Balzac, Honoré. *Splendeurs et misères des courtisanes.* Paris: Gallimard, 1948.

Bastid, Paul. *Benjamin Constant et sa doctrine.* Paris: Colin, n.d.

Beauchet, Ludovic. *Transportation et colonisation pénale à la Nouvelle Calédonie.* Paris: Revue politique et parlementaire, 1898.

Beaumont, Gustave de, and Alexis de Tocqueville. *On the Penitentiary System in the United States and Its Application in France.* Tr. Francis Lieber. New York: Kelley, 1970.

Beccaria, Cesare. *Traité des délits et des peines, traduit de l'italien d'après la sixième édition.* Paris: Bastien, 1773.

Belbenoit, René. *Dry Guillotine: Fifteen Years among the Living Dead.* Tr. Preston Rambo. New York: Dutton, 1938.

Bentham, Jeremy. *Draught of a New Plan for the Organisation of the Judicial Establishment in France.* London: no publisher listed, 1790.

————. *Panoptique: mémoire sur un nouveau principe pour construire des maisons d'inspection.* Paris: Imprimerie nationale, 1791.

————. *Sur le nouvel ordre judiciaire en France.* Paris: Patriote français, 1790.

————. *Théorie des peines et des récompenses.* 2 vols. London: Vogel and Schulze, 1811.

Bérenger, Alphonse. *De la justice criminelle en France.* Paris: L'Huillier, 1818.

————. *De la répression pénale, de ses formes et de ses effets.* 2 vols. Paris: Cosse, 1855.

Berry, Georges. *Les Mendiants.* Paris: Arnould, 1891.

Besson, Antonin. *Le Mythe de la justice.* Paris: Plon, 1923.

Bigot de Morogues, Baron Pierre-Marie. *Du pauperisme, de la mendicité et des moyens d'en prévenir les funestes effets.* Paris: Dondey-Dupré, 1834.

Biot, Dr. René et al. *Le Coupable est-il un malade ou un pécheur?* Paris: Spes, 1951.

Blosseville, Marquis Ernest de. *Histoire de la colonisation pénale et des établisssements de l'Angleterre en Australie.* 2d ed. Evreux: Hérissey, 1859.

Blanqui, Adolphe. *Des classes ouvrières en France pendant l'année 1848.* Paris: Didot, 1849.

Bloch, Camille. *L'Assistance et l'état en France à la veille de la Révolution.* Paris: Picard, 1908.

Bonger, W. A. *Criminalité et conditions économiques.* Amsterdam: Tierie, 1905.

Bonneron, Géo. *Notre Régime pénitentiaire: les prisons de Paris.* Paris: Firmin-Didot, 1898.

Bonneville de Marsangy, Arnould. *De l'amélioration de la loi criminelle.* 2 vols. Paris: Cotillon, 1855–64.

Bonzon, Jacques. *Le Crime et l'école.* Paris: Guillaumin, 1896.

————. *Des horreurs de la rélégation, des règles et des beautés de la profession de forçat.* Paris: Guillaumin, 1896.

Boucher, Philippe. *Le Ghetto judiciaire.* Paris: Grasset, 1978.

Bourdet-Pléville, Michel. *Des Galériens, des forçats, des bagnards.* Paris: Plon, 1957.

Brissot de Warville, Jacques. *Théorie des lois criminelles.* Vol. 1: Berlin: no publisher listed, 1781. Vol. 2: Paris, Aillaud, 1836.

Broglie, A., duc de. *Ecrits et discours.* Paris: Didier, 1863.

Brouilhet, Francis. *De la transportation, son organisation actuelle et ses résultats.* Paris: Rousseau, 1899.

Broussole, Paul. *Délinquance et déviance: brève histoire de leurs approches psychiatriques.* Toulouse: Privat, 1978.

Buffard, Dr. Simone. *Le Froid Pénitentiaire ou l'impossible réforme des prisons.* Paris: Seuil, 1973.

Buret, Eugène. *De la misère des classes laborieuses en Angleterre et en France.* 2 vols. Paris: Paulin, 1840.

Burnier, Michel-Antoine (ed.). *C'est demain la veille.* Paris: Seuil, 1973.

Cabanis, Pierre. *Rapports du physique et du moral de l'homme.* 2 vols. Paris: Crapart, 1802.

Cameron, Iain A. *Crime and Repression in the Auvergne and Guienne, 1720–1790.* New York: Cambridge Univ. Press, 1981.

Canler, Louis. *Les Mémoires de Canler, ancien chef du service de Sûreté.* Paris: Hetzel, 1862.

Cannat, Pierre. *Nos Frères, les récidivistes.* Paris: Sirey, 1942.

————. *La Réforme pénitentiaire.* Paris: Sirey, 1948.

Carol, Jean. *Le Bagne.* Paris: Ollendorff, 1903.

Casamayor, Louis. *Si j'étais juge.* Paris: Arthaud, 1970.

Castan, Nicole. *Justice et répression en Languedoc à l'époque des Lumières.* Paris: Flammarion, 1980.

Castan, Yves. *Honnêteté et relations sociales en Languedoc, 1715–1780.* Paris: Plon, 1974.

Castel, Robert. *L'Ordre psychiatrique: l'âge d'or de l'aliénisme.* Paris: Ed. de Minuit, 1976.

Charrière, Henri. *Papillon.* Paris: Laffont, 1969.

Chaulot, Paul, and Jean Susini. *Le Crime en France.* Paris: Hachette, 1959.

Chauveau, Adolphe, and Faustin Hélie. *Théorie du Code pénal.* 8 vols. Paris: Legrand, 1872.

Chesnais, Jean-Claude. *Les Morts violentes en France depuis 1826.* Paris: Presses Universitaires de France, 1976.

———. *Histoire de la violence.* Paris: Laffont, 1981.

Chevalier, Louis. *Classes laborieuses et classes dangereuses.* Paris: Plon, 1958.

Claude, chef de la Sûreté. *Mémoires de Monsieur Claude.* Paris: Les amis de l'histoire, 1968.

Claveau, A.-G. *De la police de Paris, de ses abus, et des réformes dont elle est susceptible.* Paris: Pillot, 1831.

Cobb, Richard. *The Police and the People.* London: Oxford Univ. Press, 1970.

———. *Reactions to the French Revolution.* London: Oxford Univ. Press, 1972.

Condorcet, Marquis de. *Esquisse d'un tableau historique des progrès de l'esprit humain.* Paris: Ed. sociales, 1966.

Constant, Benjamin. *Ecrits es discours politiques.* Ed. O. Pozzo di Borgo. Paris: Pauvert, 1964.

Corre, Dr. Armand. *Les Criminels, caractères physiques et psychologiques.* Paris: Doin, 1889.

Cuche, Paul. *De la possibilité pour l'école classique d'organiser la répression pénale en dehors du libre arbitre.* Grenoble: Allier, 1897.

———. *Traité de science et de législation pénitentiaires.* Paris: Librairie générale de droit et de jurisprudence, 1905.

Dally, Dr. Eugène. *Remarques sur les aliénés et les criminels au point de vue de la responsabilité morale et légale.* Paris: Masson, 1864.

Danjou, E. *Des prisons, de leur régime, et des moyens de l'améliorer.* Paris: Eyron, 1821.

Dauban, C.-A. *Les Prisons de Paris sous la Révolution, d'après les relations des contemporains.* Paris: Plon, 1870.

Despine, Prosper. *De la contagion morale.* Marseille: Camoin, 1870.

———. *Psychologie naturelle: étude sur les facultés intellectuelles et morales.* 3 vols. Paris: Savy, 1868.

Desportes, Fernand. *La Récidive, examen du projet de loi.* Paris: Chaix, 1883.

———. *La Réforme des prisons.* Paris: Le Clère, 1862.

Desprez, Edouard. *De l'abolition de l'emprisonnement.* Paris: Dentu, 1868.

Destrem, Jean. *Les Déportations du Consulat et de l'Empire.* Paris: Jeanmaire, 1885.

Devèze, Michel. *Cayenne, déportés et bagnards.* Paris: Julliard, 1965.

Deyon, Pierre. *Le Temps des prisons.* Villeneuve d'Ascq: Univ. de Lille III, 1975.

Dhur, Jacques. *Visions de bagne.* Paris: Ferenczi, 1925.

Diennet, Marcel. *Le Petit Paradis, récit d'Ariane Randal.* Paris: Laffont, 1972.

Donnard, Jean-Hervé. *Balzac: les realités économiques et sociales dans la Comédie Humaine.* Paris: Colin, 1961.

Donnedieu de Vabres, Henri. *La Justice pénale d'aujourd'hui.* Paris: Colin, 1929.

Dreyfus, Ferdinand. *Un Philanthrope d'autrefois: La Rochefoucauld-Liancourt.* Paris: Plon, 1903.

Dubief, Fernand. *La Question du vagabondage.* Paris: Pasquelle, 1911.

Duché, Natasha, and Ariane Gransac. *Prisons de femmes.* Paris: Denoel, 1982.

Duesterberg, Thomas J. "Criminology and the Social Order in Nineteenth-Century France." Typescript dissertation, Indiana University, 1979.

Dupaty, Charles. *Lettres sur la procédure criminelle de la France.* "En France," 1788.

———. *Mémoire justificatif pour trois hommes condamnés à la roue.* Paris: Pierres, 1786.

Dupin, André. *Observations sur plusieurs points importans de notre législation criminelle.* Paris: Baudouin, 1821.

Dupont, Etienne. *La Bastille des mers.* 5th ed. Paris: Perrin, 1933.

Du Puy, Hubert. *Vagabondage et mendicité.* Paris: Larose, 1899.

Durkheim, Emile. *De la division du travail social.* Paris: Alcan, 1893.

———. *Les Règles de la méthode sociologique.* Paris: Alcan, 1895.

Errera, Roger. *Les Libertés à l'abandon.* Paris: Seuil, 1973.

Esmein, Adhémar. *A History of Continental Criminal Procedure, with Special Reference to France.* Tr. John Simpson. Boston: Little, Brown, 1913.

Falque, Edith. *Sortie de prison.* Paris: Ed. spéciale, 1971.

Farge, Arlette. *Délinquance et criminalité: le vol d'aliments à Paris au XVIII^e siècle.* Paris: Plon, 1974.

Faucher, Léon. *De la réforme des prisons.* Paris: Angé, 1838.

Fauconnet, Paul. *La Responsabilité: étude de sociologie.* Paris: Alcan, 1920.

Favard, Jean. *Le Labyrinthe pénitentiaire.* Paris: Centurion, 1981.

Féré, Dr. Charles. *Dégénérescence et criminalité: essai physiologique.* Paris: Alcan, 1888.

Ferré, Georges. *Bagnards, colons et canaques.* Paris: Jouve, 1932.

Ferrus, Guillaume. *De l'expatriation pénitentiaire.* Paris: Gernier-Baillière, 1853.

———. *De la réforme pénitentiaire en Angleterre et en France.* Paris: Gernier-Baillière, 1853.

———. *Des prisonniers, de l'emprisonnement et des prisons.* Paris: Baillière, 1850.

Forrest, Alan. *The French Revolution and the Poor.* Oxford: Blackwell, 1981.

Foucault, Michel (ed.). *Moi, Pierre Rivière, ayant égorgé ma mère, ma soeur et mon frère. . . .* Paris: Gallimard, 1973.

———. *Surveiller et punir: naissance de la prison.* Paris: Gallimard, 1975.

Fouillée, Alfred. *La France au point de vue moral.* Paris: Alcan, 1900.

Fournière, E. *Les Théories socialistes au XIXe siècle.* Paris: Alcan, 1904.

Franck, Adolphe. *Philosophie du droit pénal.* Paris: Baillière, 1864.

Frégier, H.-A. *Des classes dangereuses dans la population dans les grandes villes.* 2 vols. Paris: Baillière, 1840.

Gaillac, Henri. *Les Maisons de correction, 1830–1945.* Paris: Cujas, 1971.

Garçon, Maurice. *Histoire de la justice sous la IIIe république.* 3 vols. Paris: Fayard, 1957.

———. *La Justice contemporaine.* Paris: Grasset, 1933.

Garraud, René. *Précis de droit criminel.* Paris: Larose, 1881.

———. *Le Problème moderne de la pénalité.* Paris: Larose, 1889.

Gérando, Baron Joseph-Marie de. *De la bienfaisance publique.* 4 vols. Paris: Renouard, 1839.

Girardin, Emile de. *Du droit de punir.* Paris: Plon, 1871.

Gleizes, Vénuste. *Mémoire sur l'état actuel des bagnes en France.* Paris: Imprimerie royale, 1840.

Godechot, Jacques. *Les Institutions de la France sous la Révolution et l'Empire.* Paris: Presses universitaires de France, 1968.

Godefroy, Thierry, and Philippe Robert. *Le Coût du crime en France en 1974 et 1975.* Paris: S.C.P.C., 1977.

Godfrey, James L. *Revolutionary Justice: A Study of the Organization, Personnel, and Procedure of the Paris Tribunal, 1793–1795.* Chapel Hill: Univ. of North Carolina Press, 1951.

Gould, Stephen Jay. *The Mismeasure of Man.* New York: Norton, 1981.

Grapin, Pierre. *Anthropogenèse et criminalité.* Paris: Legrand, 1954.

Groupe d'information sur les prisons. *Enquête dans les prisons.* Paris: Ed. champ libre, 1971.

Guillot, Adolphe. *Paris qui souffre: les prisons de Paris et les prisonniers.* Paris: Dentu, 1889.

Guizot, François. *De la peine de mort en matière politique.* Paris: Béchet, 1822.

Gutton, Jean-Pierre. *La Société et les pauvres; l'exemple de la généralité de Lyon, 1584–1789.* Paris: Les belles lettres, 1971.

Guyau, Jean-Marie. *Esquisse d'une morale sans obligation ni sanction.* Paris: Alcan, 1885.

H\*\*\* D\* C\*\*\*. *La Mort de tous les criminels.* Paris: Barrois, 1790.

Homberg, Théodore. *Etudes sur le vagabondage.* Nouvelle édition. Paris: Forestier, 1880.

Howard, John. *Etat des prisons, des hôpitaux et des maisons de force.* Tr. Langlois. Paris: Lagrange, 1788.

———. *The Works of John Howard.* 2 vols. London: Johnson, 1792.

Huchon, Henri. *Quand j'étais au bagne.* Bordeaux: Delmas, 1933.

Hufton, Olwen H. *The Poor of Eighteenth-Century France, 1750–1789.* Oxford: Clarendon Press, 1974.

Hugo, Victor. *Le Dernier Jour d'un condamné.* Paris: Hetzel, 1889.

Hunt, Herbert James. *Le Socialisme et le romantisme en France: étude de la presse socialiste de 1830 à 1848.* Oxford: Clarendon Press, 1935.

Ignatieff, Michael. *A Just Measure of Pain: The Penitentiary in the Industrial Revolution, 1750–1850.* New York: Pantheon, 1978.

Imbert, Jean. *La Peine de mort.* Paris: Presses universitaires de France, 1972.

———, and Georges Levasseur. *Le Pouvoir, les juges et les bourreaux.* Paris: Hachette, 1972.

Ingraham, Barton L. *Political Crime in Europe: A Comparative Study of France, Germany, and England.* Berkeley: Univ. of California Press, 1979.

Jéol, Marcel. *Changer la justice.* Paris: Firmin-Didot, 1978.

Joly, Henri. *Le Crime: étude sociale.* Paris: Cerf, 1888.

———. *Le Combat contre le crime.* Paris: Cerf, 1892.

———. *La France criminelle.* Paris: Cerf, 1889.

———. *Problèmes de science criminelle.* Paris: Hachette, 1910.

Joughin, Jean. *The Paris Commune in French Politics.* 2 vols. Baltimore: Johns Hopkins Univ. Press, 1955.

Jousse, Daniel. *Traité de justice criminelle en France.* 4 vols. Paris: Debure, 1771.

Junosza-Zdrojewski, Georges O. *Le Crime et la presse.* Paris: Jouve, 1943.

Kah, Philippe. *Aux enfers du crime.* Lille: Bresle, 1930.

Karr, Alphonse. *Messieurs les assassins.* Paris: Lévy, 1885.

Kock, Gerald L. (ed.). *The French Code of Criminal Procedure.* So. Hackensack, N.J.: Rothman, 1964.

Kunstlé, Marc, and Claude Vincent. *Le Crépuscule des prisons.* Paris: Julliard, 1972.

Lacassagne, Dr. Alexandre. *Peine de mort et criminalité.* Paris: Malvine, 1908.

Lalou, Jules. *Aperçu sur les motifs de la progression des cas de récidive en matière de criminalité.* Paris: Chaix, 1870.

———. *De l'emprisonnement pour dettes.* Paris: Cotillon, 1857.

Langbein, John H. *Torture and the Law of Proof.* Chicago: Univ. of Chicago Press, 1977.

Langlois, Denis. *Le Cachot.* Paris: Maspero, 1967.

Larique, Marina. *Dans la brousse.* Paris: Gallimard, 1933.

La Rochefoucauld, J.-D. de. *Le duc de La Rochefoucauld-Liancourt, 1747–1827.* Paris: Perrin, 1980.

La Rochefoucauld-Liancourt, duc F.-A.-F. *Des prisons de Philadelphie; par un européen.* 4th ed. Paris: Huzard, 1819.

La Rochefoucauld-Liancourt, marquis de. *Conséquences du système pénitentiaire.* Clermont-Oise: Carbon, 1841.

———. *Examen de la théorie et de la pratique du système pénitentiaire.* Paris: Delaunay, 1840.

Laurent, Dr. Emile. *L'Anthropologie criminelle et les nouvelles théories du crime.* Paris: Société d'éditions scientifiques, 1893.

La Ville de Mirmont, Alexandre de. *Observations sur les maisons centrales de détention.* Paris: Crapelet, 1833.

Léauté, Jacques. *Criminologie et science pénitentiaire.* Paris: Presses universitaires de France, 1972.

———. *Droit pénal et procédure pénale.* Paris: Presses universitaires de France, 1965.

———. *Notre Violence.* Paris: Denoel, 1977.

——— (ed.). *La Responsabilité pénale, travaux du colloque de philosophie pénale.* Paris: Dalloz, 1961.

Le Boucher, I. *Ce qu'il faut connaître du bagne.* Paris: Boivin, 1930.

Le Clère, M. *La Vie quotidienne dans les bagnes, 1748–1953.* Paris: Hachette, 1973.

Le Favre, Georges. *Bagnards et chercheurs d'or.* Paris: Ferenczi, 1925.

Letourneau, Dr. Charles. *L'Évolution de la morale.* Paris: Delahaye, 1887.

Le Trosne, G. *Mémoire sur les vagabonds et sur les mendiants.* Soissons: Simon, 1764.

———. *Vues sur la justice criminelle.* Paris: Debure, 1777.

Leveillé, Jules. *La Guyane et la question pénitentiaire coloniale.* Paris: Colin, 1886.

Lévy, Thierry. *Le Désir de punir: essai sur le privilège pénal.* Paris: Fayard, 1979.

Liard-Courtois, ex-forçat. *Souvenirs du bagne.* Paris: Fasquelle, 1903.

Livre du centenaire de la Société de législation comparée. *Un Siècle de droit comparé en France (1869–1969).* Paris: Librairie générale de droit, 1969.

Livrozet, Serge. *De la prison à la revolte: essai-témoignage.* Paris: Mercure de France, 1973.

Lohmann, Friedrich. *Jean-Paul Marat und das Strafrecht in der französischen Revolution.* Bonn: Rohrscheid, 1963.

Lombroso, Cesar. *L'Homme criminel*. Tr. Régnier and Bournet. 2 vols. Paris: Alcan, 1887.

————. *L'Homme criminel*. 2d French edition. Paris: Alcan, 1895.

London, Géo. *Aux portes du bagne*. Paris: Portiques, 1930.

Londres, Albert. *Au bagne*. Paris: Michel, 1923.

Lucas, Charles. *De l'état anormal de la répression en matière de crimes capitaux*. Paris: Pédone, 1885.

————. *De la réforme des prisons ou de la théorie de l'emprisonnement*. 3 vols. Paris: Legrand, 1836–38.

————. *Du système pénal et du système répressif en général, de la peine de mort en particulier*. Paris: Béchet, 1827.

————. *Du système pénitentiaire en Europe et aux Etats-Unis*. 3 vols. Paris: Bossange, 1828–30.

Lucas, Prosper. *Traité philosophique et physiologique de l'hérédité naturelle*. 2 vols. Paris: Baillière, 1847–50.

Maestro, Marcello T. *Voltaire and Beccaria as Reformers of Criminal Law*. New York: Columbia Univ. Press, 1942.

Magnan, Dr., and Dr. Legrain, *Les Dégénérés (état mental et syndromes épisodiques)*. Paris: Rueff, 1895.

Maistre, comte Joseph de. *Les Soirées de Saint-Petersbourg*. Paris: La Colombe, 1960.

Mannheim, Hermann (ed.). *Pioneers of Criminology*. Chicago: Quadrangle, 1960.

Marat, Jean-Paul. *Plan de législation criminelle*. Paris: Rochette, 1790.

Marie, Dr. Armand, and Raymond Meunier. *Les Vagabonds*. Paris: Giard et Brière, 1908.

Marion, Marcel. *Le Brigandage pendant la Révolution*. Paris: Plon, 1934.

Maroger, Mireille. *Bagne*. Paris: Denoel, 1937.

Marquet de Vasselot, Louis. *Ethnographie des prisons*. Paris: Boutarel, 1854.

Matter, Jacques. "Les révoltes des prisonniers à Paris dans la première moitié du XIXe siècle." Typescript. Mémoire de maîtrise, Univ. of Paris VII, 1975.

Maxwell, Joseph. *Le Concept social du crime et son évolution*. Paris: Alcan, 1914.

————. *Le Crime et la société*. Paris: Flammarion, 1912.

Mercier, Louis-Sébastien. *Tableau de Paris*. 8 vols. Amsterdam: no publisher listed, 1782–88.

Merle, Roger (ed.). *Les Mondes du crime*. Toulouse: Privat, 1968.

———— and André Vitu. *Traité de droit criminel*. Paris: Cujas, 1967.

Merlet, J. F. Louis. *Au bout du monde: drames et misères du bagne*. Paris: Delpeuch, 1928.

Mesclon, Antoine. *Comment j'ai subi quinze ans de bagne*. Paris: l'auteur, 1924.

Meunier, Georges. *Le Crime: réquisitoire social*. Paris: Dowy, 1890.

Michaux, Hubert-Ernest. *Etude sur la question des peines*. Paris: Challamel, 1872.

"Mimande, Paul" (pseud. of Paul-Marie La Loyère). *Criminopolis*. Paris: Calmann-Lévy, 1897.

———. *Forçats et proscrits*. Paris: Calmann-Lévy, 1897.

Mirabeau, marquis de. *Oeuvres*. Vols. 1–2. Paris: Brissot-Thivers, 1826–27.

Molènes, Alexandre de. *De l'humanité dans les lois criminelles et de la jurisprudence*. Paris: Locquin, 1830.

Moncelon, Léon. *Le Bagne et la colonisation pénale en Nouvelle-Calédonie*. Paris: Bayle, 1886.

Montesquieu, Baron Charles de. *Oeuvres complètes*. Paris: Gallimard, 1949–51.

Moreau-Christophe, Louis. *De l'état actuel des prisons en France*. Paris: Desrez, 1837.

———. *De la réforme des prisons en France*. Paris: Huzard, 1835.

———. *Du problème de la misère et de sa solution chez les peuples anciens et modernes*. 3 vols. Paris: Guillaumin, 1851.

Morel, Dr. Benedict. *Traité des dégénérescences physiques, intellectuelles et morales de l'espèce humain*. Paris: Baillière, 1857.

Mossé, Armand. *Les Prisons: exposé pratique du régime pénitentiaire en France*. Paris: Boccard, 1926.

———. *Les Prisons et les institutions d'éducation correctives*. Melun: Imprimerie administrative, 1939.

Mousset, Paul. *Albert Londres: ou, l'aventure du grand réportage*. Paris: Grasset, 1972.

Muyart de Vouglans, Pierre-François. *Institutes au droit criminel*. Paris: Cellot, 1757.

———. *Les Lois criminelles de France, dans leur ordre naturel*. Paris: Mérigot, 1780.

———. *Réfutation des principes hasardés dans le "Traité des délits et peines," traduits de l'Italien*. Lausanne and Paris: Desaint, 1767.

Niles, Mrs. Blair. *Condemned to Devil's Island: The Biography of an Unknown Convict*. New York: Harcourt, 1928.

O'Brien, Patricia. *The Promise of Punishment: Prisons in Nineteenth-Century France*. Princeton: Princeton Univ. Press, 1982.

Ollier, Jean. *Convient-il d'abolir la transportation à la Guyane?* Paris: Machalenck, 1932.

Ortolan, Joseph. *Eléments de droit penal*. Paris: Plon, 1855.

Pagnier, Dr. Armand. *Du vagabondage et des vagabonds*. Lyon: Storck, 1906.

————. *Le Vagabond*. Paris: Vigot, 1910.

Parias, L.-H. *Justice n'est pas faite*. Paris: Centurion, 1953.

Paulian, Louis. *Paris qui mendie: mal et remède*. Paris: Ollendorff, 1893.

Péan, Charles. *Le Salut des parias*. Paris: Gallimard, 1935.

————. *Terre de bagne*. Paris: Fischbacher, 1934.

Perrot, Michelle (ed.). *L'Impossible Prison: recherches sur le système pénitentiaire au XIXᵉ siècle*. Paris: Seuil, 1980.

Peyrefitte, Alain. *Les Chevaux du lac Ladoga*. Paris: Plon, 1981.

Picon, Georges. *Pour une politique du crime*. Paris: Seuil, 1966.

Pierson, George W. *Tocqueville and Beaumont in America*. New York: Oxford Univ. Press, 1938.

Pietra Santa, Dr. Prosper de. *Mazas: études sur l'emprisonnement cellulaire*. Paris: Masson, 1853.

Pinatel, Jean. *La Société criminogène*. Paris: Calmann-Lévy, 1971.

Pisier, Georges. *Les Déportés de la Commune à l'Ile des Pins, 1872–1880*. Paris: Société des Océanistes, 1971.

Prins, Adolphe. *La Défense sociale et les transformations du droit pénal*. Brussels: Misch and Thron, 1910.

Proal, Louis. *Le Crime et la peine*. 3d ed. Paris: Alcan, 1899.

————. *La Criminalité politique*. Paris: Alcan, 1895.

Quéant, Olivier. *Le Monde inconnu des prisons*. Paris: Plon, 1970.

Radzinowicz, Sir Leon and Joan King. *The Growth of Crime*. London: Hamilton, 1977.

Reinach, Joseph. *Les Récidivistes*. Paris: Charpentier, 1882.

Rémy, Henri. *Des Principes généraux du Code Pénal de 1791*. Paris: Sirey, 1910.

Renard, Georges. *L'Homme est-il libre?* Paris: Baillière, 1881.

Ribot, Théodule. *Les Maladies de la volonté*. Paris: Alcan, 1884.

Richard, André. *Le Crime*. Paris: Flammarion, 1961.

Rivière, Louis. *Mendiants et vagabonds*. Paris: Lecoffre, 1902.

Robert, Marc. *On les appelle les juges rouges*. Paris: Téma, 1976.

Robin, Elie. *La Question pénitentiaire*. Paris: Bonhome, 1873.

Rougerie, Jacques. *Procès des Communards*. Paris: Gallimard, 1978.

Rouilleault, Armand. *La Suppression de la transportation*. Lyon: Grosjean, 1938.

Rousseau, Jean-Jacques. *Du contrat social*. Paris: Garnier, 1975.

Rousseau, Dr. Louis. *Un Médecin au bagne*. Paris: Fleury, 1930.

Roussenq, Paul. *Vingt-cinq Ans au bagne*. Paris: La défense, 1934.

Roux, Jean-André. *La Défense contre le crime: répression et prévention*. Paris: Alcan, 1922.

Roux, Roger. *Le Travail dans les prisons et en particulier dans les maisons centrales*. Paris: Rousseau, 1902.

Rusche, Georg, and Otto Kirchheimer, *Punishment and Social Structure.* New York: Russell, 1968.

Saleilles, Raymond. *L'Individualisation de la peine: étude de criminalité sociale.* Paris: Alcan, 1898.

Sangnier, Georges. *Le Brigandage dans la Pas-de-Calais de 1789 à 1815.* Blangermont: chez l'auteur, 1962.

Savey-Casard, Paul. *Le Crime et la peine dans l'oeuvre de Victor Hugo.* Paris: Presses universitaires de France, 1956.

Seligman, Edmond. *La Justice en France pendant la Révolution.* 2 vols. Paris: Plon, 1901–13.

Sellin, Thorsten, and Marvin Wolfgang. *The Measurement of Delinquency.* New York: Wiley, 1964.

Stanciu, V. V. *La Criminalité à Paris.* Paris: C.N.R.S., 1968.

Stefani, Gaston et al. *Criminologie et science pénitentiaire.* Paris: Dalloz, 1970.

Sue, Eugène. *Les Mystères de Paris.* Brussels: Méline, 1844.

Syndicat de la Magistrature. *Justice sous influence.* Paris: Maspero, 1981.

Szabo, Denis. *Crimes et villes: étude statistique de la criminalité urbaine et rurale en France et en Belgique.* Paris: Cujas, 1960.

Tarde, Gabriel de. *La Criminalité comparée.* Paris: Alcan, 1886.

———. *Etudes pénales et sociales.* Lyon: Storck, 1892.

———. *La Philosophie pénale.* Lyon: Storck, 1890.

Théolleyre, Jean-Marc. *Tout condamné à mort aura la tête tranchée.* Paris: Téma, 1977.

Thorp, R. W. *Vues sur la justice.* Paris: Julliard, 1962.

Thulié, Dr. Henri. *La Lutte contre la dégénérescence et la criminalité.* Paris: Vigot, 1912.

Tocqueville, Alexis de. *Oeuvres complètes.* Vols. 1 and 9. Paris: Lévy, 1866.

Toulemon, André. *La Question du jury.* Paris: Sirey, 1930.

Tucker, Robert C. (ed.). *The Marx-Engels Reader.* New York: Norton, 1972.

Vacher de Lapouge, Georges. *Les Sélections sociales: cours libre de science politique.* Paris: Thorin, 1896.

Varant, Jean-Marc. *La Prison, pour quoi faire?* Paris: La Table ronde, 1972.

Vermeil, F.-M. *Essai sur les réformes à faire dans notre législation criminelle.* Paris: Démonville, 1781.

Vidal, Georges. *Considérations sur l'état actuel de la criminalité en France.* Paris: Rousseau, 1904.

———. *Principes fondamentaux de la pénalité dans les systèmes les plus modernes.* Paris: Rousseau, 1890.

Vidal, Jérôme-Léon. *Catalogue chronologique et analytique des documents officiels relatifs à l'administration des prisons, de 1781 à 1862.* Paris: Chaix, 1862.

———. *Coup d'oeil sur la science pénitentiaire.* Paris: Chaix, 1868.

———. *Note sur l'emprisonnement cellulaire.* Paris: Ledoyen, 1853.

Vidocq, François-Eugène. *Mémoires.* Paris: Tesson, 1828.

Villermé, Dr. Louis-René. *Tableau de l'état physique et moral des ouvriers.* 2 vols. Paris: Renouard, 1840.

Vingtrinier, Dr. Arthus. *Des prisons et des prisonniers.* Versailles: Klefer, 1840.

Voltaire, *Oeuvres complètes.* Vol. XXV. Paris: Garnier, 1879.

Wills, Antoinette. *Crime and Punishment in Revolutionary Paris.* Westport, Conn.: Greenwood, 1981.

Woronoff, Denis. *La République bourgeoise.* Paris: Seuil, 1972.

Zehr, Howard. *Crime and the Development of Modern Society: Patterns of Criminality in 19th Century Germany and France.* Totawa, N.J.: Rowman and Littlefield, 1977.

## Periodicals and Newspapers

*Annales de Normandie.* 1962, 1966, 1971.

*Bulletin de la Société Générale des Prisons.* 1877–91.

*Esprit.* 1945, 1954, 1955, 1972, 1977, 1979.

*Etudes Criminologiques.* 1925–30.

*Gazette des Tribunaux.* 1908.

*Le Monde.* 1944–82.

*La Nef.* 1970, 1975.

*Politique d'Aujourd'hui.* 1972.

*Projet.* 1972.

*La Revue.* 1908.

*Revue Pénitentiaire.* 1892–1933, 1947–80.

*Revue de Science Criminelle.* 1936–80.

*Sondages.* 1971–78.

*La Table Ronde.* 1966.

## Articles and Essays*

* Articles published in the periodicals and newspapers listed above are not listed individually.

Aubry, Dr. Paul. "De l'influence contagieuse de la publicité des faits criminels." *Archives d'Anthropologie Criminelle,* VIII (1893), 565–80.

Aylies, Raymond. "La question pénitentiaire en 1865." *Revue des Deux Mondes*, June 1, 1865, 707–41.

Baude, J.-J. "Du système pénal en France; la peine de mort, le bagne et la prison." *Revue des Deux Mondes*, Sept. 1, 1855, 1018–51.

Begouen, vicomte H. de. "Un rapport inédit de Mirabeau sur le régime des prisons." *Revue d'Économie Politique*, I (1887), 491–512.

Berlanstein, Leonard R. "Vagrants, Beggars, and Thieves: Delinquent Boys in Mid-Nineteenth Century France." *Journal of Social History*, XII (1979), 531–52.

Berlier de Vauplane. "Le cinquantenaire de Mettray." *Le Correspondant*, Oct.–Dec. 1890, 852–82.

Bizard, Dr. Léon. "Souvenirs d'un médecin des prisons de Paris." *Mercure de France*, CLXXIX (1925), 60–89, 666–86.

Brouillet, A. "La peine de mort et le pouvoir." *Nouvel Observateur*, June 27–July 3, 1977, p. 3.

Brunetière, Fernand. "Savans et moralistes." *Revue des Deux Mondes*, Nov. 1, 1891, 205–16.

Cameron, Iain A. "The Police of Eighteenth-Century France." *European Studies Review*, VII (1977), 47–76.

Caro, E. "Le déterminisme, la responsabilité morale et le droit de punir dans les nouvelles écoles philosophiques." *Revue des Deux Mondes*, Aug. 1, 1873, 531–64.

Castan, Nicole. "La criminalité à la fin de l'ancien régime dans les pays de Languedoc." *Bulletin d'Histoire Économique et Sociale de la Révolution Française* (1969), 59–68.

———. "La justice expéditive." *Annales*, XXXI, 331–61.

Chautemps, Emile. "La faillite de la transportation des condamnés aux travaux forcés." *Revue Bleue*, June 8, 1908, pp. 709–11; June 13, 1908, pp. 741–43; June 20, 1908, pp. 775–78.

Davidovitch, A. "Criminalité et répression en France depuis un siècle." *Revue Française de Sociologie*, II (1961), 30–49.

Desjardins, Arthur. "Crimes et peines." *Revue des Deux Mondes*, Jan. 1, 1891, 167–97.

Dreyfus, Ferdinand. "Le vagabondage et la mendicité dans les campagnes," in *Misères sociales et études historiques* (Paris: Ollendorff, 1901), pp. 97–135.

Durkheim, Emile. "Deux lois de l'évolution pénale." *L'Année Sociologique*, IV (1899), 65–95.

Faucher, Léon. "De la réforme des prisons." *Revue des Deux Mondes*, Feb. 1, 1844.

Garçon, Maurice. "Les bagnes." *Mercure de France*, CLXXVII (1925), 308–31.

Gatrell, V. A. C., and T. B. Haddon, "Criminal Statistics and Their Interpretation," in E. A. Wrigley (ed.), *Nineteenth Century Society* (Cambridge: Cambridge Univ. Press, 1972), pp. 336–96.

Guérin, Alain. "Attention, prison." *L'Humanité*, March 18 to April 2, 1970.

Gurr, Ted R. "Crime Trends in Modern Democracies since 1945." *Annales Internationales de Criminologie* (1977), 41–85.

Hamon, A. "De la définition du crime." *Archives d'Anthropologie Criminelles*, VIII (1893), 242–57.

Hartman, Mary S. "Crime and the Respectable Woman: Toward a Pattern of Middle-Class Female Criminality in 19th Century France and England." *Feminist Studies*, II (1974), 138–56.

Haussonville, comte Othenin d'. "L'enfance à Paris: les vagabonds et les mendiants." *Revue des Deux Mondes*, June 1, 1878, 598–627.

——. "Le combat contre le vice: la criminalité." *Revue des Deux Mondes*, April 1, 1887, 564–98.

——. "Le combat contre le vice: la répression." *Revue des Deux Mondes*, Jan. 1, 1888, 131–59.

Hennequin, Amédée. "Du travail dans les prisons." *Le Correspondant*, Sept. 24, 1848, 631–46.

Joly, Henri. "Assistance et répression." *Revue des Deux Mondes*, Sept. 1, 1905, 117–51.

——. "Le Krach de la répression." *Le Correspondant*, Feb. 25, 1896, 733–49.

——. "Le problème criminel au moment présent." *Revue des Deux Mondes*, Dec. 1, 1907, 674–708.

——. "Le problème pénal au moment présent et la peine de mort." *Revue des Deux Mondes*, Jan. 1, 1909, 173–204.

——. "Le problème pénitentiaire au moment présent." *Revue des Deux Mondes*, Feb. 1, 1910, 636–68.

Jouet, Roger. "La maison centrale du Mont-Saint-Michel entre 1846 et 1852: tentatives de réforme et conflits administratifs." *Revue de l'Avranchin et du Pays de Granville*, LXXXIV (1966), 185–237.

——. "Les montois devant la suppression de la maison centrale (1863–1864)." *Annales du Mont-Saint-Michel*, LXXXXI (1965), 108–12.

Lascoumes, Pierre, and Ghislaine Moreau-Capdeveille, "Presse et justice pénale: un cas de diffusion idéologique." *Revue Française de Science Politique*, XXVI (1976), 41–69.

Lechat, Jean. "Les prisons du Mont-Saint-Michel pendant la Révolution." *Revue de l'Avranchin et du Pays de Granville*, LXXXIV (1966), 175–84.

Lecuir, Jean. "Criminalité et moralité: Montyon, statisticien du parlement de Paris." *Revue d'Histoire Moderne et Contemporaine*, XXI (1974), 445–93.

Le Roy Ladurie, Emmanuel. "La décroissance du crime au XVIIIᵉ siècle: bilan d'historiens." *Contrepoint*, no. 9 (1973), 227–33.

Lodhi, A., and Charles Tilly. "Urbanization, Crime and Collective Violence in 19th Century France." *American Journal of Sociology*, LXXIX (1974), 279–318.

Lucas, Colin. "The First Directory and the Rule of Law." *French Historical Studies*, X (1977), 231–60.

Mackrell, John. "Criticism of Seigniorial Justice in Eighteenth-Century France," in J. F. Bosher (ed.), *French Government and Society 1500–1850* (London: Athlone, 1973), pp. 123–44.

Merruau, Paul. "Les déportés politiques en Afrique, à la Guyane française, et à la Nouvelle Calédonie." *Revue des Deux Mondes*, April 1, 1873, 689–710.

——. "La Nouvelle Calédonie et la transportation." *Revue des Deux Mondes*, Nov. 1, 1871, 178–98.

"Mimande, Paul" (pseud. of Paul-Marie La Loyère). "La colonisation pénale." *Revue des Deux Mondes*, July 15, 1893, 364–93.

Mogensen, N. W. "Crimes and Punishments in Eighteenth-Century France: the Example of the pays d'Auge." *Histoire Sociale/Social History*, X (1977), 337–53.

Nye, Robert A. "Degeneration and the Medical Model of Cultural Crisis in the French *Belle Epoque*," in Seymour Drescher et al. (eds.), *Political Symbolism in Modern Europe: Essays in Honor of George L. Mosse* (New Brunswick, N.J.: Transaction Press, 1982), pp. 19–41.

——. "Heredity or Milieu: the Foundations of Modern European Criminological Theory," *Isis*, LXVII (1976), 335–55.

Perrot, Michelle, "Délinquance et système pénitentiaire en France au XIXᵉ siècle." *Annales*, XXX (1975), 67–92.

——. "Premières mesures des faits sociaux: les débuts de la statistique criminelle en France (1780–1830)," in *Pour une histoire de la statistique* (Paris: I.N.S.E.E., 1977), pp. 125–35.

Pinatel, Jean. "La crise pénitentiaire." *L'Année Sociologique*, 3d series, XXIV (1973), 13–67.

——. "La vie et l'oeuvre de Charles Lucas." *Revue Internationale de Droit Penal*, XVIII (1947), 121–54.

Proal, Louis. "Les médecins positivistes et les théories modernes de la criminalité." *Le Correspondant* (1890), pp. 88–113, 296–322.

Richard, Gaston. "Les crises sociales et les conditions de la criminalité." *L'Année Sociologique*, III (1898), 15–42.

Salingardes, Bernard. "Les caractéristiques de la criminalité et des institutions de défense sociale pour adultes en France." *Revue pratique de Psychologie de la vie sociale et d'hygiène mentale* (1970), 145–58.

Sauvageot, André. "Dévaluation de la peine." *Revue Politique et Parlementaire*, XLVIII (Oct. 10, 1946), 17–32.

Savey-Casard, Paul. "La criminalité à Lyon de 1830 à 1834." *Revue d'Histoire du Droit Français et Étranger*, XL (1962), 248–65.

Schnapper, Bernard. "La répression pénale au XVIe siècle: l'exemple du parlement de Bordeaux." *Recueil de Mémoires et Travaux Publiés par la Société d'Histoire du Droit et des Institutions des Anciens Pays de Droit Écrit*, VIII (1971).

———. "La justice criminelle rendue par le parlement de Paris sous le règne de François Ier." *Revue Historique de Droit Français et Étranger*, LII (1974), 252–84.

Tarde, Gabriel de. "Criminalité et santé sociale." *Revue Philosophique*, XXXIX (1895), 148–62.

Valon, Alexis de. "Les prisons de France sous le gouvernement républicain." *Revue des Deux Mondes*, June 1, 1848, 728–48.

Vauthier, G. "Les prisons d'état en 1812." *Revue d'Histoire de la Révolution et l'Empire* (1916), pp. 84–94.

Wright, Vincent. "The Coup d'Etat of 1851," in Roger Price (ed.), *Revolution and Reaction* (London: Croom Helm, 1975), pp. 303–33.

Zehr, Howard. "The Modernization of Crime in Germany and France, 1830–1913." *Journal of Social History*, VIII (1975), 117–41.

Zysberg, André. "La société des galériens au milieu du XVIIIe siècle." *Annales*, XXX (1975), 43–65.

# Index